Social work practice with depressed mothers in child and family care

Michael Sheppard
with Narcyza Kelly

University of Plymouth

Funded by the Nuffield Foundation

London:

The Stationery Office

Applications for reproduction should be made in writing to The Stationery Office Limited, St Crispins, Duke Street, Norwich NR3 1PD.

The information contained in this publication is believed to be correct at the time of manufacture. Whilst care has been taken to ensure that the information is accurate, the publisher can accept no responsibility for any errors or omissions or for changes to the details given.

A CIP catalogue record for this book is available from the British Library.
A Library of Congress CIP catalogue record has been applied for.

First published 2001

ISBN 0 11 322349 8

About the author

Michael Sheppard is Professor of Social Work at the University of Plymouth, and Visiting Professor at the Centre of Evidence Based Social Services, University of Exeter.

Printed in the United Kingdom by The Stationery Office Limited
TJ2735 C10 02/01 019585

CONTENTS

Preface

This book is the culmination of work carried out over a number of years. It seeks to draw attention to the significance of depression in mothers to the practice of social workers in child and family care, and to the possibilities of enabling mothers and their families to resolve their problems and needs. In the context of child and family social work, depression in mothers has been surprisingly neglected as a factor of significance for research. In view of its extremely pernicious effects on the capacity of individuals to manage their lives in general and childcare in particular, it is of considerable importance for the conduct of practice. This is a central feature of the findings presented here. If women – who already have more than their fair share of life's difficulties – are assailed by the disabling effects of depression, how well situated are they to resolve these difficulties? How, indeed, can social workers effectively help them to resolve these difficulties without dealing with the issue of depression?

The findings presented here suggest that services are poorly organised to meet the challenge of real life situations where problems and needs cannot be neatly compartmentalised into specialised areas such as childcare *or* mental health, social *or* health services, and so on. Furthermore, if practitioners are to respond more adequately to the complex life situations of their clients, they need a structure and organisation, not to mention the appropriate skills to enable them to do so. As things stand, the structure and culture of services present obstacles to the delivery of the best possible support to these families. Furthermore, an increased preoccupation with bringing together disparate services does not necessarily help. Where, for example, hybrid mental health services are created from previously separate social and health services, this may develop greater unity *within* one area (mental health) but greater differentiation *between* areas (such as mental health and childcare).

This book arose from the efforts of several people. Vanessa Taylor was the researcher who undertook data collection in the work in County. Liz Butler conducted data collection in Borough. Narcyza Kelly carried out more work: she undertook data collection in City, tidied up the data that had been input, and also conducted qualitative data retrieval, with comments on the data produced in all the study areas.

The research project on which this book is based was devised and directed by Michael Sheppard, who also wrote all the drafts and the final version of the book which now appears. I, therefore, am responsible for any errors that may appear.

Thanks are due to a number of people. Most important were the Social Services Departments, and social workers who took part in this project. It takes a particular form of bravery to open yourself to the kinds of professional evaluation reported in this book, not to mention the time spent on research which could usefully be spent with clients. I would also like to thank Sharon Witherspoon, Assistant Director of the Nuffield Foundation, and some anonymous reviewers who helped in the development of the research proposal leading to this book. The helpful and supportive relationship of the Nuffield Foundation to researchers is particularly valuable when carrying out large projects, such as that reported here.

This book is dedicated to my biggest supporters, Lauren and Jo.

Michael Sheppard

Part one
Context and study

1

1 Introduction

Prevalence of depression in social work practice

Depression has been called 'the common cold of psychiatry'. Embedded in this statement, it appears, is an attempt to draw attention to the frequency with which people suffer from this mental health problem, which is certainly important. However, colds, while they may be unpleasant and irritating, do not provide the physical equivalent of depression. We may – using lay language – say 'I feel depressed', and in so doing indicate that we are really fed up, unmotivated and 'down'. This, however, hardly gives expression to the impact on sufferers of clinical depression.

Depression of this sort can be devastating. People speak of their world closing in, of being in utter despair, and of being cut off from others, even the closest of friends and relatives. Life loses meaning, while the sufferer has a very poor perception of themselves, at times reaching a point where they can see themselves as worthless and even evil. Depression is associated with a pessimistic view of the world, the past, and the future. A general sense of hopelessness can emerge. A perception of an inability to influence important events of their lives – of being out of control of things – can emerge, at times reflecting the reality of the depressed person's situation. In this context, and as the person sinks into depression, it can be hard to rouse themselves to do anything, and they might take to their beds, becoming reluctant to leave them. Everyday problems can grow from molehills to mountains, fuelling a sense of powerlessness. Additionally, or sometimes alternatively, a rage can develop, as the individual rails against the perceived injustices perpetrated on them by the world. Increasingly trapped in a personal world characterised by anger, hopelessness and a sense of helplessness in terms of influencing the direction of their lives, depressed individuals can contemplate suicide as a positive way out of their predicament, sometimes reaching the point where suicide is attempted, and even achieved.

Depression, therefore, is not best analogised as the psychiatric equivalent to the common cold. Neither does it present auspicious circumstances for caring for oneself or raising children. An interest in the issue of depression in relation to childcare social work practice (and which led to this book) grew, a number of years ago, from various converging issues which were apparent from the research literature. These included the knowledge that, in general, women have primary responsibility for childcare, an awareness of the impact of depression on childcare, and the obvious link between social disadvantage and the increased likelihood of depression. All these factors are examined in detail early in this book. However, a more direct appreciation came from social work practice, where, for those with some degree of mental health expertise, it was obvious that depression was characteristic of many mothers on child and family care caseloads.

The research reported in this book represents the third stage in the process of examining the issue of maternal depression and its significance for child and family care social work. The first stage involved an extensive review of literature focusing on the link between maternal depression and childcare problems. It became apparent that, although the issue of maternal depression had not been given much attention in research on childcare social work practice, evidence taking in a wider focus demonstrated a strong link between childcare problems and the presence of maternal depression. This link, together with mediating factors such as social support and social disadvantage, was identified in a series of studies (Sheppard 1993a, 1993b, 1994a, 1994b, 1994c). It became very apparent that the groups at highest risk of depression – women with children, those in large families, with poor support and in socially deprived areas – characterised those on child and family care caseloads. There was, then, a strong *prima facie* case for high rates of depression amongst mothers in families on childcare social work caseloads.

This in itself would be an obvious cause for concern. However, one defining characteristic of families on child and family social work caseloads is their high levels of problems and needs. The presence of depression, it would seem likely, would impair the capacity of the women to overcome their problems. In already inauspicious circumstances of social deprivation and familial difficulties, depression could have a severely disabling effect on the capacities of women to overcome their problems.

The second stage of the depression project was to begin to examine the issue of depression in social work practice. The research sought to discover some initial or provisional answers to some basic questions: how great is the frequency of depression in mothers on child and family care social work caseloads? How does this compare with other population groups? Does it vary greatly between rural and urban areas? Do social workers recognise depression, and how do they respond to its presence?

The initial answers were provided through an exploratory study, comparing two teams, one rural and one urban, reported in a series of papers (Sheppard 1996, 1997a, 1997b, 1997c, 1998). Although the size of the study was restricted, the findings were clear and remarkable. Amongst the more significant were findings that between a third and two fifths of mothers of families on childcare caseloads suffered clinical levels of depression. This outnumbered by a ratio of over three to one the proportion of clinically depressed women seen by health visitors in the same geographical areas. This was interesting because health visitors tend to see, when compared with social workers, and in terms of their socioeconomic make–up, families that are more representative of the general population. However, there were further intriguing findings. Neither health visitors nor social workers were particularly accurate in their identification of depression. Social workers, though, showed a strong tendency to make negative errors (that is, to fail to identify depression when it was present) rather than positive errors (identifying depression when it was not present). Nevertheless, it was families with mothers suffering depression who had the most severe and enduring problems. There was a significant association between child abuse and the presence of depression and these families tended to receive the most long term intervention. This greater severity of problems, it should be remembered, was not found in comparison with the general population, but when compared to other families whose problems were severe enough to be on child and family social work caseloads.

This second stage of research provided some important initial answers. However, it was short in a number of respects. Firstly, although the combination of the study, together with the *prima facie* case made by examination of the wider literature, strongly suggested depression was a significant factor, it was not really large enough to be conclusive. Secondly, although the broad contours of practice had been shown through the study, considerably greater detail, particularly on the nature and reasons for social workers' practice strategies, was required. Thirdly, the voices of the women themselves were silent. A more definitive study was needed, supplementing the research from the second stage of the project with a more extensive analysis, focusing on these broad areas.

Overview of the book

The work reported here constitutes the third stage of the study. It brings together, with findings from the second stage, findings from a much more detailed multi-method study of maternal depression. As a result, the study contains data from three local authorities in different parts of Britain, covering both rural and urban areas. As the reader will discover, the data strongly confirm the widespread experience of depression in mothers of children on child and family care social work caseloads, and raises important questions about the context for the organisation and conduct of practice. Broadly, it seeks to evaluate the processes of social work intervention in terms of their appropriateness for the needs of the mothers in particular and their families.

The rest of Part one of the book places the study in context. Chapter 2 focuses on a number of diverse themes which are brought together to provide the background to the study. These include the policy context, the link between maternal depression and childcare problems, the key ways in which the responsibilities of childcare practitioners are framed by legislation and policy, the negative cognitions of depressed people, and our existing understanding, through research, of mental health issues in social work. Chapter 3 provides details on the areas chosen, the methodology used, and the rationale for both of these.

Part two focuses directly on the issue of depression and the ways in which it was experienced and understood by the women and their social workers. Chapter 4 focuses on the women's experience of depression. This provides data on the ways in which they were aware of themselves as depressed individuals, the effect on them of their depression, their past experiences of abuse, and the way this was seen to be related to their current depression, and the effects of the depression, as they saw it, on their children and childcare. Chapter 5 outlines the ways in which social workers made sense of the women, and the extent to which this reflected a sense that depression was a defining factor in understanding the women and their situation. This showed that the 'character issue' was at the heart of social workers' construction of these women, and that these constructions could be broadly divided into three: the 'genuinely depressed', the 'stoics' and the 'troubled and troublesome'.

Part three examines the social workers' views of these mothers' needs, the responses they made, and factors influencing these responses. Chapter 6 outlines the main problems and needs identified, divided into broad areas of social problems, adult relationship, adult health, parenting and child problems. Chapter 7 focuses on social workers' responses to these problems and needs, showing the social workers to have responded to these situations primarily in terms of social and childcare problems, and support for the mother as parent, rather than as an individual with needs in her own right. Chapters 8 and 9 go on to explore key factors underlying these differentiated responses. Chapter 8 examines the organisational context, identifying four key features: the priority systems adopted for work, the effects of care management, the key focus on the child (and interpretation of the notion that the welfare of the child should be paramount) and the limited confidence amongst social workers in their skills dealing with mental health issues. Chapter 9 looks at the use of mental health services. Here the focus is on the gap which exists between mental health and childcare services, arising from different expectations and priorities, together with the difficulties engaging mental health services with mental health problems in a child and family care client group.

The book goes on to examine intervention strategies with different groups which make up the child and family care client group. The spotlight here, in Part four, is on the nature and rationale for the intervention strategies developed. Three broad intervention strategies became apparent. Two concentrated on child protection, the first in which child abuse was the dominant consideration, and the second where family support was the main focus. The third involved families with children with disabilities. Chapter 10 examines child protection–child abuse strategies, which at their heart carried a major dimension of authority. This major theme of intervention contained other facets of support, in which managing risk through control and decisions about care are considered. Chapter 11 concentrates on the second child protection strategy, that which involved a strong focus, within the general realm of child protection, on family support. This involved social workers helping mothers directly by providing emotional support and parental coping strategies, and indirectly through management of care. Chapter 12 is about intervention strategies with families with children who had disabilities. These form a separate group, in that child protection was not the main concern. The core strategy issue for this group was the question of resource provision, which was generally less available than where child protection was a concern. This chapter focuses on the perceived strengths of the mothers in adversity, and the effects of this perception, together with limited available funds, on resource provision. This entails an examination of the limited direct and indirect work carried out with these families, which generally had low priority in resource provision.

A characteristic of the different strategies identified in Part four, which follow on from Part three, is the way in which intervention was defined most significantly, by issues other than the depression of the mothers, and the responses which would go some way to meet those needs. The intervention strategies are not, therefore, primarily defined in terms of maternal depression, but in terms of child protection and child disability. The consequences of this, and other dimensions identified earlier in the book, are apparent in Part five, which looks at women's experiences of receiving intervention.

Chapter 13 focuses on women's experiences of child protection–child abuse intervention strategies. The issue of partnership (and its considerable limitations in these cases), the sense of entrapment which emerged in the women's dealings with social services, and the guilt–inducing effects of that involvement, are all features of the women's experience of this intervention strategy. The issue of control was at the centre of women's experiences of this intervention, and many did not have any perception of partnership in a meaningful sense. Women often felt blamed unfairly, that they were themselves victims of the system, and they had a pervasive sense of being trapped.

Chapter 14 examines the issues involved in receiving child protection–family support intervention. A central feature in this chapter is the issue of partnership, as well as the qualities and skill of practitioners that were considered to be important in intervention. Some of the women found the work of social workers as supportive as it was intended, and such women spoke highly of their experiences of intervention. However, the women's depression often provided a barrier to working in partnership. Evidence is consistent with the diffidence on the part of the woman emerging from the depression, and the limited skills and awareness of depression on the part of social workers, combining at times to undermine the possibilities of working in partnership. Often women felt angry and marginalised while social workers did not respond positively, unaware of the women's dissatisfaction.

Chapter 15 is concerned with the experiences of women with children with disabilities. The overwhelming issue identified amongst this group was the impact of limited resources. There was a widespread feeling of desperation (contrasting in some respects with the 'stoics' attributions frequently made by their social workers). The problem of limited resources overwhelmed every other consideration, including the professional qualities and personal characteristics of the social workers. Partnership did not even emerge as an issue for many of these women, since there was not sufficient contact to begin the process of working in partnership.

The range of feelings emerging from groups experiencing all three intervention strategies – of marginalisation, absence of control, entrapment, blame and feelings of being victims – are all elements associated with depression. Depression, in other words, was not simply something which was 'brought into' the situation by mothers, but which could be exacerbated by their experiences of intervention. Indeed, there is evidence that child protection procedures could induce feelings of depression on the part of these women.

Part six makes conclusions and recommendations, which appear in Chapter 16. At the heart of this is the concept of 'entrapment' which is developed to describe relationships between these women and their social workers in pursuit of their childcare responsibilities. It brings together the outer workings of the childcare system with the inner workings of the women's minds, in terms of the way they felt in this situation, and in the light of their previous experiences. This entrapment had various dimensions, including the impact of life experiences and the culture and organisation of service provision. It often had the effect of marginalising the women's own needs as individuals in their own right. Recommendations are made, from the organisation of service delivery to the conduct of partnership and the nature of skills required to carry out practice. It is, however, absolutely clear that depression in mothers is a major facet of social work practice in child and family care, and that much could be done to make the human services more responsive to these women's needs. After all, if these women are not around to care for their children, who is?

2 Themes in maternal depression, childcare and social work

Many of the most influential studies of social work practice in child and family care are based directly on issues derived from policy expectations, the ways social work practice emerges or is defined through these policies. Thus, for example, we have studies of partnership, of processes of child protection, and of need (e.g. Birchall 1995; Gibbons et al. 1995; Thoburn et al. 1995). The focus of this study is not directly on these policy based dimensions of practice, but rather on a feature of women's lives which, on the basis of inference from previous studies outside social work, and early emerging evidence on social work practice, is likely to be of considerable significance for the conduct of practice. This is, on the one hand, practice by childcare social workers working with depressed mothers and, on the other, the women's experience of that practice.

While, however, policy did not provide the direct focus of the study, it provided its context. Where we are interested in issues of practice, we are bound to be concerned with those policy features which seek to underlie that practice. The somewhat tangential relationship between policy and the subject of this study means that, in relating it to practice, it is necessary to draw initially on quite disparate themes. In the first place, there is the question of why we should be interested in maternal depression when looking at child and family care practice. What, in other words, is the connection between depression and childcare which should make it a subject of interest? A second dimension relates to the conduct of practice, and research on that conduct. In particular, how far is practice conducted in a way which indicates sensitivity to issues of maternal mental health, and depression in particular? A third feature is: why should there be an issue about depression? What are its characteristics which might, in principle, make it an important issue for the conduct of practice? Is there anything about it which might be expected to affect the woman's engagement with social services? Fourth, what do we know about mental health issues in childcare practice, and maternal depression in particular? What, in other words, should be the start off point?

However, it is necessary first to contextualise this by examining the key policy dimensions. What is it about policy and practice expectations which should make parents, and mothers in particular, a focus for attention? This is the first issue to be given attention.

Policy Context

The legal framework for practice, provided by the 1989 Children Act, places great emphasis on the provision of family support by social services. This developed against the background of a trend, in the 1970s and early 1980s, of increasing use of compulsion by social services in the care of children, and the emphasis, in the 1975 Children Act, on the provision of substitute care to promote children's welfare. Reaction to well publicised child deaths 'almost certainly' (Packman 1981, p. 178) had far reaching effects on childcare policy and practice. Under the 1975 Act, ties between children and parents could be more readily broken, by, for example, the assumption by local authorities of parental rights over children who had been continuously in care for three years, while more children could be freed for adoption through wider grounds for dispensing with parental consent. This was seen, according to Fuller and Stevenson (1985) as 'a potential discouragement to preventive and rehabilitative work with parents'.

The reaction against this emphasis on parent–child separation is evident in the mid 1980s. Official documents stressed both the centrality of the birth family and the significance of support and prevention. The DHSS *Review of childcare Law* (1985, p. 47) placed considerable importance on working with children living with their families, where work

> ...could be regarded as having two main aims: to provide 'family support' to help parents bring up their children and to seek to prevent admission to care or court proceedings, except where this is in the best interests of the child.

In promoting these aims, it was suggested that respite care or reception into care could actually be a positive step and should not be regarded as a last resort (p. 48). It should be part of a range of services for family support enabling children to stay with their families, or live independently in the long term.

The Children Act introduced a number of concepts linked with a greater emphasis on the birth family. According to Fox Harding (1991, p. 229) 'on balance it appears that the Children Act, while containing both paternalist and pro–birth family provisions, leans more heavily on the latter perspective'. The responsibilities of local authorities in relation to family support revolve around the related provisions that (a) the family is generally the best place for the child, and that (b) parents have responsibilities towards the child.

In relation to the first of these, official guidance comments that 'all the provision reflects the Act's philosophy that the best place for the child to be brought up is usually in his own family and that the child in need can be helped most effectively if the local authority, working in partnership with the parents, provide a range and level of services appropriate to the child's needs' (Department of Health 1991a, p. 1; Department of Health 1989). Parental responsibility refers to the collection of rights, powers, duties and responsibilities given by law to parents, placing great emphasis on birth parents, and which are not affected by separation or divorce (s 21 (6)). Even where courts intervene in family life, the duty of both parents to contribute to the child's upbringing remains (Department of Health 1989, p. 1).

The Act displays a central concern with prevention. It gives local authorities duties to provide for children in need. According to the Department of Health guidance (1991a) the definition of need, involving three categories – a reasonable standard of health or development, significant impairment of health or development, and disablement – is 'deliberately wide to reinforce the emphasis on preventive support and service to families' (p. 5). In pursuit of prevention, under section 17 (1) local authorities have a general duty to provide a range and level of services appropriate to children in their area who are 'in need', to safeguard and promote their welfare, and as far as is consistent with that aim, promote their upbringing by their families. Second, the Act assumes that families, in general, are capable of caring adequately for children, but that, on occasions, they have difficulties resulting in inadequate care for their children. In this situation, if they seek help from local authorities, they should meet with a positive, non–stigmatising, response. Prevention, in these circumstances, may include the provision of voluntary care (now termed accommodation), as well as advice, guidance, assistance, counselling and home help services. Prevention, then, permeates every stage of support, including accommodation.

More recent developments serve to emphasise, not always in a social work context, this general commitment to family support. The clearest statement of this lies in the consultation document *Supporting Families* (Home Office 1998), where there is a commitment on a wide basis to helping parents in the difficult task of parenting. Two particular areas were considered to stand out: a gap in support in the vital early years between birth and early school, and the limited availability of information on parenting support. In line with this a variety of developments were proposed, including a national parenting help line, enhanced role for health visitors, and 'Sure Start', an initiative to help families with children in their early years.

Consistent with the emphasis on family support, parental responsibility and prevention, partnership is considered very important (Department of Health 1991a; 1995a). For parents, partnership in effect means working with them in catering for the needs of the children with whom social services are involved. The initial emphasis is on voluntary arrangements, which build on the family's strengths and minimise weaknesses, in a way that 'enhances the parents' capabilities and confidence so that they may provide effectively for the child's welfare' (Department of Health 1991a, p. 11). This is the preferred alternative to compulsion. Even where a child requires accommodation, or is likely to suffer significant harm (s 31 (9) and (10)), local authorities should try to work with parents to achieve agreements to the child's accommodation. Only when faced with a lack of co–operation should the need for care proceedings or emergency protection be considered. However, even where compulsion is required, practitioners are expected, as far as possible, to work in partnership (Department of Health 1995a). There is considerable concern that, despite difficulties arising from the authority role of social workers and the effects of child protection procedures, practitioners should nevertheless seek to foster partnership with parents.

Further developments following the election of the Labour Government in 1997 involved an important emphasis on inter–agency and inter–professional collaboration. This is of particular importance for a focus both on adult mental health and childcare issues. There was a clear policy objective, outlined in most detail in the white paper *Modernising Social Services* (1998) to bring down the 'Berlin Wall' between health and social care, which prevented an appropriate response to needs. Their concern was to develop a system of integrated care which meant that individuals would be able to receive services appropriately in both health *and* social care. Much of the concern was with structural restrictions based on organisational separation and budgeting responsibilities, but there was also a drive to integrate practice more effectively. However, much of the government's thinking, while concentrating on bringing agencies together, involved focusing on discrete areas, for example, greater integration in either mental health services or childcare provision. There was little emphasis on integrating better both agencies (social and health service) and discrete areas (childcare and mental health) (see e.g. Department of Health 1998). Thus while priorities in childcare meant regarding the welfare of the child as paramount, priority in mental health was given to the adult severely mentally ill (Department of Health 1991a; Department of Health/Social Services Inspectorate 1994).

Depression and childcare

The legislation and official guidance stress the importance of supporting parents as far as possible in the care of children, and also of parental responsibility and partnership. One group of particular significance in this respect is mothers who suffer from depression. This is because, on the one hand, there is a close relationship between maternal depression and childcare problems, which provides a *prima facie* case that such families would appropriately receive family support services. On the other hand, the features of families subject to social work intervention indicate they are at high risk of maternal depression. On the whole, women retain primary responsibility for child rearing, and this is the case with those referred for childcare social work intervention, where many families are characterised by single parents or are broken or reconstituted (Packman et al. 1986, Hardiker et al. 1991; Sheppard 1998). However, the capacity of mothers to care adequately for their children is severely affected by the presence of depression.

This is of particular significance for social work intervention. It is well established that women are subject to rates of depression about twice that of men (Weissman and Klerman 1977). Equally well established research shows female depression to be linked to social disadvantage. Studies have shown that rates of maternal depression are particularly high in deprived urban areas, characterised by poor environment, housing difficulties and frequently dislocated social relationships (Moss and Plewis 1977; Richman 1977; Richman et al. 1982). Brown and Harris (1978; Brown, Ni Brolchain and Harris 1975) found four times as many working class as middle class women in their urban community study suffered depression. A key vulnerability factor was motherhood: having one child aged under six or three under 14. This picture of social disadvantage resembles closely that of families subject to childcare social work intervention (Gibbons et al. 1990; Hardiker et al. 1991; Sheppard 1998). Characteristics extensively identified include high levels of unemployment, receipt of income support (indicating low incomes) and financial problems.

Alongside this, the central concern of child and family care services with parenting and childcare problems indicates further the significance of maternal depression. Extensive research has shown important relationships between childcare problems and depression in mothers. A general impairment in role performance, including communication problems, lack of involvement, guilt, resentment, and mother–child friction have been found in mothers of children up to age 18 (Sheppard 1994a).

Maternal depression is associated with emotional and cognitive problems in children. Amongst those of pre–school age, and when compared with children of mothers who are not depressed, these include temperamental difficulties and crying in infants, lower mental and motor development, poor concentration span, delays in expressive language development, more limited involvement in play activities (though this is in part because of the lack of mother's involvement in play), and when actually involved, a more limited degree of concentration on these activities. School age children of depressed mothers display more somatic complaints, more negative cognitions about themselves and greater rates of child depression. When adolescent depression is associated with maternal depression, it is more closely related than maternal depression alone to adolescent social and cognitive functioning (see e.g. Cox et al. 1987; Forehand et al. 1988; Welner and Rice 1988; Murray and Stein 1991; Murray 1992; Murray et al. 1993).

Consistently greater problems in child behaviour and conduct have been found amongst children of depressed mothers, both amongst pre–school children and those of school age. In pre–school children, task competence is generally lower, as is their persistence in relation to challenging tasks. School age children are involved in more conflict and fighting, both at home and at school, and are also more frequently withdrawn and less interested in usual activities (Welner et al. 1977). Adolescents tend to have poorer relations with their parents, more behaviour problems at school, perform less well academically, and are more frequently involved in illegal behaviour (Caplan et al. 1989). There is some evidence that maternal depression shows greater association with child behaviour problems as children get older, and that when parental conflict (a well known feature of families involved with childcare social services) occurs as well as maternal depression, this is associated with more severe child behaviour problems (Ghodsian et al. 1984; Goodyer et al. 1993).

There is a great deal of evidence that mothers' judgement of their children's behaviour is negatively affected by depression (Sheppard 1994a). There is a tendency for depressed mothers to rate their child's behaviour more negatively than other assessors, such as teachers, or standardised instruments, when they are used. Indeed, it is probably the case that depression has a direct effect on mothers' perception of child behaviour (seeing it more negatively) and an indirect effect (through the effects of depression on the quality of parenting) on actual child behaviour (Pannacione and Wahler 1986). Of course, there could be a vicious circle in which the responsibilities of parenting, and in particular the behavioural problems of children, leave women demoralised and contribute to the generation and maintenance of their depressed state (Sheppard 1994a).

Depressed mothers are more likely to use corporal punishment, to express hostility and irritability towards their children, and to involve themselves less in play with young children. Parents of adolescents appear more likely to have communication problems, lack of involvement, and feelings of guilt and resentment (Weissman et al. 1972). Some evidence suggests that children of moderately, rather than severely, depressed mothers are at greater risk than other children of child abuse and physical aggression (Zuvarin 1989; Whipple and Webster-Stratton 1991).

Social construction of practice

Clearly there is an important relationship between childcare problems and maternal depression. How far, then, is practice conducted in a way which enables social workers to show awareness of this issue, and focus constructively on it? One interesting feature is the relatively limited attention given to maternal mental health in the most authoritative studies on childcare practice. In this respect they reflect the conduct and construction of practice. The framing of social services responsibilities, derived directly from the law, provides the key to the ways in which childcare practice is conducted and constructed. Two central elements were identified by the Department of Health (1995b) summary of research which make this clear: that of children 'at risk' of significant harm, relating in particular to section 47 of the Children Act, and the provision of services to families with children 'in need' (relating here to section 17).

In child protection, the nomenclature of abuse provides the 'conceptual space' (Bulmer 1979) through which focus of concern and nature of task are defined. The language of child protection has a profound impact on practice. Hence the main categories – physical, sexual and emotional abuse – provide not just the key areas of concern, but the basis for the ways practitioners formulate their thoughts. This is clear from the category 'grave concern', which was removed as a category of child abuse in 1991, with the result that the apparently 'inexorable rise' (Gibbons et al. 1995, p. 11) in number of those on child protection registers was checked, and the rate fell in 1992. The variable use by local authorities of the term, furthermore, was associated with differences in numbers on the child protection register (Farmer and Owen 1995; c.f. Gibbons and Little 1993).

While, however, the practice of defining children as 'at risk' or 'in need' provides the focus for childcare practice, its content is not always clear. Gibbons et al. (1995) found that about 40 per cent of local authorities had not formulated specific criteria with which to define child abuse categories, jeopardising consistent management of cases including the threshold for registration. Colton et al. (1995) found a similar situation with definitions of need (c.f. Williams, 1997), with the result that social workers were using their own interpretations, which could vary widely. Aldgate and Tunstill (1995), concentrating on the local policy rather than practice level, noted how systems of priority were used to distinguish those in need who would qualify for services when resources are scarce. The greatest priority in these community 'need groups' was given to those defined as children at risk of abuse and neglect, children with disabilities, and children who have offended (all given priority by more than 60 per cent of authorities). By contrast, 'focus of problem is on the parent' was given priority in only 35 per cent of authorities. In general, these priorities reflect a focus on the child rather than the parent, even though the quality of parenting may be integral to the child's well-being.

Much of the most authoritative research on the process of intervention has concentrated on child protection processes. At the point of investigation and conferencing, much of the focus is on establishing the fact of abuse, verifying the claims made in child abuse referrals or allegations, and identifying the perpetrator (Farmer and Owen 1995, p. 8; Gibbons et al. 1995, p. 49; Thoburn et al. 1995, p. 52). Assessment of risk then takes place, and the initial case conference is a 'critical phase in the construction of risk' (Farmer and Owen 1995, p. 86). This process served the purpose not just of protecting the child, but to manage practitioners' anxieties about the possibility of misjudgement (Farmer and Owen 1995; Department of Health 1995b).

Establishing the fact of abuse is generally undertaken in the context of problems and needs (Thoburn et al. 1995; Gibbons and Little 1993). Farmer and Owen (1995), on the basis of their small intensive study, commented that background information was often crucial as a means for establishing the fact or risk of abuse. However, this was not knitted together in a coherent explanatory framework, which meant that it served further to emphasise the ubiquity of abuse as an issue, rather than constructing the situation in a way which made abuse less dominant.

The most frequent areas for discussion at case conferences were areas such as child behaviour and development, mother's behaviour and attitude, father figure's behaviour, attitude and parenting skills (all in at least two thirds of cases). The mental health of either parent was considered in only 15 per cent of cases, one of the three areas least considered. Where it was an issue, however, Gibbons et al. (1995, p. 56) found children were more likely to be conferenced and registered if parental mental illness was recorded in the notes. Farmer and Owen (1995) found that registration was nearly always the outcome when the mother was identified as having mental health problems.

In many cases, social workers' actions were directed towards the child. Farmer and Owen (1995) found that where the main focus was the mother, the central concerns remained with the child. This general theme is evident from Thoburn and colleagues' (1995) work on partnership. Colton et al.'s (1995) study of need was more equivocal, but nevertheless not encouraging. One third of those interviewed said they had not received help with 'bringing up children' and most of the rest found it difficult to say how they had been helped. Of twelve areas of support identified, only 'emotional support' focused unambiguously on parental need, and this was undertaken with only just under a third of cases. Research on prevention (Hardiker et al. 1991) shows a similar picture again. Child centred interventions such as management and control of children, child neglect and physical care of children were frequent subjects for research, whereas studies on parents as individuals were considerably rarer.

The cognitive world of the depressed person

Why should depression be an issue of concern in this context? First, there are clearly some families where parental mental health is an important consideration for the conduct of practice. Furthermore, we have also seen the important connection between childcare and mental health problems. There is, of course, an additional dimension: that family support, which includes a strong emphasis on helping parents, is also a key consideration for practice.

However, there are particular facets of depression which suggest that it will have an important effect on the mother's capacity to engage constructively with practitioners. The depressed woman lives in a psychologically impoverished world, characterised by what Beck (1976) has termed the 'negative cognitive triad': a negative view of the self, the world and the future (Blackburn, 1988; Blackburn and Davidson 1990). She has a pervasive sense of helplessness and hopelessness, and pessimism about opportunities to effect any positive change. Rowe (1983) has used the metaphor of a 'prison' to capture the sense of imprisonment within the unrewarding personal world of the depressed woman. It can lead to a tentativeness in her behaviour predicated on her sense of pessimism.

A negative view of self is generally regarded as core to depression (Gilbert 1992). Becker (1973) contrasts low self-esteem with 'inner sustainment', a kind of psychological and emotional robustness which resides within the individual. This is a belief in oneself which sees one more easily through life crises and even sharp personality changes. Low self-esteem, by contrast, bestows an inner fragility, which can have a paralysing effect on action and which leaves the individual particularly vulnerable in adversity. The kinds of problems suffered by many women subject to social services intervention, particularly in the form of social disadvantage, and the day to day difficulties of managing in this situation, provide circumstances of particular vulnerability for depression. Likewise, involvement of childcare services, with the implicit negative judgement of the mother's parenting capabilities, provides a further cause for such vulnerability.

Low self-esteem, a sense of personal worthlessness, is closely associated with a sense of failure. Chodoff (1974) suggests two ways in which this can emerge. On the one hand there are those who feel themselves to be unloved and unlovable, and for whom interactions contain the constant fear of rejection, criticism and blame. In ambiguous situations, such women are more likely to see themselves as criticised or blamed. On the other hand is the sense of having failed to live up to one's own expectations. In general, this is associated with perfectionism, of setting unachievably high standards for oneself. However, in situations of adversity, even the achievement of reasonable expectations may be very hard. Brown and Harris (1978) note this as a feature of women with large families (three or more aged under 14) who are vulnerable to depression. This failure to achieve either one's own, or perceived others', standards can leave women particularly at risk of depression. It is rather obvious how women in families who seek, or less willingly are involved in, child and family social services, will often have feelings of failure, which reflect either their own, or others', perceived criticisms of their standards of parenting.

Vulnerability to depression is frequently seen as rooted in childhood experiences. Bowlby (1977), for example, considers that early maladaptive attachment experiences between parents and children can have a crucial impact on the emergence of depression. Becker (1973; Freden 1982) refers to this as a failure to develop 'basic trust' leading to a concomitant failure to develop inner sustainment noted earlier. Maladaptive behaviours can include parental unresponsiveness to the child's care-eliciting behaviour, active disparagement or rejection, or threats of abandonment to control the child's conduct. The large research study by Bifulco and Moran (1998) goes considerably further than this, identifying a strong relationship between the experience of abuse in childhood and depression in adulthood. This involves a span from the shockingly mundane, involving persistent coldness, disinterest and criticism which undermined the confidence and self-esteem of the women as they grew up, to examples of the most serious sexual abuse and violence, as bad as anything seen by social workers in the course of their practice.

Others, such as Bibring (1953) and Seligman and colleagues (Abramson et al. 1978) emphasise the absence of control felt by individuals in seeking valued experiences. Such lack of control can emerge through, for example, the failure of care-eliciting behaviour to gain a response from parents. Through this, the child develops a sense that their aspirations are beyond their best efforts, and a feeling of helplessness can emerge. This is generalised, so that there is a tendency to feel out of control in even mildly challenging situations. It is also associated with perfectionism, in which women are unable to achieve high standards which they set themselves, which then leads to a sense of failure.

Those in the tradition of Freud emphasise object loss, which could be the loss, not just of a material object, but includes symbolic loss, such as that of a role or relationship (Klein 1975). Again, the attachment issues mentioned earlier could also be conceptualised in terms of the loss of a sought-after relationship, one which is needed in child development. Freud emphasised the development of high dependency needs which emerge because of the feelings of anxiety about the stability of relationships, and fear of the loss of those relationships. However, the dependency feelings carry with them also feelings of frustration and hostility in view of the individual's ambivalence about their own dependency needs in relation to particular individuals.

As adults these dependency needs can manifest themselves in reliance on relationships which are not necessarily suitable, and may involve conflict and violence. Merely hanging on to a relationship, however unsuitable, becomes a goal of those with low self-esteem. The frustrated care experiences of the mothers, as children can make them particularly vulnerable to threatened losses of relationships, threats to self-esteem, or extra dependency demands made by others. As Reder et al. (1993) comments, this can also involve the care of their own children. These stresses can provoke anxiety, feelings of being out of control, with explosions of anger, or attempts to control or punish the person evoking the insecurity. Such parents, in other words, may be unable to tolerate the child's own immaturity and dependency (Kelmer-Pringle 1978; Reder and Lucy 1991).

These different dimensions indicate the ways in which adult low self-esteem can influence the situation of the depressed mother subject to social work intervention. The sense of lack of control, feelings of failure, and high dependency needs, are all facets which, in theory, might manifest themselves in situations where social services are involved in ensuring adequate care of their children. They also provide some understanding of why women might find it difficult to respond to the needs of their children in a consistent, need-satisfying manner. Where their 'self' is subject to such strong and variable feelings, it is not necessarily easy to respond to the needs of the children.

Social circumstances and cognitions

For some, low self-esteem can operate as a classic trait disposition. The relation between the way they view the world (the negative cognitive triad) and its affective result (depression) is broadly trans–situational, i.e. is largely unaffected by the woman's circumstances. Whether they are in adversity or not, they are liable to have low self–esteem and be vulnerable to depression. A trait disposition involves schemata, which are stable beliefs and theories about oneself, other people and the world in general. Such people would be pessimistic and lack confidence, these negative traits being largely unaffected by positive events and circumstances in their lives. Whatever their circumstances, however positive their situation, such people would retain an outlook characterised by the negative cognitive triad.

In others, events and environment exert a greater influence on self–esteem and the development of depression. For these individuals, feelings of low self–esteem emerge in the context of perceived adverse circumstances (which carry a contextual threat, to draw upon Brown and Harris 1978). Amongst some individuals such triggers can emerge from a wide range of situations of varying severity. Amongst others, there is greater discrimination in the kinds of situations which are likely to trigger depression. Brown and Harris's (1978) well known work on depression indicates that depression mostly emerges in women in the context of very adverse situations indeed, situations which carry considerable contextual threat. These they define as severe life events and major difficulties, those to which considerable significance is attached by the woman (Brown and Harris 1978; Brown et al. 1986). The link they found between depression and disadvantage – specifically social class – showed that provoking agents of severe life events and major difficulties have a significant place in the causal chain leading to depression. Of particular importance for us, they found that motherhood, particularly single parenthood and having a large family with three or more children aged under 14, conferred particular vulnerability on disadvantaged women.

Brown and Harris's (1978) model places considerable importance on the environment, and the difficulties of maintaining self–esteem in situations of extreme adversity. Of course, this vulnerability can be rooted both in childhood experiences and extreme adversity, which in adulthood would mix cognitions developed through childhood experiences and their current circumstances in a cocktail which would be lethal in terms of depression. For mothers whose children were the subject of social work intervention, widespread adversity clearly confers some vulnerability to depression. It is possible that the experience of social services involvement would further increase the likelihood of depression since it would be expected that this would constitute a 'role event' (Brown et al. 1986), one which presented considerable contextual threat to the women in a role of major importance to them. The same could be said of child protection procedures. For those with adverse childhood experiences, the vulnerability to depression, it might be expected, would be even greater.

There is then a continuum, in which vulnerability to low self–esteem is represented, at one extreme, by a form of 'trait model' – a fairly consistent set of views leaving them with low self-esteem. At the other extreme would be a contingency model, in which environment plays the major part on the emergence of depression (Kuiper et al. 1988). Between these two would be variations in the balance between trait and environment in producing depression. In either case, whether emerging from current adverse environment, or past childhood adverse experiences, women would be vulnerable to depression.

The tentativeness which can emerge through these feelings of pessimism and low self-esteem could, it might be expected, make engagement with social services during intervention rather harder for depressed women than others. There is evidence of an association between depression and difficulty in assertiveness. Depressed women frequently either fail to express an opinion about potential issues of conflict, or may do so in a tentative and ineffectual way (Barbaree and Davis 1984). Assertive behaviour may be cognitively inhibited by the non–assertive individual's desire for approval, a sense of failure, and the idea that their views are worth little. This could present difficulties in engaging with social services in relation to childcare with, it might be inferred, implications for partnership.

Mental health issues

These diverse themes – the policy imperatives towards working with and supporting parents in birth families, the clear link between maternal depression and childcare problems, the social make–up of social services clients which put them at high risk of depression, the practices which have a tendency to construct families through certain social categories, and the psychological dimensions of depression – suggest strongly that maternal depression has a significant place in child and family social work practice. However, there has been a tendency, until very recently, for mental health and childcare issues to be approached quite distinctly from each other, both in practice and research on social work. The division between mental health, or more broadly, adult and childcare services, has led to specialisms which have the tendency to separate, rather than bring together, mental health and childcare. Research on childcare and mental health, in social work and social services, at any rate, has tended to be carried out separately. Childcare research at times mentions mental health issues without giving them a major place in the research.

Most of the mental health research relevant to interests at the centre of this book, has focused on prevalence rates in social services. Fisher et al.'s (1984) research used a heuristic device for defining mental health problems in individuals, without being limited by departmentally defined boundaries. They found that, using their definition, the majority of individuals with a mental disorder were not recognised as such through departmental definitions. They were more socially deprived than other clients, and mental health problems were a significant element across all client groups.

Fisher et al. (1984), however, did not use standardised instruments, so the accuracy of their findings is not clear. Notwithstanding this, other research has confirmed the wide prevalence of mental health problems across client groups. Huxley and colleagues (Huxley and Fitzpatrick 1984; Huxley et al. 1987, 1989), in studies using standardised instruments on social services clients not restricted by client group, found a quarter of newly referred and consecutively allocated clients were 'cases' (i.e. suffered a mental disorder), and over half were either definitely or borderline mentally ill. Corney (1984a) found two thirds of intake team clients were 'cases', while depending on the threshold, or cut off point between mental health and illness, Cohen and Fisher (1987) found either 35 per cent or 52 per cent of area team clients were 'cases'.

Despite variations in prevalence, these studies share a common finding that mental illness is a significant aspect of social services work, including that outside specific mental health work. However, social workers' capacity to identify mental health problems is limited. Although social workers have been found to do this in between half and two thirds of cases they showed no more than chance ability to diagnose correctly (Corney 1984a; Cohen and Fisher 1987; Huxley et al. 1987). Fisher et al. (1984) found that social workers' approach to mental health issues was largely pragmatic. They were suspicious of a 'medical' approach related to a concern about the deleterious effects of labelling. Huxley et al. (1989) concluded that it is important for social workers to understand the nature of mental disorder, and to be able, broadly, to recognise and account for it in their practice.

Despite these findings there has been little focus on parental mental ill health in child and family care. Where it has occurred it has been marginalised, and often relied on social workers' own assessment of its presence. Packman and colleagues (1986), for example, found 30 per cent of mothers whose children were considered for care were thought to suffer from some form of mental disorder. Gibbons et al. (1990), using the malaise inventory, which does not distinguish clinical disturbance, found over half of those referred to social services suffered some sort of malaise. Sharland et al. (1995), focusing specifically on alleged sex abuse, found high rates of mental illness, although theirs was a small sample.

The research on child protection procedures, to which we have already alluded, suggests the likelihood of high rates of mental health problems, without this being a major and consistent subject for attention. Indeed, the process of investigation itself at times had negative effects on mental health, where, as Thoburn et al. (1995, p. 55) put it, parents often experienced 'overwhelming feelings of fear and despair' (cf. Farmer and Owen 1995, p. 61–2). However, awareness of such issues was unlikely to be helped by the absence of clinical involvement. Doctors were the least likely profession to be represented at conference, with GPs being the least attendant of all (Gibbons et al. 1995, p. 69; cf. Birchall 1995; Farmer and Owen, 1995). Dingwall et al. (1983) highlighted the need for both social *and* clinical assessment, yet Farmer and Owen (1995) found the latter underrepresented, and certainly less than was the case when Dingwall et al. undertook their study.

There have been a few small scale studies of parents of children in care, using standardised instruments. Quinton and Rutter (1984) found that three times as many mothers whose children were receiving care for at least a second time had a current mental illness than a matched group of families who had never required care for their children. Most commonly, this was depression or anxiety, frequently associated with personality disorder. Isaac et al. (1986) found that, overall, half the mothers and a third of fathers were significant 'cases' using the General Health Questionnaire.

Research by Sheppard is the only work which has examined social work practice in child and family care teams, using standardised instruments. Studying both rural and urban areas, he found (Sheppard 1997 a and b; 1998) a prevalence rate specifically for depression of 36 per cent with minor and non–significant variations between rural and urban areas. This was about three times the rate of depression in a health visitor cohort over the same area focusing largely on mothers with at least one child aged under one year. He found also that, compared with non–depressed mothers, they were likely to suffer considerably more social and familial problems, and to have more intensive and long term intervention. Maternal depression was also significantly associated with child abuse. However, social workers showed a tendency not to recognise the presence of depression.

There is little detailed work directly on the conduct of social work practice with depressed women in general, and more specifically with depressed mothers, particularly in child and family care. That which exists, focusing on mental health specialists, suggests suitably skilled practitioners may make a difference. Cooper et al. (1975) and Shepherd et al. (1979), examining general practice attachments, found social work helped chronic neurotic clients significantly with both clinical and social adjustment scores. A more complex picture was found by Corney (1984b) in relation to depressed women. She found no overall difference was made with social work intervention. However, those with symptoms of more than three months' duration (acute on chronic), and with poor contacts and major difficulties with partners, benefited significantly from social work help. Sheppard (1991) focused on mental health centre users, primarily women suffering neurotic disorders, and found interpersonal skills to be critical to the experience of intervention. The ability to listen, to empathise, provide information and advice, and to help them release pent–up feelings were of considerable importance. With extended intervention, most clients felt social work helped at least prevent deterioration, and even avert suicide.

Moving forward

The disparate themes outlined indicate both that maternal depression is a factor in a significant proportion of those subject to child and family care intervention, and that there is little research on the matter. There are three broad limitations on existing research. First, even that investigating this particular issue was essentially only exploratory, providing no more than a few broad facets of intervention. Second, there has been little study of the nature of and rationale for social workers' practice strategies when conducting intervention. Third, there has been no focus on depressed mothers' experience and their perceptions of intervention.

These issues need to be placed within further important policy and practice questions which emerge from earlier comments. In particular there are key questions about the extent to which involvement with social services is itself a depression–inducing experience, the extent to which the women are able to engage positively in resolving their problems when weighed down by the psychological facets of their depression, the degree to which they are themselves able to engage in partnership, and the extent to which the support actions of the social workers enable the women themselves to feel supported. Beyond this are the general dimensions for social work practice, in particular the extent to which the effects of the authority role – with social work powers in relation to child protection – may have an impact on depressed mothers.

A central concern, therefore, is to examine in greater detail the practice strategies employed with social workers in relation to depressed mothers, and the mothers' experience of that intervention. More specifically, these may be resolved into the following issues:

❏ How far, and in what ways, did social workers identify maternal depression as a facet of familial, parenting and childcare problems?

❏ How did mothers experience their depression as a facet of their lives and as part of their familial problems?

❏ To what extent did social work intervention focus on the mother's own needs as an individual, rather than childcare problems and her needs as a parent?

❏ How far were social workers able to operate in partnership with the depressed mothers, and what factors influenced the quality of partnership?

❏ To what extent were mental health professionals involved with these depressed mothers, and how far was this involvement incorporated as part of the social workers' practice strategy?

❏ What was the depressed mothers' experience of intervention: in particular the quality of the relationship with the social worker; their helpfulness, and the relevance of intervention to their perceived needs; and the extent to which practice actions were perceived as supportive?

All these are issues which, on the basis of the themes we have examined, appear to be of some significance for social work practice with depressed mothers in child and family care. The next concern, then, is to outline the study and its methods.

3 Context, study and methods

Where we are concerned, as is the case here, to draw lessons from research which (a) have practical implications and (b) may be widely applied, it is important to understand the extent to which generalisations from the findings may be made. The issues of gaining access and study characteristics therefore become of considerable significance.

These two issues were closely related. Access to busy social services departments for research purposes is frequently not easy. There were, furthermore, no widespread statistics on a local authority basis on the subject of the study, maternal depression. It was not clear, therefore, what might constitute representative authorities. In the event the opportunity for access, (i.e. the agreement of a local authority to be involved in the research) became a major consideration. Permission was sought from a number of authorities who felt research would place too great a burden on their staff. Nevertheless, when seeking local authority involvement, certain key characteristics were identified as important. The researchers were concerned to have two authorities which were geographically separate, where routine day to day influences on each other would be minimised (through, for example, common local professional training programmes). A further criterion was that, in certain key characteristics (such as the division between adult and childcare services) the authorities were similar to most authorities in England and Wales. It was also important that one of the authorities should have a NEWPIN (New Parent Information Network), a voluntary facility specifically set up for depressed parents to provide them with support.

In the end, involvement of authorities fitting these criteria was gained, and the characteristics are described below. One of the authorities had a population which was predominantly white, while in the other, ethnic minorities constituted a major component of the local community. It is worth noting that both study areas were urban, although, as we shall see, rates of maternal depression, though higher, were similar to those of a rural area which was the subject of earlier study.

Study areas

The study was undertaken in two urban local authorities; one a London borough and the other a city in the South of England. Each had certain characteristics in common with most other social services departments, and were similar in many characteristics in their service delivery. Both were divided into, on the one hand, adult services, which included adult mental health social work, and, on the other, childcare services. As a result there was a degree of specialism by age, and to some extent, in a more detailed way, by client group, which was underwritten by the organisation of the departments. Both areas were also characterised by an organisational division between health service based psychiatric provision, and the local authority based childcare social services provision. A third characteristic common to both areas was the provision of childcare social work services which concentrated on the family unit, rather than more broadly based community development services. This did not mean such services were unavailable to either area, but that the bulk of social work services was undertaken through work with children and families, either through direct action by the social worker, or indirect resource, including human resource mobilisation.

Borough

Borough was a London local authority with a population of 231,000. It was a mix of affluent and middle class owner–occupied, often leafy residential areas, and areas of considerable deprivation, with overcrowded and often poor quality accommodation. Nearly half the households with dependent children were owner–occupied, a similar proportion were rented from the local authority or housing association, and the rest were privately rented. Lone parent households constituted over a quarter of all households with dependent children. The overwhelming majority of lone parents were women, two thirds of whom were without paid employment. The overall rate of unemployment was 14 per cent.

It was within commuting distance of central London, and most employed adults worked outside the borough. In view of the area and working patterns, it is unsurprising that, of those employed, the overwhelming majority (four fifths) worked in banking and service industries, while most of the rest were in manufacturing and construction. In terms of social class, using census definitions, two fifths of those working were professional/managerial, a similar proportion were skilled manual and non–manual and the rest were partly skilled or unskilled.

The population was ethnically mixed, with just under four fifths being white. The largest group within the substantial black population were Caribbean (10 per cent), African (4 per cent) and other (2.5 per cent), totalling one sixth of the population. Of other minority ethnic groups, Indian comprised just over 1 per cent and all other groups totalled 4.5 per cent of the population. Just over a quarter of households were families with dependent children, fairly evenly divided between those with one dependent child and those with two or more. Pre–school children comprised almost a third of all children.

Borough sought to develop all their services for children and families within a broad policy of need identification. They regarded the response of child and family care services to be part of more specialised services for those with deeper or more long term difficulties, compared with the more universal services for other families less in need. Although they had been influenced by care management as an idea – in particular in an emphasis on seeing the social worker frequently as a manager, rather than provider, of care – Borough had not instigated a rigid division between purchaser and provider services.

Borough had eight social work teams whose primary focus was on child protection. These were sited in four district offices, or 'service units'. This study was based on the work of two of these four service units. All the social workers in these teams considered themselves to be extremely busy, with far more referrals received than they could deal with. They felt that in recent years the rate of referrals had increased, and with this, the seriousness of the problems with which they had to deal. The service units were based within the areas which they served, designed to have easier access to service users than if they were centrally sited. Each team was managed by a service unit manager, as well as two senior social workers, together with a number of social workers under each of the seniors (average eight). Each team had access to a childcare co–ordinator whose role was to chair child protection conferences, provide advice to social work staff, raise standards, and monitor and audit cases.

Social workers felt, to varying degrees, that they had autonomy in the conduct of their cases. All recognised some scope for making their own decisions, and many felt that they were operating in partnership with their managers. A few felt, as part of a wider disillusionment with practice, that their actions were determined by managers to a greater extent than they would have liked. In some areas, there were clear procedures to be followed, such as child protection procedures, registration or accommodation. Where managerial control was not directly exerted, this was often because the social workers were themselves aware of managerial expectations, and their practice actions were informed by this knowledge.

Managers were able to exercise considerable influence over the conduct of practice. Some of this was overt. The teams studied in Borough operated a duty system, from which referrals given sufficient priority were allocated by the managers. Influence was exercised on a day to day basis through the discussions of practice actions, whether informally or formally through supervision. They very much saw their role as ensuring that the provisions of relevant legislation on children, in particular the protection of children, were properly implemented in the everyday practice of social workers. One manager in particular emphasised the importance, for quality assurance, that files were kept properly up to date. An example of managerial control was where cases were 'drifting', or where more purposive intervention was considered (by the manager) to be required.

Social workers took turns in taking the role of duty officer, where they received all the referrals. Most referrals were unallocated for longer term intervention, and those that were, following an assessment, were those regarded as most serious. Borough, at the time of research was in the process of developing eligibility criteria, through which it would be possible to allocate priority on a more consistent basis. At that time, however, such criteria were not in operation, so that allocation of scarce resources was based on individual decisions. Nevertheless, even without generally applicable eligibility criteria, referrals allocated for longer term intervention were those characterised by the most serious problems, informed by considerations of need, risk and protection of children.

Children with disabilities were the responsibility of a specialised team within the overall childcare service provision. Individual specialist social workers were sited within service units which provided the bases for other childcare social workers, and they covered the same geographical areas. This was deliberately consistent with the idea, enshrined in the Children Act, that a child with disabilities is, first and foremost, a child. Their responsibilities included registration of all children with disabilities, although, like other childcare social workers, their resources were limited, with priority based on assessment of need and risk.

Some importance, at the policy level, was attached to the interface between childcare and adult mental health services. The department had set up a policy sub-group focusing on child and family mental health. However, this was, at the time of the research, at a rather early stage of development. There was a specific commitment in the *Children Plan* of Borough, however, to focus on the interface between child protection and mental health services to ensure that their specialist mental health approach did not militate against the whole needs of the family. As things stood at the time of the research, there remained considerable organisational separation between specialist adult mental health services and childcare social service provision.

One of the more interesting elements in Borough was the presence of two NEWPIN (New Parent Information Network) facilities. This was a voluntary sector service whose specific focus was on childcare and parenting support (Cox et al. 1991; Cox 1993). NEWPIN worked with parents, or other main carers, suffering from depression or feelings of isolation, with the aim of keeping families together and supporting them through difficulties. Their stated purpose, largely through using volunteers (although they had paid co-ordinators), was to combine peer group support and counselling for parents. Although outside the mainstream of mental health provision, both facilities were part funded by Borough. The presence of NEWPIN, with its focused support for depressed mothers, provided one reason for carrying out research in Borough.

City

City was a local authority with a population of comparable size to that of Borough, containing just under a quarter of a million people. It was, at the time of the research, part of a large, predominantly rural local authority with a population of over a million. Soon after the completion of research City became a unitary authority. City was one of the larger urban areas in England, but was some distance from other urban areas. It had a population covering a spectrum from some of the most deprived areas in Britain, to areas of considerable affluence. A significant feature was its association with the armed services, which was still strong although less than it had been in the past. City provided a major centre of employment for those in a large rural hinterland, as well as urban residents.

City was composed of an overwhelmingly white population (over 99 per cent of total), in this respect differing most markedly from Borough. The rate of unemployment was similar to that of Borough, at 13 per cent. Far fewer (36 per cent) of the working population, when compared with Borough, were employed in the service industries of banking, transport, distribution and catering. A high proportion – nearly two fifths – were involved with other service and tourist industries, while just over a fifth were employed in manufacturing and construction. A quarter of those employed were professional or managerial, two fifths were in skilled (manual or non-manual) occupations, and marginally over a fifth were in unskilled or partly skilled occupations. Nearly one in ten were in the armed forces.

Nearly two thirds of households with dependent children were owner-occupied, a rather higher proportion of total than that of Borough. Nearly four fifths possessed at least one car, a little more than Borough. Just over two fifths of these households had one dependent child, the rest having two or more. Compared with Borough, proportionately fewer – 14 per cent – of households with children had single parents. Like Borough, however, the overwhelming majority (over 90 per cent) of lone parents were women, nearly two thirds of whom were not in paid employment.

City's childcare policies and practices were profoundly influenced by two factors: a commitment to care management of a sort which entailed a strong purchaser–provider division, and the significance of child protection. There had been some concern about the former. Some of City's managers and workers had found the emphasis on the systematic process of assessment, planning, review and evaluation of practice to have been positive developments. However, there had been concerns that it had been 'de-skilling' , and it had become harder to provide families with the direct services which children and families needed, in view of the 'red tape' involved in the system, and a concentration of 'provider' (direct work) skills amongst social workers on the 'purchasing' side. A rigid distinction had, by the time of the research, proven impossible to implement, with much direct work with children carried out by social workers themselves. When City achieved unitary status soon after, the commitment to a purchaser–provider division had been abandoned. In practical terms, therefore, expectations of a mix between direct work by the social worker and indirect work through other resources were similar to that of Borough.

The issue of child protection related to the obvious statutory responsibilities of the local authority, finite resources, and the increased barrage of referrals which had occurred in recent years. City managers tended to place practice, including family support, within the realm of child protection, rather than child protection within the framework of family support. However, the strong commitment felt to supporting families meant that, like Borough, one of the teams in City was able to point to a reduction almost by half of the number of children on the child protection register in recent years. Managers expressed a desire to reduce the extent of child protection procedures where they were not absolutely necessary, because of concerns about their perceived deleterious effects.

At the time of the research, City had seven teams, which were not of equal size. The study was carried out with two of these, covering a large area of City, and about one third of its population. Like Borough, these teams were sited in their area, enabling easier access for potential service users. Each team had one team manager, with overall responsibility for the team, and two practice supervisors, whose role was to supervise and advise social workers, as well as allocate referrals as appropriate for further assessment and longer term intervention as appropriate. They in turn were responsible to a district manager. One team had twelve full or part time social workers and the other had thirteen. All the teams operated a duty system, rather like Borough, in which social workers took turns on the duty rota. While case allocation was undertaken by the practice supervisor, this was done in consultation with duty workers.

Unlike Borough, City had a well developed set of eligibility (for service) criteria, in the light of which allocation was made. This was a means of rationing scarce resources on the basis of risk and need, and an attempt to develop consistency in the allocation of priority. Cases were divided into four categories: category A was danger of physical/emotional harm, likely to result in serious injury, abuse or death; category B was danger of family break–up, or leaving chosen environment; category C was where intervention would enhance the quality of life; and category D was where families would benefit from intervention, but nonetheless could maintain an acceptable quality of life. In general, only category A cases were allocated for longer term intervention.

Like Borough, there was a strong sense that social worker autonomy was circumscribed by managerial influence and the limits to resources meant that opportunities for preventive work by social workers were practically non–existent. The focus of work was therefore on individual children and their families. Unlike Borough, there was no separate team for dealing with children with disabilities, although within each team were social workers who specialised in this area. The practical effects, given the integration of similar social workers with child and family teams in Borough, were that the two authorities were, on the whole, similar in their approach to children with disabilities.

While Borough had plans for greater integration of childcare and mental health services in future, City had no such plans at the time of research. The two services were quite separate, and managerial expectations of collaboration with mental health services were quite low. There was one open access mental health centre in the city centre, which, however, largely took referrals from individuals or others in their informal social network. Some social workers and managers, in any case, felt that mental health problems were closely related to disadvantage, and advocated (without carrying this out) community based approaches, including anti–poverty strategies.

Conduct of the study

The focus of the research, detailed earlier, can be presented in terms of two general themes: (a) what were the key characteristics of social work practice, and how did the social workers account for their actions? and (b) how did women experience this intervention – what did it feel like to be on the receiving end? From these two general themes it was hoped to be able to draw conclusions of significance for practice. These themes required the collection of data from both the social workers and the depressed mothers. However, having identified the study settings it was necessary also to identify the study cohort – that is, the depressed women.

This was a two stage study. The first was a 'screening survey' in order to identify depressed mothers. From these caseload cases the initial aim was to obtain a sample of about 80 families where the mother was depressed. However, as is evident below, close to 100 were eventually identified. The families were ordered randomly, through the use of random numbers, and initially contacted by the social services department to gain their agreement to be interviewed. If they refused, the next woman on the list was contacted, and this went on until the requisite sized sample had been obtained. Where the women agreed, they were subsequently contacted by the researcher who arranged an interview. Where the woman was found to be depressed at the first screening interview, a second, 'follow–up' interview was arranged to explore in more detail the woman's experience of intervention. A more detailed follow–up interview was also carried out with the social worker of these depressed women. Women were offered £10 for involvement in each of these interviews. It was stressed throughout that the interviews were confidential and that the research was carried out independently of the social services department.

Slightly under three fifths of the women contacted agreed to be interviewed at the first stage, and there was a further slippage with both social workers and mothers in the second phase interviews, as a result of which the following interviews were undertaken (Table 3.1):

Table 3.1 Interviews conducted with depressed women

First phase	women contacted	378
	women interviewed	223
	social workers' 'case' interviewed	223
Second phase	women interviewed	87
	social workers' 'case' interviewed	95

The first stage interviews involved the use of structured questionnaires. Women were screened for depression using the Beck Depression Inventory (BDI), which distinguishes between depression whose severity may be regarded as 'clinical' and 'non–clinical'. The BDI does not yield a discrete diagnosis, but rather measures depression as a dimension of psychopathology that cuts across diagnostic categories (Beck et al. 1988). The interest, in this research, in partnership with social services in general, and social workers in particular, initially involved the use of the Quality of Partnership Instrument for Mothers (QOPI(m)), which measures partnership across a number of dimensions: partnership morale, participation in decision making, involvement in decision implementation, receipt of information, consultation and degree of conflict. The third instrument used was the Parent Concerns Questionnaire through which women's perceptions of their problem were measured across five areas: social, adult relationship, adult health, parenting and child problems (Sheppard 2000).

Table 3.2 Rates of depression in six districts

	Borough		City		Sheppard 1997a (County)		Total
District	A	B	C	D	E	F	
Total cohort	73	45	52	53	66	50	339
% Depressed	43	44	44	42	38	34	41

Table 3.2 shows the rates of depression identified in the screening interviews in the four teams studied and in two teams which were the subject of earlier studies. Overall, slightly more than two fifths of these mothers suffered clinical depression, involving a significant proportion of all families on child and family care caseloads, and a very high rate of depression indeed. The remarkably similar rates of depression in City and Borough, although slightly more than in the previous study, are nevertheless broadly consistent with the high rates recorded in the earlier study. District F was a rural area.

Seventeen of the mothers in the cohort were black Africans and/or Caribbeans (18 per cent), two were Asian (2 per cent) and five (5 per cent) were from other racial groups. Many of the depressed women were lone parents: 52 families (54 per cent) had single mothers, and a further 29 families (30 per cent) were reconstituted.

Nearly three quarters of the 93 depressed mothers whose benefit status was known (67) were in families reliant on benefits alone. Compared with the City and Borough population as a whole, therefore, this was a group containing more ethnic minorities, more single parents and far more deprivation, as measured by receipt of benefits. Only a small proportion of families had both birth parents.

Follow-up interviews were undertaken with 87 of the 97 women identified as depressed. Those who did not take part either refused (two women), were uncontactable (four women), were too depressed to take part, or in hospital (three women), and one was dying. The interviews were largely semi-structured and designed to allow exploration of a range of issues around key themes identified in the research, and which were developed by the women in interview. The concerns in this research were with the women's perceptions in several broad areas: the importance of depression in the generation and maintenance of familial, parenting and child problems; the relevance of intervention to their own perceived needs (as opposed to those of their children); the relevance of the quality of partnership; and the quality of the relationship with, and helpfulness of, the social worker.

While an interest in policy- and practice-driven concerns represented one facet of this study, it was also important to develop issues on the basis of the women's own accounts. Obviously, such interviews were inevitably interactive, and without this the 'rules' of conversation would have been broken, rendering the interviews strange experiences for the women. Two methods employed through the women's accounts could be used as 'sources in themselves' for identifying issues: summarising information already provided in order to reflect back and check our understanding of the women's accounts, and building on issues which emerged from the interviews through further exploration of these issues. In addition to the semi-structured, more exploratory, interviews, the Arizona Social Support Interview Schedule (ASSIS) was used (Barrera 1981, 1985), an instrument designed specifically to measure social support for women with children. Its use provides information on types and source of support, the degree to which women were socially isolated, and the extent to which they were in conflict with members of their social network.

Social workers also went through a two phase process. The study aimed for social workers to be interviewed within a week of carrying out the screening interview with the mother. However, it transpired that it was only possible, on the whole, to interview them within two weeks of the mother's screening interview, with a small proportion taking up to three weeks. The focus was particularly on their views of the women's problems and the quality of partnership. The former was achieved using the Social Assessment Schedule for depression ((de)SAS), an instrument similar to the PCQ, but designed for use by social workers (Sheppard 1999). The latter involved the use of the social workers' Quality of Partnership Instrument (QOPI (SW)), an instrument structured in the same way as QOPI(m), but with questions directed at the social worker rather than the mother. These data were collected for all 223 women interviewed at the first stage.

A follow-up interview was undertaken with the social worker of families of the mothers identified as depressed. The gap between second stage mother interview, and second stage social worker interview was similar to that of the first stage. Of the 97 depressed women, social worker interviews were completed in relation to 95. However, in one of these cases the social worker had not met the mother, and the information gained was limited. In two other cases, the social worker had left before the interview could take place. The interviews with the social workers were, like those of the mothers, semi-structured. They followed the same principles as those with the mothers and we sought to explore with them the nature of the family's (in particular the woman's) problems; the rationale behind their practice strategy, including in these the main reasons for social services involvement with the family; the ways they sought to relate to the mother; and the extent to which they sought to draw on mothers' opinions in developing their practice strategies.

The approach

One of the underlying elements in the approach to this study was a methodological commitment to triangulation. This is based on the straightforward idea that coming at a problem from a number of different angles is liable to provide a more accurate representation, or closer approximation, to what is actually being studied, than employing only one method (Denzin 1978; Brewer and Hunter 1988). The use of different methods, in other words, enables the cross-validation of the data collected. The processes described show the study was triangulated in two ways: first, by the use of a combination of both qualitative and quantitative methods, and second through the use of different sources of information, from both the social workers and the depressed mothers.

Thus, for example, one of the strengths of the use of qualitative data derived from interviews is that it allows exploration, enabling us to gather rich data through which the subjects' understanding of their situations and interactions could emerge (Burgess 1993). This was important, as we shall see, for example, with the mental health attributions of social workers, and the concepts of exclusion and entrapment which emerge from some of the mothers' accounts. However, various scholars have suggested that some kind of counting, even if relatively simple, should occur with qualitative data, in order to gain some kind of idea of the magnitude of significance which can be ascribed to particular findings (Miles and Huberman 1994; Silverman 1985; Layder 1993). This is essential when carrying out evaluative studies of this sort, which have considerable potential practical importance. The use of quantitative data, alongside qualitative data, facilitated still further our capacity to understand the magnitude of the issues which emerged, as well as providing information in its own right.

We intended, however, to triangulate still further, through the use of documents, and specifically by use of the most recent case reviews. This was because we were concerned to balance the retrospective accounts of social workers, gained through interviews, with data gained from reports written specifically for practice purposes during the conduct of intervention. This opportunity for checking the validity of social workers' accounts was denied us, however, for revealing reasons. A large proportion of reviews, and all those in Borough, used the 'Looking After Children' instrument, developed specifically for reviews of looked after children, which focused entirely on the children and their needs (Parker et al. 1991). These were also used as guides for reviews of many of the children who were not looked after. This instrument, widely used by local authorities, precluded the possibility of gaining information in an area of considerable interest to us: social workers' thinking specifically about the mother. The lack of attention to the mother provided both an interesting form of triangulation on the later findings related to social workers' focus on the mother, and, in view of the instrument's widespread use, findings which are likely to have general implications.

There are, however, limits to triangulation, and this is particularly evident when working with interviews with social workers and clients in child and family care. The very nature of practice in this area, where social workers are involved in actions which women may see as extremely threatening (such as those relating to child protection), or where they have different expectations of childcare, or feel defensive about their parenting, can have a tendency to generate conflict. The result can be that social workers' and women's perceptions about practice actions and interactions may diverge considerably. For example, actions which social workers consider vital to child protection (and hence legitimate), such as the removal of a sex abusing partner from the home, might, for some women, be regarded as unjustifiable, particularly if they are inclined not to believe the partner is, in fact, an abuser.

Under these circumstances, it is legitimate to seek to understand the intentions and purposes underlying social workers' actions, and the ways in which women experienced those actions. Both are of considerable importance in themselves. It may be, for example, that actions which social workers sought to undertake in a sensitive way were, for various reasons, not experienced sensitively, and the outcome was less positive than intended. In such circumstances, one could seek to explain these differences in terms of factors which may have led to outcomes other than those intended. One of the key issues confronted in this research relates to factors which would or would not enable women to engage positively in the process of intervention. It is through understanding the differences between social workers and mothers that we can begin to understand those factors which enable or inhibit such involvement.

It is, therefore, not a simple matter that the researcher should always seek to validate information gained from one source by finding confirmatory information from another. If it were, this would confer upon the study too simplistic a process. Differences in perspective can be revealing, but a theoretical sensitivity is required to enable us to make sense of these differences (Hammersley and Atkinson

1995). Layder (1993) is helpful in this respect, distinguishing between different levels of social analysis. In his terms, this study was primarily concerned with 'self' and 'situated activity'. Where the self is the focus, it involves the intersection between biographical experiences and social involvement. In 'situated activity', the emphasis shifts away from the individual towards the emergent dynamic of social interaction. 'Setting' denotes a research focus on the intermediate forms of social organisation, such as social services, which provide the immediate context for social activity.

The accounts of the social workers and mothers can only fully make sense where the social service setting for interaction is taken into account. Much of the practice examined here, for example, involved child protection. At times these mothers were 'captive clients', that is women who would rather not be involved with social services, but who have little alternative. In a situation replete with potential for conflict, there is ample opportunity for strongly differing views, and high levels of criticism by mothers about social workers (and vice versa).

While, therefore, it is clearly essential to take notice of the women's and social workers' accounts, a deeper understanding is achieved by placing them within the higher order of a contextual understanding of 'setting'. This derives from the position of social worker as state functionary, which defines, to a considerable degree, the nature and meaning of social workers' tasks, and their interaction with the women. The child protection function, most obviously, helps us to understand better the conflict which may emerge between social workers and the mothers. Of course, this may well not explain all conflict (why, for example might some social workers and mothers work well together while others do not?). Nevertheless, it provides the vital context in which it is possible to begin to understand some of the issues this study is concerned with. While its focus and data operate largely at the level of situated activity – in seeking to understand the accounts of mothers and social workers – they will be contextualised where appropriate, by reference to expectations generated by the setting for this particular situated activity. Such expectations can include, for example, the prevailing model of social work practice (such as an emphasis on care management), or the systematic ways in which practice differs according to the category of case (for example, differences between families with disabled children and child protection cases).

There were other factors which bore upon the issue of research validity. One of the advantages of conducting 'retrospective' research (i.e. obtaining accounts from social workers of their practice, and the women of their experiences of the practice), was that this helped them to impose a coherent impression of the intervention and its rationale. The retrospective nature of the research could also allow them to provide a *post hoc* interpretation of their actions which did not provide the rationale for their actions at the time. This does not have to be done in bad faith, merely that understandings would change over time. One particular concern was with a possible 'Hawthorne effect'. This is where the conduct of the research itself has an impact on the findings. In this case, detailed interviews with social workers only occurred in relation to women found to be depressed, and an important fear was that social workers would, *ex post facto*, seek to explain their own actions in the light of that knowledge of the woman's depression. This was a particular risk in the absence of documentation of reviews. However, reflecting on the interviews, social workers seemed to strive to be honest in their accounts of their practice actions. In particular, they frequently did not consider the woman to be clinically depressed, or considered the depression to be, at most, of marginal significance to their conduct of the case. It would appear, therefore, that knowledge of the woman's depression did not exert a major impact on the social workers' accounts.

The presence of depression, furthermore, invokes particular issues for the women's accounts, which Brown and Harris (1978) call the 'search after meaning'. This refers to cognitive processes in which the women seek, also *ex post facto*, to make sense of their depression. Here, events which might not have any specific relationship to their depression, could be mentally organised retrospectively in such a way that helped the woman account for her depression. This could have exercised an impact on the research. However, the study was not seeking to identify causal factors in the manner of Brown and Harris, although it did seek to contextualise the depression. Furthermore, although depression was ever present in this cohort, it was not the single overwhelming factor in most cases, which, in general, were characterised by multiple problems.

Need

Even where there is no explicit reference to need, it provides an underlying concept, or overarching term, depending on your perspective, which organises much of the current thinking about intervention. One of the concerns of this research relates specifically to need: the extent to which social workers focused on the mother's own needs, as opposed to her needs as parent, but the general concern with needs pervades much of the analysis. Need, then, is an implicit notion underlying much of this research.

However, the issue of need is not here regarded as one that may be usefully separated from the range of issues which are the subject of this study. This reflects the position taken, that it emerges from the various elements of analysis of women's problems and social work responses. In taking this view, there is a commitment to the notion of a differentiated concept of need, outlined in some detail by Sheppard and Woodcock (1999). They argue that there are two notions of need as an operational concept, one a deficit model, and the other, which they develop, a differentiated model. The deficit model entails the idea of falling below some expected, universal standard. This is one which has been common in the social work literature, with statements that an individual is 'in need', or that social services should respond to need (Shaw et al. 1991; Dartington 1995).

Sheppard and Woodcock suggest this causes considerable problems. For example, some have created 'need areas', which include, say, sex or other forms of abuse (Shaw et al. 1991). Children, however, hardly 'need' sex or any other abuse, which are more appropriately defined as problems. Likewise it is odd, linguistically, to think of 'responding to need'. If George needs radiotherapy for his cancer, the 'need' (radiotherapy), is itself a response to a problem (cancer). Sheppard and Woodcock refer to the idea of 'problem based needs'. They suggest a better understanding of need is as a differentiated concept involving three constituent 'sub-concepts', of problems, support and resources. Thus, for example, we may argue that Janet suffers depression (the problem), for which counselling may be provided (a form of support), by a psychotherapist (resources).

These distinctions underlie the approach in this book. Thus, the focus in the first instance is on problems (on which needs are based), with a subsequent examination of the types of support required, and the manner in which this is, or is not, provided. This approach provides a way in which it is possible to organise the data coherently. Hence it is useful for pragmatic reasons, but it is also consistent with the conceptualisation of need.

Part two
Depression

2

4 Depression: the women's experiences

Gaining some idea of the lived experience of depression as the women themselves understood it provides an obvious starting point for a study where depression provides its central theme. The women, to be sure, did not always ascribe a central place to depression in their accounts. Indeed, depression might be understood as a perfectly reasonable response to difficult circumstances in a group characterised to a large degree by social deprivation. Nevertheless, where the women felt sufficiently depressed, the possibility of their finding it more difficult to sustain relationships, for example, or carry out their ordinary daily activities, is clear. Indeed, their depression could take over as their primary focus, making it difficult to concentrate on everyday activities which might otherwise have been straightforward.

In this chapter we will focus on facets of the ways women experienced their depression: in particular as an aspect of important relationships in childhood and adolescence, their current relationships, and those involving their children. We were particularly interested in the ways the women themselves associated these relationships with their depression. We will begin, however, with the ways the women understood their depression.

Women's reflexive awareness of depression

Not all the women identified themselves as being depressed, but an overwhelming majority considered they had some kind of severe emotional problem. Marginally under four fifths of the women (69/87) considered themselves to be depressed. A further eighth (11/87) considered themselves to be anxious or distressed, but not severely enough to be depressed. This depression recognition was more widespread among the women, as we shall see, than social workers. The presence of depression for some mothers was in some respects the overwhelming and routine experience of their everyday life. In some cases, their depression was chronic and did not easily respond to treatment, as with one mother for whom pharmacological intervention had little impact. Although she was able to present a 'face' to the outside world, which served to mask her depression, there was no easy way out:

> I find it weird that I am taking anti-depressants, and I am still depressed, and I don't find it weird. I think what the doctors don't get is that being depressed is a natural state of mind for me. They try and heighten my mood — it just brings me to another level of depression. And even the days I smile and laugh, and behave as if the world is alright, I am actually still depressed.

For many, depression was a 'normal' feeling, so understandable that it did not occur to them to think of it as a psychological or psychiatric state. Their social and personal circumstances were so deprived and entrapped that not to feel some emotional response would be odd. Hence the rather odd, reflexive statement by the woman that 'I find it weird that I am taking anti-depressants, and I am still depressed, and I don't find it weird'. One woman appreciated the chronicity of her depression only when it got worse:

> I wasn't depressed, then within the last six months I've been depressed. It's probably a bit more than that. I probably would say that I've been depressed the whole way along. It hasn't really surfaced until the last, say, year.

For other women, although their experience of depression was long term and chronic, it nevertheless peaked periodically. The concern about depression, where it was periodic, could develop into a semi-constant apprehensiveness about its recurrence, which affected the woman even during relatively 'good' times. One woman commented that 'generally, I feel that there is an underlying risk that things can get very bad, very quickly. I live with depression, but I don't actually feel it that often'. Another attributed her problems, including those which led to social services involvement, to her depression, which thus had an overwhelming impact on her life:

> My problem is basically with my depression. I am a very, very depressed person. I could have a few months lovely. You wouldn't think that I am depressed, that I have any problems. And then bang, it hits me. Especially when I am due on. It hits me like a ton of bricks. I am crying. I can't stop.

One woman expressed very clearly the withdrawal that lay at the heart of many of these women's experience of depression. This woman was caring twenty four hours a day for a disabled child and she just 'snapped'. She presented a graphic description of the extent to which depression dominated her life.

> I do not have boundless energy, and I just could not get out of bed. I was so tired. I didn't feel like I had anything left to live for, like there was no life left in me. I needed a break.... It is withdrawing from everything. Yes, I stopped eating for about two months, and I got really ill...and basically, what I was going to do...was to go into hospital. But I am not prepared to take an overdose or cut myself.... So I thought the only way I could do that, was to stop eating and collapse, and end up in a hospital on a drip. That was going to be my holiday.... You kind of go brain dead.

For others, however, the suicidal thoughts — and sometimes intent — were very real: 'I could be suicidal for months' and 'I wanted to kill myself — I could go into the cupboard, I have got a packet of painkillers'.

Some women were aware of the extent to which depression could alter their perceptions, something evident in earlier quotes. The degree of self awareness, which was by no means universal, added a further dimension to women's reflexive awareness of themselves as depressed. This could take the form of magnifying trivial matters quite out of proportion to their importance, or finding them quite impossible to cope with:

> I think that perhaps I have emotional problems that are kind of extra....
> Well, I suffer from depression a lot, you know...yes a hell of a lot. So things
> that might be quite trivial are quite difficult to me — I think he [partner] is
> sometimes at a loss.

At their most extreme, distortions, by some women's admission, could take the form of paranoia. One woman, referring to her experience of negative cognitions characteristic of depression, explicitly recognised these exaggerated distortions. 'I suppose it made me paranoid, maybe I am just imagining things, or something. I have not been very on line. You imagine all sorts of things when you are depressed.' This could, for some, become overwhelming, as with one woman, who wished she could just be 'swallowed up'.

> I can't think of the word. I suppose I mean, depressed all the time. People
> think I can't cope, though I do manage to get through it all. I find every-
> thing a struggle, the whole shebang. I hate the world. I hate — if I had my
> way it would be just me in a hole with a lid on it.

The descriptions these women gave indicate the extent to which, in principle, depression could impact on them. They describe feelings of guilt, self-blame, of hating the world, of lethargy, even difficulty getting out of bed, distorted and negative perceptions, of finding everything a struggle, and even suicidal ideas. These, we shall see, were associated with extreme social problems and disadvantage. It is, perhaps, unsurprising that such undermining cognitions were associated with those problems. However, things, at times, went further back than that.

Past experiences

The experience of abuse during their own childhood and adolescence was described by over half (51) these mothers and their social workers. The definition of abuse is, in some respects, problematic, and it has been claimed that it is a social construction, with variations in different times and places (Department of Health

1995b; Gibbons at al. 1995). However, careful studies have shown the reality of the impact of abuse, including, in particular, its long term implications for depression (Lynch and Roberts 1982; Bifulco and Moran 1998). We cannot, therefore (and social workers do not), dismiss abuse as something simply socially defined and relative to the particular values predominant in a society.

Regardless of this, however, there is the problem, on a case by case basis, of consistently identifying where abuse has taken place. The women themselves were often aware that they had been abused as children, and their accounts make plausible these claims, as we shall see. We were nonetheless guided by the work of Bifulco and Moran (1998) who have provided clear definitions of each of the various types of abuse. Where the women's accounts corresponded with what Bifulco and Moran (1998) have termed 'moderate' or 'marked' abuse, these situations were defined as involving past abuse. This is consistent with the definitions and data in their study, where they found highly significant relationships between past abuse of a moderate or marked degree, and adult depression in women.

These experiences seem to have been highly significant for them, in that many were recalled with great vividness, and were at times accompanied by distress when talking about them during interview. On the other hand, some of these experiences, which could be quite horrific, were described in a matter of fact manner. The women sometimes directly connected these experiences with their own feelings and actions as adults. However, even where such connections were not directly made, it is difficult to believe that they had no impact on their adult life, even where they suggested that they had worked through their feelings. As Bifulco and Moran (1998) note, these can diminish or eliminate the kinds of psychological robustness which enables women to deal with challenges brought by their lives.

Some women expressed the way in which they had been systematically undermined by childhood abuse, which had a profound impact on their adult lives. One woman expressed it as follows:

> I used to cut my wrists when I was younger.... I didn't feel I had any purpose in life...I would hurt myself, like stopping eating. It is one of my behaviour cycles, but I put that down to the abuse I had when I was a child as well. I have had eating problems for a long time now. I am not bulimic, but I get, I do start getting anorexic, and I am a bit like a skeleton now. I have lost 7 pounds in ten days.... I think it is my anger with myself. I think I am punishing myself. I don't like myself very much at the moment...because I have allowed things to happen in my life which shouldn't have. That I have put myself in a [violent] relationship which I knew was going nowhere.

This was not merely a description of the woman in adulthood, but an expression, as she saw it, of the effects of the abuse she experienced in childhood and adolescence. This woman was able to recognise her own anger which underlay her anorexia, and the importance of having control of her life. Her relationship with herself had been profoundly and negatively affected by past abuse, and this was affecting all parts of her life.

Women could also recognise a link between their own past abuse and their current negative behaviour. Their experiences had a brutalising effect which in turn could make them brutal to others. One woman admitted to brooding at times over her childhood experiences and that this could generate a fearful anger, which could present a danger to her children:

> Sometimes I get really down, thinking about what happened to me. I know what happens, 'cos I get angry and short tempered. I know I shouldn't do it, but it's hard. One minute I'm not talking to anyone, the next I can really lose it. Once or twice I've really hit [son], and it's not his fault — he's not really done much.

This woman was able to recognise her own responsibility in her violent behaviour, connecting it with past abuse, although according to the social workers, this was not always the case, as we shall see. However, others were even more proactive in their response. They felt that their own experiences of childhood abuse had made them more determined than ever to prevent the same abuse occurring to their own children. One woman, involved with social services because of her daughter's disability, commented that 'I can't honestly remember the last time I smacked her across the legs, it's such a long time ago. Whether it's right or wrong my part, I don't know. Because I went through, the hidings that I took'. This woman, it should be noted, was in a position of considerable adversity, with constant demands of care placed on her as a result of her child's disability.

Women described experiences of all kinds of abuse. Their own childhood emotional abuse could at times have a mundane or routine feel about it. What this, and other more graphic emotional abuse had in common was that its profoundly undermining nature arose from the creation of feelings of rejection and low self-esteem. In general, this occurred within the family (although some had themselves experienced care), leaving the women feeling profoundly excluded within the family. It could include statements which were persistently critical, while failing to praise when (as children) the mothers achieved anything. They could also involve zealous and over-strict behaviour which showed little understanding of the child. The preferment of brothers or sisters could be painful, as in this example of a fostered child.

> Because I was always told that I wasn't wanted and felt left out. I was compared to my sister, and I was always put down, so I have never felt any confidence...from about nine years old I was told. I used to sit and wait for my mum to come and get me — she never came. She was supposed to come back and get me in six weeks. I didn't know nothing, but when I was told that she, I was just sitting there waiting.

This rather poignant picture of a child waiting shows the impact of the double rejection she experienced at the hands of both the foster parents and mother. Some women were able quite graphically to recount incidents which left serious emotional scars. One woman, who described abuse within her family over many years, highlighted it though her experience, as a child, of virtual imprisonment. This she found to be a terrifying experience, precipitated by an argument over a boyfriend. This traumatic experience was vividly recalled:

> Put it this way, he locked me in the cellar. I can't remember how old I was. He locked me in the cellar for 24 hours. He didn't let me out till the next day...[it was an] old cellar. And it was really dark in there. Lots of rats and mice running around and all. He locked me in there and that's the kind of person he is. I was screaming in there. I was banging on the door, asking to let me out, and he wouldn't. Mum went along with it. Didn't say anything. I was probably 12 or 13, and it was an argument.... He didn't like this lad calling for me.

Many women recounted incidents as children which would undoubtedly have been classed as physical abuse had they been brought to social services' attention, including quite severe beatings on a regular basis. One woman spoke of the way she was hit even when she was very young, and the way her mother was 'off with us all'. Another described the loveless and violent home in which she was brought up, and she felt this restricted what she had subsequently been able, emotionally, to give her own children.

> My children...I can't, most of the time, give them anything.... I think it goes all the way back to when I was a child. My own experiences of family life. My parents outwardly had a beautiful home. But there wasn't any love in the home. My father. I was frightened of my father. He was quite violent. He would beat us with a belt for the slightest reason. And he used to beat up my mother. You would never know...if she had a black eye she would say she went into a door.

Physical abuse was not simply about violent behaviour but could also include cigarette burns, as in the following case.

> I feel isolated and I have got my depression back again.... I have only just started talking to my dad again, and I am angry with my mum for my childhood...I was burned by my mum when I was six ... they took me into care. ...she got me back. Then when I was in my teenage years I remember I was not allowed to have boyfriends or anything. I can't remember ever having a happy childhood or anything. I could not go out. She used to make us do paper rounds. I would only get £7.50 for a paper round and she would want a fiver for my keep. Stuff like that.

This woman recalled her early life in terms of serious changes and mundane abuse building on the physical abuse which precipitated her initial reception into care. Interestingly, she explicitly related her current depression to her early life experiences, and she was not the only woman to do this.

Sexual abuse was recounted by various women, often of persistent and extreme severity, and at times alongside other forms of abuse such as beatings or social isolation. This could stretch into their adult lives, with the sex abuse they experienced as children being 'reprised' in the form of rape and violence. The effect could be devastating:

> My dad used to abuse me by asking me if I still loved him, and if I wanted to sit on his lap. If I wanted money for sweets I gave him a kiss.... But his hands used to wander everywhere, on my top and on my bottom, all over, my legs and in between my legs and that...it started when I was about five or six...it would still carry on if he had a chance.

This abuse could have, as with this example, a permanent effect, inducing longer term trauma, rather than some relatively transient event. Such was the case with the following woman, who had not begun to come to terms with the appalling and persistent abuse that she suffered as a child, and a reconstituted familial context which made her drinking quite understandable (she was considered by social services to be an alcoholic). She reflected bitterly on her involvement with social services:

> I mean, abuse your children? to be with social services? I have been raped when I was 18. Sexual abuse as a child [by] my next door neighbour. I can't face any more [breakdowns]. The [social workers] didn't know.... My mum used to be afraid to hit me when [dad] was around. One time she hit me and I went into a convulsion. She didn't hit me after that. Drinking...was in the family. My stepdad was a drinker, [brother] was a drinker, [sister] is a drinker. I am a drinker.

Others also described the most horrific abuses which accompanied sexual abuse, including persistent 'hidings', being beaten with belts and broomsticks, and even by red hot pokers.

Many of these women experienced multiple abuses, with, for example, physical and emotional abuse at the same time. Some were clearly aware of the effect of this abuse on their adult life and current behaviours. Women described themselves as feeling 'very, very insecure', unable to relate properly to families and friends, or to carry out their parenting role as they would have liked. One woman explained how her childhood experiences had a direct and inhibiting effect on her as a parent, including a general lack of closeness to her children as well as specific functional abilities:

> I suffered sexual abuse at the hands of four people in my life, two of them relatives. And trying to deal with that, and an abortion, as a result of rape, has been very hard...it's still in my life now.... That's why my partner and I split up, because I was taking half of it out on him. I didn't even know I was doing it...and that is part of the reason I am not so close to my children...I got to the point where I could bath them. I couldn't put cream on them when they had nappy rash...can't cuddle them, the children.

Another woman described being beaten regularly, and a kind of psychological terrorism by her own mother who sought to frighten her when she was young by taking out light bulbs and 'making scary faces'. She was also sexually abused by both her mother and her father. She ran away from home when she was a teenager, unable to take the abuse any longer:

> I escaped when I was 14, and I walked the streets for many months. Lived on the streets, begged, borrowed and stole. Basically…it wasn't my fault. It was 'survival of the fittest'. I was on the streets, I would say, for about two years…. I [became] very hard and aggressive. No-one could speak to me. I didn't want to know.

Cumulatively these experiences, on the woman's own admission, had made her much harder and aggressive, qualities which were still present when she was interviewed. Although the woman saw herself as something of a survivor, she nevertheless proclaimed herself as being 'very angry and bitter'. She also had strong feelings of being punished and, of course, was prone to depression.

Effects of depression

Not all women considered their depression related to effects on the conduct of their lives. Where they did, however, the effects were, over the whole group, wide ranging. At the heart of this was a sense of meaninglessness in pursuing the kind of things which might otherwise seem important, even if routine. One key element was their inability to carry on with their lives. Management of the home could be a casualty:

> Awful. I didn't even want to get out some days. You know, I just couldn't be bothered with anything. I couldn't be bothered with tidying up, and that's not like me at all. I'm a bit of a housework freak really…. I let the children play, don't get me wrong, they do make a mess, but…wait for them to go to bed and then re-tidy again. But I just couldn't be bothered to do that.

Everyday activities like shopping could also prove problematic, when the mother was preoccupied by familial worries.

> I'm standing at the cross and I sometimes think, why the hell am I so forgetful — supposed to put this thing in the bag before I left, or my bill. Oh, I got to run back now, and I'm standing there, and the light would be changing for me to cross the road, and I stand there [the lights change]…and I nearly get knocked down by that, you know.

The same could happen to paid work, although few women had jobs: 'I just couldn't face work. I didn't care to go to work. And I didn't actually care about anything at all'. These different facets illustrate how, for some women at least, their depression could undermine their capacity to function effectively across a range of routine but important areas of their lives. Where this was the case with relatively straightforward tasks, more demanding areas were equally undermined.

There were a number of direct effects, which the women attributed to depression, on their capacity to engage with others. One woman saw a complete change in herself which cut her off from her past sense of self and her current relationships. This woman sums up well the sense of withdrawal from relationships:

> I'm not as bubbly, I'm withdrawing into myself. I could have a laugh and a joke. But now I can't communicate. I can't...'cos I don't think there's nothing to look forward to, getting dressed... I could feel people that visit me, my mum and that, and they're looking at, God, what's the matter with her. But I weren't caring. I was just sitting there, and that's it.

Another woman described the effects of depression across all her social relationships. She related this in turn to her abusive and violent partner:

> I don't socialise. I don't ever go out with my friends having a birthday coming up.... Before I met him, I would go out once or twice a week with her to socialise with people, but I don't do that any more. It makes me feel like I've got nothing to look forward to in life.... The other day, I took her [young daughter] for a haircut. 'Cos he hadn't got the keys for the flat, he was going mad. He walked in, and I'm on the phone to the housing lady, he was screaming, shouting.... I am depressed, but he's got a really serious problem.

This woman was in a vicious circle, related, it seems in part, to her abusive relationship with her partner. Her depression contributed to a growing isolation which left her with feelings of hopelessness and in turn reinforced her depression.

Poor familial relationships as with the partner above, could contribute to depression, but they could also emerge as a result of depression. One woman discussed the strained nature of her familial relationships:

> I feel isolated, and I've got my depression back again. I don't get on with my family very much. I've only just started talking to my dad again after three years, and I'm angry with my mum for my childhood. I hate this area. I'm not much good at going out, so I tend to stay in a lot more.

While partners could be the cause of considerable grief, they could also suffer the effects of the depression. One woman admitted, 'I guess I take my depression out on him now, rather than the kids. I take it out on him a lot'. In another case the partner was the object of real aggression, in part because of his attempts to be supportive, or perhaps because he feared for the woman if she were left alone:

> He thought I needed help. The more he cuddled me, the more I hated it. One day I felt like I could have killed him. Was because he wouldn't leave me alone. If I went to the toilet, he would be there: are you OK? I just felt there was no way I could escape him.

Such misplaced supportiveness could have placed this man in some danger, in view of her potentially explosive frustration. In another case, in a change she put down to depression, a woman became increasingly intolerant and tetchy about behaviour which she had previously found attractive in her partner. As her depression gave her a greater need to talk about her feelings, his reluctance to engage was perceived in a negative light:

> When we are with each other, it's me who does most of the talking. In the old days, I used to respect him for it, but it became, not the effect that I want...he is just not on that level, where you — we do talk, but is things like what kind of day you had, more on a conversational level — to tell him about my day must be a bit boring...then when we do talk, he just looks blankly at me.

Depression could contribute to deteriorating relationships with partners. Although this woman recognised her partner was trying, she was also intolerant because his best efforts did not have the effect of meeting her needs as she saw them:

> We just argue about everything. Maybe because I'm here all the time. I get so depressed.... I wish he would try to achieve, and help me, and try to understand me, what I want. I think it's hard, he's struggling, really struggling to get weekends [to be with her], finding that really hard.

At its worst, women attributed to depression effects which went beyond the everyday and the routine. One extreme example of this was of a woman who felt the need to shoplift when she was depressed:

> I know I am bad when I get depressed and I will go and shoplift...it's always been a thing. When I get caught, it's because I want to get caught. It sounds stupid.... Instead of just, it's like I punish myself more. 'Cos I've been out, and thought they're going to stop me. Instead of putting things back, I let them stop me. It's been going on for years.... People might take drug or drink. That is my release.

Others, less dramatically, but still importantly, had physical reactions. One woman commented that 'my health deteriorates pretty quickly.... I end up with ear infections, bilious attacks, abscesses and so on', while another said that 'you get to the stage where you become a bit of a hypochondriac. I have imagined myself with all sorts of illnesses. Cancer. Everything'.

Children

Many women were aware that their behaviour frequently had a negative effect on their children. Not all the women were, however, and these were at times the same women whose children social workers felt were at greatest risk. Indeed, some mothers actively blamed their children for inducing their depression in the first place (this was different from a recognition, amongst parents of some disabled children, that their child's disabilities and their effects, generated their depression). They placed the blame on the children themselves. As one woman said, 'There are some children who are just naughty children...and you need help' and another, having given up on her daughter, commented that 'that child has hurt me to such a point, I don't want to know anything now. I don't care to know anything'. This feeling was reiterated by a further mother who even recognised the inaccuracies, or inappropriateness, of her own perceptions of her child:

> Occasionally I lose my rag. Because he is such a little monster umm, I mean it's very frustrating. I mean, he might be a typical three year old, but to me he is a little sod.

Even those who recognised the negative effects of their behaviour did not always attribute it directly to depression. However, many did link their moods, their behaviour and problems they had with their children. Aggression towards the child, in various forms, was a feature of some women's depression. Where depression led to aggression, women generally talked of reaching a point where they 'snapped', and simply could not cope with their children any more. When that happened, some children could be at risk, even if the mother basically loved them. One woman, who said she could not cope, described the emotional chaos which accompanied this process of distress, despair and aggression:

> I just lost my temper one night.... I just flipped, and I don't know exactly what happened, but I remember slapping her around the face, and she was laying down and I slapped her. And the next thing, she had a hand mark, and it was a very bad hand mark, and I said, that's it, 'cos I didn't even realise how hard I'd slapped her or anything.

A theme of this aggression, whether verbal or physical, was the woman's inability to deal with her own emotional turmoil. Often this was a persistent problem accompanying the depression. Women could again show a reflexive awareness of the situation, this woman commenting on the way that she felt angry that she was getting angry.

> I was breaking down every day, shouting at the kids, snapping. There was nothing that they could do right at that particular time. And it was weeks and weeks I was like that. She [my daughter] was going through a really bad patch. It [the situation] was making me really angry.

Some women felt guilty for not being 'proper mothers', that they were not able to care for their children adequately, unable to respond properly to their needs, and that this was a direct consequence of their depression. One woman found it difficult to cope

> ...sometimes, that is the frustrating thing, because I know what is happening to me...and I know what I want to be like. I feel the children are affected. I feel I don't know what is true or not true then. I feel I am not giving them what they need when I am going through these depressions.

This kind of behaviour was often associated with feelings of lethargy, of not being able to perform their parental role properly. One woman commented that she would consistently tell her child to 'go away and play' simply to avoid having to do anything, leaving the child with persistent feelings of rejection. This lethargic, neglectful, parenting was often associated with role reversal, where the priority the woman gave to her own needs meant that the child was primarily responding to her rather than vice versa. One mother commented in this way, like others, that when 'I felt panicky I would call him (son), and he would help to calm me down. But he wasn't being a child any more. It was as if he was the adult and I was the child. He was taking over, and it just wasn't fair on him'.

The unpredictable and at times volatile behaviour of the mother could give the impression of not caring about the children. The aggression and withdrawal could send signals that the mother was not really interested in the children, signals which the children were likely to pick up. This was not just about her behaviour in front of the children, but about the way she needed to focus on herself, and in the process, divest herself of the children. The unpredictability was likely to be difficult for children to cope with. One woman displayed this unpredictability, first in wanting her children in care, then immediately wanting them back:

> Yes, when I had the breakdown, I just couldn't [care for the children]. It was like people were looking at me. Even now I don't go unless I have to. And...I sat there and thought I don't believe this. I might as well have them at home.... I missed them like hell. I wanted them back.

The effects of unpredictability were described by another woman:

> I have sat down and spoke to him. He has told everybody that I didn't care about him. When he came here, I said what's this I hear, I don't care about you. Of course I care about you. I live for you. I said if it weren't for you, I probably wouldn't be here. Because the way life has treated me so far, sometimes I feel like being six foot under.

The woman did not say what his reaction was to the responsibility she had given him for her well–being. However, some women were aware of the psychological damage their own depression had on their children. One commented on her daughter's own depression and self–neglect. The effects were forcibly brought home to one mother: 'I was very depressed and crying, she wanted to talk to me and I really, talk to her about her, and she was saying she wasn't loved'. This negative cycle – of depression, negative effect on children, and on mother potentially reinforcing the depression – could become destructive for both mother and children.

The depression took its toll on the women's capacity to focus on their children. However, in a further form of role reversal, some mothers expected their children to 'understand' their depressed behaviour, in particular withdrawal, even when aware how unfair this was. Although it was a great deal to ask of the children, one woman still pursued this strategy:

> And if the kids are home from school, then I keep telling them to go out of the room, and to leave me alone. Which isn't fair on them, but they seem to know that when I get down these days, that I need to be on my own.

Care could be a refuge for the mother who felt the child was out of control, or who blamed the child for their problems. There were few accounts (four) where the woman felt her depression directly triggered care. One woman felt that care was the best place for her child. He needed care because she was unable to look after him adequately herself, in view of the effects of the depression:

> I just want him to stay where he is, and be happy. 'Cos when he's happy, I'm happy. I've missed him, but I haven't really been up to it. Because I am so down, he could just go 'boo' to me and I'd end up shouting. I have to be really on top of myself, strength and everything, to keep up with him.

If he were not in care, she would neither be able to cope, nor be sure that she would not be aggressive and undermining towards him.

Key points

There are clear themes in the mothers' accounts: that they recognised they were depressed, and that this depression was placed in the context of their past and current relationships, including those with their children. Of course, as we have pointed out earlier, their accounts could have been affected by a search after meaning, whereby they interpreted their past and current situations in a way which enabled them to make sense of their depression. Also, the negative outlook generated by their depression may have made them more pessimistic than otherwise about these relationships. However, the findings presented here about past abuse are in line with those of Bifulco and Moran (1998) and we are focusing here on mothers in situations which could quite objectively be regarded as inducing turmoil. These were families characterised by severe disadvantage, most of whom were involved with social services because of concerns about the adequacy of their parenting, including the possibility of more extreme actions by social services. It would be odd, indeed, if the accounts did not reflect this.

Some authors have expressed concern about a 'cycle of abuse' thesis, whereby the parent (in particular the mother) becomes the hapless reproducer of her own abuse as a child by then perpetrating abuse on her own children. The problems with this were identified some time ago by Sheppard (1982). The findings presented here should not be interpreted as a simple rendition of a cycle of abuse thesis. There is nothing about these data which suggests that women cannot take charge of their own lives, react against their own abuse, and thus prevent the cycle beginning. There is evidence of this even amongst this cohort. However, the cohort is biased, in the sense that we are not choosing a sample reflecting *all* women who had experienced abuse. We are focusing on families with childcare problems, many of which involve abuse. A considerable proportion of these did experience abuse in their own childhood, and the data here are consistent with a view that experience of abuse in childhood, while not inevitably precipitating a cycle, can make it more difficult to care adequately for children as adults.

1 Most women who were depressed considered themselves so, and almost all felt they had some kind of emotional disturbance. For many depression was a normal feature of life, so understandable that it did not require them to think in psychiatric terms. Many women mused reflexively on their depression.

2 Many of these women were characterised by withdrawal, lethargy and sometimes suicidal ideas. Trivial things sometimes took on enormous importance, and some women recognised they could distort situations.

3 Past abuse was described by over half these women. This could have a profound effect on their adult lives, including a dislike of self and anorexia. It could also have a brutalising effect, in which mothers could take out their feelings on their children. In other cases, it could make them determined not to behave in the same way as their parents. Alternatively, it could have a direct effect on the women, making them, as parents, hard, angry and bitter.

4 The women's experience of past emotional abuse was widespread, and could be quite mundane and routine, such as persistent preferment of brothers and sisters, undermining their confidence and self esteem. There were also vividly remembered and aggressive forms of emotional abuse.

5 The types of past physical abuse suffered by the women were as varied and wide as identified in childcare social work. It could involve periodic beatings, or cigarette burns, and was generally associated with feelings of having been in a loveless home.

6 Past sexual abuse was described by the women in ways as bad as that which would have involved social services intervention had it occurred today. Some women gave harrowing and graphic descriptions, and it was sometimes accompanied by emotional or physical abuse.

7 The effects of depression currently could make it hard for women to carry out their everyday lives. They could become lethargic, unable to shop or (in the rare cases where they worked), go to work. Depression often made it difficult to engage with others. Women were often withdrawn, often chose violent relationships, sometimes were unable to take support from relatives, and were at times argumentative.

8 Some depressed women blamed their children for their problems. However, many linked their depressed mood to poor parenting, which could place their children at risk, particularly when they experienced uncontrollable rage.

5 Social workers' mental health attributions

Although all the women in this study were depressed, not all of them were understood in terms of their depression in any significant way by their social worker. One measure of the importance attributed to depression lies in the extent to which it was considered to be the primary problem in these cases. In only 13 of the 95 cases where social workers responded was the primary problem identified in a way which could be considered to be depression. In these cases social workers saw the primary problem as psychosis, clinical depression or acute psychological distress in the women themselves. Other problem areas were considered primary with a far greater frequency. Child problems were primary in 26 cases, parenting in 18 cases, adult relationship also in 18 cases, and social problems in 14 cases. Physical health problems were considered primary in six cases.

Of course, depression could have been a feature of the situation without necessarily being considered the primary problem. However, taken together, these data strongly suggest that social workers frequently did not conceive of these cases primarily in terms of women's depression, as more detailed analysis of the data shows. There was a major 'fault line' which existed between families where maternal depression was considered a major element and those where, for a variety of reasons, it was not. Where the woman was considered depressed, there was likely to be a more sympathetic response to her situation. Where she was not, the response was liable to be more explicitly or implicitly condemnatory, focusing on her inadequacies or ill deeds.

There was, then, both a descriptive or explanatory element to the social workers' judgement, and a moral dimension. It is important, however, to appreciate that the moral dimensions of judgement did not undermine the descriptive or explanatory dimensions. It would, for example, be hard not to present in moral terms a coldly calculating violent episode against a child. Indeed, we would expect it to be influential in thinking about intervention: if you referred to a mother as cold and calculating then you would not simply be making a moral judgement but also providing information which could help inform your future practice.

When social workers did identify depression, they often alluded to it in their accounts in a way which formed an explanation of the situation and helped reach a coherent undestanding of it. Social workers took their cue in this respect from different sources. Sometimes it involved an outside referral or assessment, or it could be based on the social worker's own judgement. Social workers commented, for example, on outside assessments:

> We received a referral from their new health visitor and then contacted …they commented on similar things: that mum is suffering from depression, and that there were relationship problems. And there was also a DSS investigation of fraud.

Others made their own assessment:

> Initially [mum] turned up at the office with her two children, saying that she didn't want them any more, and could we take them off her. She was very depressed and upset, and really felt she couldn't handle it any more, she wanted her life back.

> [She was] so unmotivated…she cannot sustain anything for a length of time. She almost forgets what you say to her. You go to see her and she has intended to do this and that, you go back the next time, 'Oh no, nothing got done, it's too much for me'. She just cannot sustain anything difficult.

This woman's behaviour could easily be construed as exasperating by the social worker, yet, instead of condemning her as a malingerer, the social worker was basically sympathetic to her plight. This was primarily because it was viewed as an aspect of depression.

Social workers described the women in such a way that there was a clear moral–predictive dimension: that is, they made moral judgements, and these judgements also implicitly (sometimes explicitly) had implications for future intervention, in particular relating to the welfare of the child. It was possible to identify three distinct groups: the 'genuinely depressed', 'troubled and troublesome' and 'stoics'. The data here are based on social work responses on 94 mothers, since in one case the social worker had not seen the woman.

'Genuinely depressed' mothers

The 'genuinely depressed' mothers' group totalled 52 women. Where depression was both recognised, and seen as a key feature of the case, social workers tended to manifest a sympathetic response towards the mother. Depression did not have to be perceived as the only problem, or even the most fundamental – which might, for example, be poor coping or persistent experiences of abuse – but it was conceived of as a major dimension of the total picture. In these cases the mother was perceived in some senses to be a victim, either of the effects of the depression itself, or of factors which underlay the depression. One social worker commented on the long term suffering of one woman, in the context of which the depression seemed quite understandable:

The main problems are, I think, a lot of it is to do with mother's state of mental health. This has been assessed.... Mum's had mental health issues from, well, since she was a child, she was sexually and physically abused by her elder brother, and wasn't able to communicate this to her family. There were self–harming incidents and attempted overdoses.

In other cases the social workers recognised more contemporary causes:

It was social problems that were leading to her becoming depressed.... Like poor housing, poor relationships, she was in a violent relationship, she seems always to be going through violent relationships...she has difficulties coping with stress generally, and when she experiences stress she tends to express this through the development of depressive symptoms and allegations of harassment.

Whether the result of contemporary or past circumstances, the women were considered in some senses to be trapped by their experiences, with the unsurprising consequence that they became depressed. A key to this was that their problems were not seen to be their responsibility. They may not be good mothers, and they may need support, but the depression was perceived to be the result of factors which lay outside their control, hence the victim status with which they were accorded. Beyond this, however, the social workers' descriptions of mothers and explanations of their depression were loaded with moral content – in other words, they were making moral judgements about the women.

Mother's character

The mother's character was a frequent focus for attention. Although the mother may, for example, have been neglecting her children, involved in violent relationships, or finding it generally very difficult to cope with her life, it was not these facets which dominated social workers' judgements. One significant feature was where social workers considered the mother to be caring. Where a mother's own life was characterised by a devastation visited upon her by her depression and its causes, a capacity to continue to care about her children was a cause for positive comment. It showed at least an attempt to understand her own child's needs, even though her own may have been overwhelming and she may have found it hard to sustain progress:

Without a doubt you can work with [mum] some of the time. She comes across as a very caring mother in many respects. And then allows this negative thinking to take place, which is prolonged. It is not just a one–off, when you get somebody on a bad day. It is prolonged over weeks and months. And she sustains it for that length of time. So it is very hard work with somebody who can give such mixed messages.

Women who worried about their children were also viewed positively, for similar reasons. This took matters one stage further, for their anxiety often focused on the effects of their own parenting on their children: 'I remember her saying that she had mental health problems and that she was worrying about the impact of this on her child'.

These were women who were prepared to recognise their problems, even where such recognition meant seeking help when they could no longer cope. As a result they tended to be seen as co-operative clients, where their intentions at least were to do the best they could for the child. Indeed, they could be forward looking, aware of potential problems for their children.

> I think the current issue is [mum's] mental health, and what the long term prognosis is for her. Both as an individual adult woman and as a parent. Because she worries a lot about what will happen to her child if she becomes ill. And the pattern, if she develops a pattern of becoming ill, needing to go to hospital and coming out again, I think that's a very big worry for her.

Another emotion received well, or at least sympathetically, by social workers, was guilt. Although guilty feelings are an aspect of clinical depression, whether or not they are reality-based, their manifestation, particularly in relation to the children, could be construed more specifically as critical appraisal of inadequate parenting. Many mothers with children with special needs were inclined to feel guilt, and where mothers in child protection cases felt similarly, social workers were more likely to respond sympathetically to the needs of the mother as well as the children. As one social worker said:

> What I am getting at is, I think that someone like [this mother], other mothers like her, are often so filled with guilt and enormous amounts of unresolved loss processes whether it is anger, guilt or other kinds of feelings, that they get turned upside down.

Capacity to elicit sympathy or compassion

Whether or not they felt able to address the issue of depression in their practice, or, indeed, they felt there was any immediate resolution to the family's problems, the social workers felt able to express compassion for the women as human beings. One social worker commented, 'I was concerned for her I really was concerned. Because she was so flat', while another said:

> There is some element of concern for her as in a human being, who deserves respect and pity. I do feel, sometimes that compassion is a difficult thing to address, and I do feel sometimes that the work I do is ineffectual in addressing her depression. I sort of think of that as more of a medical — I do what I can with understanding that I have of depression which is limited I suppose, by...[the doctor's] standards.

The compassion for women identified as 'genuinely depressed', therefore, was facilitated by an empathy with the problems which depression generates, not so much in general, but for *this* woman in particular. It was a recognition that depression was not simply about distress, for which sympathy might be relatively easy to elicit, but involved less attractive characteristics, including, for example, apathy and anger, factors which could undermine their capacity to work with their problems, or even to have a reasonable relationship with the social worker:

> It is very difficult for somebody who is depressed to, you know, to see the value of anything that somebody is saying to them, and even if they know in their own mind that, yes, perhaps that will work, very often there is a feeling of apathy, and I don't want to do it anyway, and just wait and see what happens.

These women's status as 'deserving' clients was further emphasised by the language used to describe their psychological or emotional state. In particular, adjectives such as 'vulnerable' or 'fragile' enhanced an understanding of women in a supportive rather than critical way:

> I am also aware that mum needs support as well. And I think if it were not for mum's fragility, there would be less work input than there is now. We are recognising that mum is a very needy person herself. And we need to keep liaison with the health service about her emotional state. Her repeated feeling that she is on the verge of giving up.

This helped the social workers to frame the childcare problems. Rather than an aggressive or neglecting perpetrator the woman would be seen as needy in herself, and, where some optimism existed about working with her, these needs would be significant in practice:

> When mum is saying that [her daughter] can't come home...I can see what she means and I would not want to push her over the edge. It's such a thing for her that it would be very wrong pushing [her] home, and we would make her very ill and it wouldn't help [the daughter] either.

Another dimension related to the effort they were seen to be prepared to put in to resolve or ameliorate their problems. This effort for change was considered praiseworthy given the difficulty the women had in summoning the energy to do so. One social worker said, 'I think she is more aware now, of the possibility of change than she was originally.... But I know when I go out of the door, the odds become unattainable for her...all the problems crowd in and she becomes overwhelmed'. Another commented on a more successful, but still slow moving effort. There had been change:

> ...although it's been very very gradual. Although if you compare now to last year, it's probably a big change.... More recently...she has been quite open saying she feels quite depressed, and she's been able to seek counselling, where in the past she hasn't felt able to say that she can't cope, because that would mean exposing herself and make her feel weak.

This was, at times, complemented by a desire not to take action which was too draconian. In one case, there were clear child protection issues, and it was necessary to accommodate the children. Because of the depression, however, 'we decided not to go down the child protection route, which we could have done in view of the injuries'. Instead the social workers sought to provide the woman with 'time and space without the children to get better' before the children were returned to her.

'Troubled and troublesome'

In other cases, depression either went unrecognised, or was given a much more peripheral place in social workers' understanding of the situation. In these cases social workers were much less likely to respond sympathetically to the behaviour of the mothers, and they were more likely to be defined in terms of negative characteristics. Rather than seeing the behaviour to be in some respects a feature or result of depression, they were taken as 'actions in themselves', evidence of the mother's intentions or character, to be used to help the social worker make judgements about how best to work with the family or protect the children. Their visible problems, rather than an interpretation of these problems in the light of depression, were seen as the primary issue, and judgements were made accordingly. We have called this group 'troubled and troublesome' (total=28).

Of interest here is the relationship between this group, and the women identified as having been abused in the past.

Table 5.1 Relationship between past abuse and social workers' mental health attribution

	Genuinely depressed	Troubled and troublesome	Stoics
Past abuse	24 (46%)	21 (75%)	6 (43%)
$X2=6.0$ $df=2$ $p=0.03$			

Table 5.1 shows clearly that women in the 'troubled and troublesome' group, based on social workers' descriptions, were significantly more likely to have been abused in the past, although we should note that this was far from an exclusive relationship. In view of the characteristics ascribed by social workers to the mother, and their implications for practice, this link would seem to have some importance.

Needy mothers who placed their needs first

Some mothers were seen as overwhelmingly needy. This judgement contained two elements: the women had great problems themselves (regardless of the child's problems), and they were self-regarding, concerned primarily with themselves and their own needs. The result of this was that they found great difficulty even considering the needs of their children, and were certainly unable to do so where they clashed with their own needs. This was a clear warning sign for many social workers, where a lack of focus by the mother on the child's own needs could have serious child protection implications.

This self–regarding feature of these women's behaviour is clearly illustrated from the following example:

> She is very, I don't know, she is very needy. She wants people to be around doing things for her. She wants to talk to people about herself. Although she will say that she hates intervention, she actually thrives on it, she wants more intervention. We don't know why, where it all stems from. But she is certainly very needy in terms of wanting attention. And that is more important for her often than her children, and meeting the needs of her children.

In these cases, social workers were not entirely without some bounded sympathy for some women's plight. Their neediness was at times seen as an indication of their own internal psychological trauma, uncertainties and insecurities:

> I feel in two minds. I am sympathetic [to mum and her mental health state], and I do think she's ill, and that's why I don't want to put any pressure on her. On the other hand, I find it quite hard. I think she's scapegoating [her daughter], and expecting her to behave like an adult and expecting [her] to understand her. Then I feel like saying 'come on a minute, she's only young and she's a child, and [she's] not really able to think like that'.

Alongside the guarded sympathy, this social worker is clearly describing some classic features of role reversal, where the child is seen to be serving the mother's needs rather than vice versa. However, such neediness can elicit censure, where the behaviour and demands made upon the social worker became exasperating:

> I have on occasions 'bent over backwards' for this woman. The amount of times we have had her wiping her nose on our trousers, and snivelling into our shirts. We have hugged her. But she is so needy. Sometimes she just needs a hug and we go round there. She has had the gas cooker on, she hasn't got a clue what she is doing.... It is really worrying.

On some occasions, social workers felt their best hope, in terms of the child's own psychological needs, was to work with the children themselves to help them cope with their mother, rather than to attempt to instigate change in the mother's behaviour. The mothers were, at least for the time being, lost causes. In one case, where the mother's focus on her own needs was associated with a daughter who had become verbally and physically aggressive, the social worker described her strategy as:

> ...working on [mum] accepting the fact that she is still the parent, she is still the adult, and that she is the one who instigates all this.... What we

> have been doing is trying to equip [the daughter], to be aware that her
> mum may never read her emotional needs. Because her mum is so needy
> herself.

In this case, the social worker is directly attributing the child's problems, at least in part, to the mother's neediness.

Malicious and manipulative mothers

Some women were also seen as downright malicious. While needy women were thought, in some respects at least, not to be fully in control of themselves since their needs were so great, this was less the case with malicious mothers. They were characterised rather by an unsympathetic, sometimes even vicious approach to others. Many of these women were involved in child protection cases, and the focus for their malicious behaviour was their children. Their actions were described not as those of a woman under stress, but at times even had an alarmingly routine quality. Their depressed mood, if recognised, did not elicit sympathy, because it was overwhelmed by other factors which were implicitly or explicitly regarded to provide a more profound understanding of their character. One such case was reported by a social worker:

> On the first visit she was saying, if you don't take these children, I'm going
> to hurt them. Can't cope. I'm depressed. On the second visit she showed me
> injuries, that she had whacked one of them on the back with a belt, she had
> stamped on the leg of another one. All the children were there, she was
> calling them all the names under the sun. They were all completely sobbing.
> At that point, I decided they needed to be accommodated.

The sheer scale of the damage done to the children was alarming enough for the social worker to consider immediate accommodation the safest option. This woman was clearly being described as dangerous, and her non-coping was not passive, but violent, representing a real threat to the children.

This malice could take forms other than direct physical violence. One woman whose relationship with her children was regarded as abusive, had promised her son that having obtained her social security money from the post office, she would provide a small amount for football socks, so that he could play a match with his friends. He clearly regarded his mother with some trepidation and was waiting anxiously for the money:

> When she came in she sort of ignored him and then he sort of tactfully tried
> to say, you know, can I have my money for my socks, and there was just a
> whole, are you sure you don't want – the whole barrage – she took a
> handful of money...and threw it across the room at him. And he had to
> scrabble around the floor to pick it up with tears rolling down his eyes and
> just ran out the door.

The social worker graphically paints a picture of malice in the form of humiliating the child. Under these circumstances, the paramountcy of the welfare of the child came to the fore, not simply because of the obvious risks, but because of the acts of commission, that the abuse was an active, rather than passive matter, and that there was a degree of intent to hurt which underlay some of the actions.

Some of these women were considered quite violent, and this violence could be directed against the social workers themselves. Such violence could, in principle, be that of a misguided attempt to protect their relationship with their children, in the face of the perceived threat of social workers in their authority role. However, social workers also considered these women to be aggressive in themselves, and this aggression could be as easily directed at their children as the social worker. One social worker expressed considerable indignation at the aggression to which she was subject, and distinguished clearly between the aggression she experienced, and the anger expressed by those she regarded as primarily distressed:

> I am happy to deal with distressed people…but I am not prepared to put up with that abuse, you know. And often, yeah, I do find it distressing, because I then think — I then have to question, am I stopping contact with [her daughter] because mum is abusing to me? Do you see what I mean? So I have that dilemma.

In this case the behaviour had practical consequences, even though the social worker remained determined to try to be as fair to the woman, under considerable provocation, as she could.

Their willingness to 'play the system' (which was seen as manipulative and directed at the social worker), to get what they wanted, was seen as one aspect of this overall 'hardness', which could also be manifested elsewhere. Basically, such women were seen as those who didn't care:

> A lot of time I have gone out of my way to help her or write a letter to the court because she has not paid the fine, or whatever. You will pass her the letter, or you will drop her off back home after running her round a lot, and she will just get out of the car, and close the door and just walk off, and you sort of think, you ungrateful bugger.

Self–destructive and incompetent mothers

Some mothers were described as manifesting behaviours which were self–destructive or otherwise incompetent. For rather different reasons these women's depression was not considered central to the social workers' understanding of the case, and there was considerable pessimism about their capacities to care for their children. Like needy mothers, these women's behaviour tended to be viewed as primarily self–centred with little or no thought for the needs of others, including their children. Amongst those who were self–destructive were substance abusers, those with eating disorders (particularly anorexia nervosa) and those with suicidal ideas. Each of these threatened the women's capacities to cope with the challenges of their own lives, let alone care for their children.

A key feature was that, even when the social worker recognised depression to be an aspect of the case, it was seen as peripheral. One social worker rather dismissed its significance with one mother:

> Oh God, who knows in a sense? I think the main problem in the family is mum's severe dependence on alcohol.... That is the thing that is very hurtful for [her son] as well. He is the last of four children, where she has done the same to all four children. Umm, and I think that up to why [mum] drinks.

Amongst this group were addicts, and the need to feed their habit – whether it was drugs or more commonly alcohol – overwhelmed all other aspects of their lives. Their behaviour, furthermore, undermined their capacity to take greater control of their own lives. Such behaviour could leave the social worker perplexed:

> Ultimately I don't know what the answer is. It is the issue of treating her as an adult, which she is. Perhaps it would be easier to safeguard against this thing [drug use] happening with children. You would always assume that a responsible adult would be able to say, I don't need any more of those etc. But that is what [mum's] problem is.

Persistent drug use was, as far as the social worker was concerned, undermining this woman's capacities to care adequately for her children, and indeed, could endanger them. Yet like other addicts there was little motivation for 'kicking the habit'. Underlying this, in some cases, were the same kind of uncertainties and insecurities which characterised needy mothers. However, whether or not such psychological trauma underlay their substance use, social workers were more likely to see them primarily as addicts.

Mothers who were learning–disabled were seen as less self–obsessed than self–destructive mothers, yet nonetheless their own limitations presented problems in coping with the challenges of their own lives. They may have been depressed, and this, where recognised, may have evoked some sympathy, but the learning difficulties, rather than the depression, were seen as the key to understanding and resolving the problems of the woman and her children. These mothers were likely to have difficulty in understanding and communication (something which was evident in some of the research interviews), and this presented a serious impediment to their capacity to engage in problem resolution. Some of these women, furthermore, were implicated in the abuse or neglect of their children, and limits in their social competence could make them seem to have difficult or alienating behaviour when seen by their social worker.

'Stoics'

A small group of women (total=14) did not fit easily into either of the above groups. These were women, who, although depressed, did not express their depression clearly, and even attempted to cover it up. Instead, many of these women sought to present themselves as capable and coping parents. The result was that social workers were likely to ascribe less serious problems to them, and less likely either to recognise their depression, or to consider it had a significant bearing, from the practical viewpoint of intervention, on their child and familial problems. This was particularly the case with depressed mothers of disabled children.

One social worker worked with a family with a child with cerebral palsy who needed 24 hour care. She recognised the devastation that was visited upon the parents by their daughter's disability, and mused about their parenting:

> How do they cope? They cope, they cope…. The only two things they have ever contacted me about was when they were having trouble with the housing association, who installed her cooker…then once because they wanted a taxi to the hospital, they had to take her to the hospital three times a week.

Some social workers were aware of this, and made efforts to give some practical recognition to the women's needs. However, this was far from universal, and social workers felt a number of mothers seemed unable to ask for help for themselves, and hence did not receive any. Mothers who put on a 'good show' or 'kept smiling', in taking responsibility for the care of their children were always in danger of having their depression and other needs ignored, minimised or dismissed.

One social worker commented on a disabled mother of a disabled child, who was the subject of constant malicious complaints by neighbours about the care of her children:

> She's not a person who phones social services 'I need this and I need that'. Things have to be really bad…. People like that are really proud and self reliant, so you have to respect it…she isn't a person who would ring about trivialities.

However, this same social worker nonetheless minimised the woman's distress: when asked if the woman was stressed, she said, 'I don't know. Stress is everywhere. We are all stressed out and it's a blanket term these days. Everybody has got stresses'.

In some cases, social workers did attempt to provide support, but the enormity of the events with which the mother had to deal meant that they had to show considerable stoicism in adversity. This was the case for one woman whose son died of leukaemia, but was reluctant to 'let people in' to help her. She soldiered on to continue to care for her other children, even though her partner periodically went off, leaving her to look after the children herself. When offered medical support, she replied, 'I don't want medication, I'll manage'. She responded to the social worker's support, even though the social worker lacked expertise in this area by her own admission, and the woman was aware of this.

In some cases the stoicism was a cultural issue. One woman, for example, was an immigration overstayer (she had stayed longer than her visa allowed) and was finding it difficult to cope with her children and the shortage of money. Despite this, she believed she was not entitled to any financial support, so she would take no money from her social worker, even throwing it on the ground when it was offered to her. The social worker commented that she 'didn't know how she survives'.

Key points and summary

While these groups represented, as a whole, distinctive ways in which social workers defined the women, there were certainly some characteristics of other groups where they merged with each other. For example, while social workers may have defined many women as 'troubled and troublesome', some of these women may, while fitting this dominant definition, have had some of the characteristics of the 'genuinely depressed' group.

On reflection, this distinction is not surprising. A very high proportion of these women had brutalising lives, and while their depression is an understandable outcome of these experiences, it could also effect deep psychological damage on the women themselves. It is here that the relationships between these women's own past experiences of abuse emerge as an interesting factor in relation to social workers' own judgements of them. Those whom social workers were likely to regard in the least sympathetic light, and to be the most problematic, were the 'troubled and troublesome' group, which had a significantly higher proportion of women who had themselves suffered past abuse. This suggests a relationship between past abuse and current characteristics. It should be noted, however, that close to half the other two groups contained women experiencing past abuse. It would be wrong, therefore, to regard the data in this cohort as indicating a discrete and univariate relationship between past abuse and current categorisation by social workers.

Nevertheless, some writers on personality disorders in adult life draw attention to the effect of early negative experiences as a precursor to exactly the kind of self-regarding behaviours, and limited capacity for empathy, which social workers described in these 'troubled and troublesome' women (Bowlby 1988). Such a disorder would not preclude feelings of depression, and could indeed be consistent with the focus on self frequently identified by the social workers. On the other hand depression itself can go hand in hand with self-absorption, and periods of anger and aggression. While, therefore, personality disorder may be a feature of some of these women, the depression itself can produce outcomes which are less likely to invoke sympathy than self-criticism, guilt and low self-esteem.

1   Social workers did not always understand the women and their problems in terms of their depression. Indeed, this was rarely considered the primary problem. Social workers described women in a 'moral-predictive' way. This involved moral judgements about them being good or bad, deserving or undeserving as people or parents. The predictive elements had implications for case management.

2   The largest group comprised the 'genuinely depressed' mothers. Depression was seen as a major dimension of the total picture, and mothers were seen in some respects as victims, trapped by past or present experiences.

3   The 'genuinely depressed' mother's character, a major concern, was generally viewed positively, and judgements were based on the way such mothers related to their children. Those who were seen as caring, worried about their children and the effects of their behaviour on them, who had feelings of guilt, and who were seen as co-operative, fell into this group.

4   The capacity of 'genuinely depressed' mothers to elicit sympathy was another characteristic. There was a recognition that less desirable characteristics such as apathy and anger were part of the depression. There was as a result an optimism about working with these mothers who were seen as deserving.

5   'Troubled and troublesome' were the second main group. Depression was more peripheral to social workers' understanding of these women. They were likely to be seen more negatively, and as dangerous in terms of the child's welfare. They were more likely to have experienced abuse in their own childhood.

6   Some of these mothers were seen as having overwhelming needs of their own. They were perceived as generally placing their own needs before their child's, and role reversal occurred at times. Some were considered manipulative or malicious, making unsympathetic, even vicious approaches to others, most significantly their children. Self-destructive or incompetent mothers were unreliable and self-regarding, often substance abusers, particularly with alcohol. Their unpredictable, addictive behaviour was generally seen as dangerous for their children.

7   'Stoics' were the third, and smallest, group. These mothers were seen, by contrast, to be very self-reliant and resilient. They might seek to 'cover up' their depression, and did not so frequently seek help.

Part three

Problems, Needs, Responses

3

6 Problems and needs

The families of depressed mothers had very high levels of problems and needs. It is also worth noting the highly interrelated nature of these women's problems. The extent of these difficulties is quite clear from Table 6.1 which shows, in terms of broad areas, the degree to which most families suffered problems in each of these areas. Most families were experiencing problems in most areas. These were, as a whole, 'multi–problem families'.

Table 6.1 Broad problems and severe problems

	Problems	Severe problems
Adult social	88 (94%)	54 (57%)
Adult relationships	86 (91%)	58 (62%)
Adult health	76 (81%)	41 (44%)
Parenting	73 (78%)	48 (51%)
Child	91 (97%)	74 (79%)

The most widespread were, unsurprisingly, child problems. However, child problems were only considered primary with marginally over a quarter of families, and other major problem areas were considered primary as follows: health (19 per cent), relationship (19 per cent), parenting (19 per cent) and social (14 per cent). Indeed, while social workers were able to identify a single primary problem, they generally saw a number, or group, of problems as being of particular significance.

The previous chapter, however, raises further issues. One of the implications of the differentiation of depressed women into separate groups is that they were likely to be characterised, at least in some respects, by different problems and needs. While, therefore, this chapter will examine problems of the depressed women as a whole, areas of difference between the subgroups will also be identified.

Social workers had a practical, action–oriented way of constructing problems. Their way of defining these families' problems was constructive in terms of moving towards action. The problems were not identified without some sense of what might be undertaken in order to ameliorate or resolve them (this theme will be developed in this, and further, chapters). The implications of this 'action orientation' will be discussed in detail later in chapters on intervention strategies. Nonetheless, it should be noted that whether or not the problems were resolved or ameliorated, they were always constructed in a way which would allow social workers, in principle, to link with a response. By defining problems in a concrete way, they were able to pave the way for direct action. This link between problem and response represents two dimensions of need, which have been identified earlier in terms of an interconnection of problems–supports–resources. For analytic purposes, therefore, a distinction may be made between problems and responses to those problems, but social workers themselves were invariably at pains to link the two in practice.

Social problems and needs

Poverty, financial and housing problems

Social problems cover an area of largely instrumental, practical issues, although they could include relationship questions, as with problems with formal organisations. Amongst the problems in this area are: financial, housing, home management and criminal behaviour, either by the woman, or others close to her. Financial and material problems were widespread in this deprived group, and were the most frequent of all social problems. Nearly three quarters of depressed mothers were in families relying on state benefit (67/93 for whom these data were known). Marginally under two thirds had financial problems and a quarter were considered to have severe financial problems. These occurred within a social context of considerable disadvantage.

This widespread poverty was recognised by social workers in general as a serious impediment in women's attempts to resolve their problems. Many of these women found themselves in debt, and the high reliance on state benefit made it very difficult to pay off this debt. Its impact was clear in the material effects in the home. Social workers were acutely aware that some homes did not have carpets, were barely furnished, and that at times there was little food in the house. Mothers frequently requested money for food vouchers, or for utilities such as the electricity meter. A few families had problems requiring extra financial expenditure such as new bedding for children with enuresis, or travel to visit children in care or partners in prison. Families with disabled children sometimes had particular financial demands, such as travel expenses to hospital, or adaptations to their homes. Indeed, time could be lost from employment, although the high unemployment levels in general represented a further impediment to surmounting financial problems.

One of the key issues in this respect was single mothers who were largely reliant on state benefit. Single parent families constituted over half (54 per cent) of those with depressed mothers. Single parenthood was not generally viewed by social workers as a problem in itself. Most of these single mothers (88 per cent) lived entirely on benefits, and were usually seen by social workers to be seriously impoverished. While most mothers had support from friends, and to some extent relatives (although there were problems with conflict in their networks), the type of support which might have been expected from a stable, live–in partner, was clearly not available. Care should be taken to avoid idealising partner relations. These were often unreliable and inadequate for the women's needs, with partners 'living off them' and making their situation worse. However, where the combination of poverty and single parenthood was associated with an understandable poor self–esteem, this lack of emotional and practical support could be a serious disadvantage for these women.

Family size also contributed to poverty. Brown and Harris (1978) have argued that large family size – specifically three or more children aged under 14 – contributes to depression because it is hard to fulfil adequately the mothering role, and this has an impact on self–esteem. Nearly half the mothers in this cohort (46) had three or more children. This was often combined with low income, and living in cramped conditions and impoverished circumstances. These mothers, social workers generally recognised, had difficulties in budgeting on limited incomes for such large families. Although social workers might seek to support these families with section 17 money, the poverty was often important, for social work purposes, for its effect on children. Children were, at times, deprived of the kinds of activities widely available, including recreational and entertainment activities, playschool and holiday outings in summer.

Housing problems were also widespread, and closely connected with poverty. Over four fifths (83) of these families lived in rented accommodation, nearly three fifths (58) in council housing. Housing problems were experienced by two fifths (39) of these women and for 15 per cent this was severe. Some of these mothers were in arrears in payment of rent, and were under threat of eviction. Houses were at times overcrowded, particularly where there were large families, were often in poor areas disliked by the mothers, and could be in poor condition. Social workers recognised that these mothers were frequently unhappy with their homes, but were prevented from being able to seek new homes by poverty and financial problems.

There was a variety of environmental problems which were related to housing difficulties. Many of the women lived in run–down areas, with poor, sometimes unhygienic housing, including problems of damp. The neighbourhood could be subject to vandalism, and areas affected by violence created a housing problem, in that women could be anxious to move. Another feature was where women had poor relationships with neighbours, or were in conflict with them, creating a desire to move. Housing problems could be related to health problems: fifteen of the 39 women with housing problems (nearly two fifths) either suffered long term ill health problems themselves, or their partner did. Sometimes these problems related to the poor quality of the housing, or their ill health was exacerbated by it.

Indeed, poor housing provided the backdrop for a range of other problems. In particular, where there were large families, the overcrowding did not help familial relations, and could create points of conflict. The feelings of entrapment could leave the woman feeling miserable, and exacerbate depressed feelings. Home management difficulties – an extensive problem area in its own right, occurring with two fifths of families – were also exacerbated. It was difficult for the woman to feel houseproud because she simply wanted to get away from the house.

Those who lived in council accommodation did not have free choice as to where they should live, often having limited opportunity to move. Waiting lists were generally long, and gaining priority for rehousing difficult to achieve. Mothers on waiting lists were only given minimal choice for rehousing, and often had to wait a long time for allocation. Social workers often recognised that housing was unsuitable for these families, yet generally felt they had limited powers to influence what was to be done regarding rehousing.

Criminal behaviour

Criminal behaviour, although not as frequent as other problem areas, is interesting because it throws up significant differences between the three groups of 'genuinely depressed', 'troubled and troublesome' and 'stoical' women. Just under a sixth of women (15/94) were themselves engaged in criminal activities. Only two had obvious criminal records, such as shoplifting or possessing a firearm. Social workers were aware also of fraudulent activities, such as moonlighting while on benefits, or illegal marketing of cigarettes or drugs. Some mothers were also prostitutes, which, as well as being a criminal activity itself, could place the mothers in considerable danger. In general, there was some sympathy felt by the social workers for women in these positions, which they considered arose largely because of their poverty.

Drug abuse, together with alcohol abuse, was a problem for one fifth of mothers (19/94). A large majority of these were alcohol rather than drug problems. However, where drug abuse occurred, this was frequently a serious problem for childcare, and was also illegal. An additional potential for theft existed where the women were poor, and needed to maintain their habit. All the women with these problems (both alcohol and drug) were in the 'genuinely depressed' or 'troubled and troublesome' groups, and none were amongst the 'stoics'.

Of real significance were problems associated with criminal behaviour of the close adult family, usually the partner's. Over one third of women (33/94) had these problems, none of whom were in the 'stoics' group. Nearly half the 'troubled and troublesome' group (13/28) and two fifths of the 'genuinely depressed' group (20/52) had these problems, significantly more than the 'stoics' (Kruskal–Wallis test p=0.01). There was a range of ways these partners were involved in such activities. Violence, including domestic violence, was a frequent problem, as was involvement in drug use. They were also at times petty criminals, involved in theft or burglary. Like the mothers, they were at times involved in moonlighting while on benefits.

Domestic violence is a relationship issue as well as one of criminality. In general, this was violence by the partner to the mother, both verbal and physical. Many of the women found it difficult to escape from these relationships, and they could have serious implications for childcare. Children living with this aggression and hostility are hardly being brought up in the optimum environment, and this could affect the quality of care and their emotional stability. However, this could go further, and there were cases where violence against women was matched by violence towards the children, or where children were caught between parents when violence was occurring.

Social relationships

Partners

Adult social relationship problems were widespread amongst depressed mothers, as shown in Table 6.1, and three fifths of these women suffered at least one severe relationship problem. Social relationships was a key area where there were considerable variations between the different groups. Problems with partners were extensive, occurring for nearly three fifths of these women (54/94) and were severe for nearly a third (30/94). In view of the number of single parents, these data include problems with ex–partners. This reflects, in part, conflict and disagreement over care of the children, where the natural fathers remained in contact. However, for some mothers, who could be very needy, not having a partner presented a problem in that they felt the need for that kind of support.

However, this needy state meant, as far as the social workers were concerned, that some women remained with unsuitable partners, who could be abusive, unsupportive and undermining. Some mothers were seen as 'just needing to have a man around' and as feeling unable to cope on their own: 'a bad man was better than no man at all'. Mothers were considered unable to break away from men that were clearly making them unhappy, or were a danger to their children or themselves.

These data link with those on women suffering sex abuse or violence. Nearly three fifths (35/94) were subject to this violence. Perhaps more importantly, there were significant differences between the groups, with the 'troubled and troublesome' group suffering this problem to a considerably greater degree than other groups. Exactly half this group suffered sex abuse, and a third (9/28) suffered it severely. This compares with two fifths of the 'genuinely depressed' group, of whom under a sixth (8/52) suffered it severely. The 'stoics', on the other hand, experienced no sex abuse or violence (Kruskal–Wallis test, p =0.005).

It was, therefore, the 'troubled and troublesome' group who were subject to the most extreme problems with partners, followed, to a much lesser extent, by the 'genuinely depressed' group. In addition to those women stuck with unsuitable partners, were those who moved from one unsatisfactory or abusive relationship to another. These problems were often seen as a function of the mother's own attitudes or psychological state. Some mothers had their own problems with, for example, anger management or alcohol dependence. Where this was the case, although the partner contributed to the problem, the women were themselves seen to play a significant part.

The women's choice of partner, and their own contribution to partner problems, at times had both historical and contemporary significance. Abusive relationships as adults were in some cases continuations of abusive experiences these women had in childhood. There were deep psychological issues which were expressed through their depression, and acted out in their needy and unsatisfying relationships. On some occasions, not to be overstated, it was because of their involvement with these men, and their abuse, that the intervention of social services was required for child protection.

Familial problems

Problems with extended family occurred with three fifths of the women (58/94). Here again, there were major differences between the three groups. Only three of the 14 'stoics' had these problems, compared with just over three fifths (33/52) of the 'genuinely depressed' group and nearly four fifths (22/28) of the 'troubled and troublesome' group (Kruskal–Wallis test, p=0.001). The latter group tended also to have more severe familial problems.

One of the major issues here was with over–protective or domineering birth families who did not leave the mothers to lead their own lives. This was a particular problem for mothers with their own physical or learning disabilities, and the protectiveness is, in some ways, an understandable reaction to the women's own distress and their childcare problems. Even genuinely supportive family — usually mothers or sisters — were sometimes a problem, being seen as undermining the mother's confidence and her role as parent.

Such relationships could be insidiously undermining, but problems could be more overt. In some cases there was serious conflict between family members and the mother, which could take the form of persistent arguments, or the avoidance of the provision of support when needed. These again tended to be with those who were also most likely to be supportive, female relatives. As with partner problems, many of the most serious problems had considerable longevity, having occurred over a number of years. The conflict was part of undermining relationships which sapped the women's self–confidence, and did not help in their development of parenting competence.

Social isolation and loss

A further dimension of the fractured relationships frequently suffered by these women were problems in their wider relationships. Nearly two fifths of women had a problem of lack of relationships and social isolation, a quarter of these (24/94) severely. Although there was a tendency for 'troubled and troublesome' women to have these problems to a greater extent than the other groups, this difference was not significant. This isolation could be a major problem for these women, affecting their capacity to receive reliable and consistent social support, and limiting the possibility of their engaging in social activities. Both of these could provide background factors which would make adequate care of children more difficult, and sliding into depression, or worsening depression, more likely.

Social workers frequently recognised psychological difficulties as a factor contributing to isolation. Mothers who were depressed often lacked the motivation to sustain relationships, and unless they had a partner, family or friends who would visit them at home, they spent considerable time on their own. Henderson (1984) has pointed out, however, that the personality of the depressed person can make it difficult to make and sustain relationships, as they can often seem defensive, short tempered or withdrawn. Where this happened, it was likely to engender considerable self–doubt which could contribute to the maintenance of depression.

The other main factor contributing to social isolation was poverty. As has been shown earlier in this chapter, reliance on state benefit and the presence of financial problems was widespread. Poverty made it difficult for women to go out, to socialise with friends, and to undertake activities of interest. This could engender a feeling of entrapment, in that women found it extremely difficult to break through the poverty to develop social relations when they were reliant on state benefit on such a wide scale. On low incomes the choice can be between using some of the money for recreational purposes and not letting the children go hungry.

Loss was an important area also, suffered by over half the cohort (51/94), and a severe problem for a quarter. One obvious loss area was where parents had children accommodated or placed in care, for some mothers a devastating experience involving the loss of self–esteem and parenting competence which accompanied the loss of the child. Women suffered a sense of loss in other diverse areas. Some women, who went from one relationship to another, or who no longer had a partner, could feel this loss strongly, especially those defined as needy. Others were parents with disabled children. For some of these parents, although social workers recognised they generally loved their children, their sense of loss of the 'normal' child whom they had hoped for was a persistent feature. Indeed, these parents had a sense of loss that they were unable to pursue paid employment or outside social relationships to the extent they would have liked because of childcare responsibilities. Some women whose children had been abused, particularly sexually abused, felt the loss of the relationship they would otherwise have had without this trauma.

Parenting: parent–child relationships

This, of course, was an area of major importance, since much social work involvement arose because problems with parental competence placed the children 'at risk' or 'in need', in terms of expectations of social work involvement. It was also an area which, equally importantly, had highly significant variations between different groups. Exactly three quarters of these women had parenting problems, which were considered serious with half the women. Parenting problems could be underlying features of child problems, but particular difficulties with children, for example where they were disabled, could contribute to difficulties in parenting adequately. Having stated that, it is very clear that parenting problems were not as severe for 'stoical' mothers as for the other two groups, particularly those in the 'troubled and troublesome' group.

Table 6.2 Depressed women and child abuse

	Forms of abuse					
	Child abuse (including register)	Emotional abuse	Physical abuse	Neglect	Sex abuse	Child protection register
Number	53 (56%)	27 (29%)	24 (26%)	23 (24%)	18 (19%)	30 (32%)

Table 6.2 shows over half these depressed women to have children whom the social workers considered to have suffered some child abuse, although only about a third of them were on the child protection register. The implications of these figures also are that many of these families had children suffering multiple abuses, involving more than one area (such as emotional *and* physical abuse, neglect *and* sexual abuse, neglect, physical *and* emotional abuse etc.).

There were also some differences between families in the ways their problems were perceived. In some families, the child problems were not, on the whole, seen to be so much an issue of parental incompetence. This was most obviously the case for families with disabled children. These came to social services' attention generally because of the child's disabilities rather than parental misdemeanours. On the other hand, the majority of families were involved with social services because of the inadequacy of the parenting which could place the child at risk. In some cases the mothers would be seen as wholly or partly culpable because of aggressive, volatile or neglectful behaviour. In other cases, the women could be overwhelmed with their own problems, which could both lead to and include depression, severely reducing their capacity to care for their children.

Much of the social workers' concern with these families revolved around the issues of parental competence and abuse. Over half the women had children known to have been abused, and 16 were on the child protection register. Again this problem was a feature of families with 'troubled and troublesome' mothers. Nearly four fifths of these mothers had children who had been abused (22/28), compared with half the 'genuinely depressed' mothers (27/52) and only 30 per cent (4/14) of the 'stoics' (X^2= 10.4, df=2, p=0.005). These abuses were significant, associated as they were with a range of parenting and child emotional and behavioural problems. There were a number of cases of abuse to children by partners, including those of sex abuse. Where there were schedule 1 offenders in the house, mothers were at times confronted with a choice: between keeping her abusive partner and losing her children, or getting rid of him. For some of these women, who could be very needy (particularly in the 'troubled and troublesome' group) this could create an acute dilemma. Where mothers were reluctant to separate from partners under these circumstances, this was seen by social workers as a significant problem.

A feature which generally linked the areas of parental competence and abuse was the ways in which the children were being neglected. The neglect of children could take various forms, and interestingly these showed highly significant differences between the three groups of mothers. The most frequently identified problem was the lack of guidance provided to children, which occurred in two thirds of these families (60/94), and which was severe in two fifths (38/94). Lack of guidance occurred in related ways, including right or wrong behaviour, setting clear behavioural boundaries, and taking action where children misbehaved. Parents might not know where their children were and generally were perceived to be exercising insufficient control over them. This problem was particularly severe for women in the 'troubled and troublesome' group, where nearly 90 per cent (24/28) had this difficulty. This compares with two thirds of the 'genuinely depressed' group (34/52) and only two fifths of the 'stoical' group (6/14). These differences were highly significant (Kruskal–Wallis test, p=0.02).

Another area which featured neglectful behaviour was in the provision, or lack of it, of positive affection towards the child. Two fifths of the women (37/94) expressed direct hostility towards, or criticism of the child. This is an area which tended to go beyond neglect to physical and emotional abuse. Children were subject to high levels of criticism. Women could express themselves towards their children in undermining, esteem–reducing and aggressive ways, in a manner which paid little attention to the children's own needs. This was far less frequent in mothers of disabled children (two out of 14), although overall differences between the three groups were not significant. An area of more obvious neglect was that of limited attachment and bonding, and a general lack of concern about the children. This could take various forms, but was represented largely by a high degree of indifference to the children, their emotional needs and their safety. A third of women (30/94) had this problem, one fifth (19) severely. This was a problem almost absent in the 'stoical' group, only one woman having it. However, it was a problem for three fifths of the 'troubled and troublesome' women (17/28) and a fifth of 'genuinely depressed' women (12/52). Variations between these groups were highly significant (Kruskal–Wallis test, p–0.0008). This indifference towards children was, therefore, overwhelmingly more a problem with the 'troubled and troublesome' women.

A very basic area of neglect, which could verge on physical abuse, was in relation to the physical care of the children. Interestingly, this was the least frequent of the parenting problems, occurring in marginally over a quarter of cases (25/94). The relative rarity of this problem may reflect the extreme nature of parental incompetence required for care to be inadequate. It included problems such as inadequate concern about hygiene, adequacy of clothing and lack of care of the children when ill. At its most extreme, young children could become ill or suffer severe sores because of the absence of adequate physical care. Part of the reason for the relatively low frequency of this problem is that it is more likely to emerge with younger children. This inevitably restricts the proportion of families which could be affected. Despite the relative infrequency of this problem, there were significant differences between groups. None of the women in the 'stoical' group had a problem in this area. On the other hand over a third of the 'troubled and troublesome' group (10/28) and over a quarter of the 'genuinely depressed' group (15/52) provided inadequate physical care for the children, again a significant difference (Kruskal–Wallis test, p=0.04).

Neglect was also expressed in limited involvement with the child, which occurred with just over a third of mothers (33/94) and which was severe for just under a sixth (15/94). This referred to women who showed little enthusiasm for their children's interests, where they had limited communication with the children and sometimes even limited contact. It could show itself with younger children in difficulties or disinterest in involving themselves with their child in play, and with older children, ignoring them, and leaving them to their own devices. In this respect, it could be similar to lack of provision of guidance. Again, there were highly significant differences, whereby this problem was greatest for the 'troubled and troublesome' group, followed by the 'genuinely depressed' group. Lack of involvement was a problem for only one of the 14 'stoics', compared with nearly a third of the 'genuinely depressed' group (24/52) and two fifths of the 'troubled and troublesome' group (11/28) (Kruskal–Wallis test, p=0.008).

A further area was unrealistic expectations of the child. This referred to expectations of children inappropriate for their ages, such as expecting them to undertake tasks they were too young for, or have an understanding more appropriate to older people. One obvious way this could emerge is with 'role reversal' in which children would be expected to make their needs secondary to those of their mother, or parents, rather than vice versa. This was a problem for two fifths of the women (38/94), and a severe problem for one fifth (19/94). Although differences were not significant, the 'stoics' were noticeably less likely to have such expectations, only three (of 14) of them having this problem, compared with 15 (of 28) 'troubled and troublesome' women and 20 (of 52) 'genuinely depressed' women. This was a severe problem for a higher proportion of these two groups than for the 'stoics' where none of the women were considered to be severely affected.

Child problems were an unsurprising accompaniment to parenting problems. They could be an effect, or cause, of parenting problems, or sometimes both. Three problem areas were the most frequent identified. Nearly three quarters of the mothers (69/94) had children with emotional problems, including persistent distress, depression, anxiety and disability. A similar proportion of children had behavioural difficulties such as habitual defiance, aggressive behaviour and tantrums, which occurred in 71 cases, or cognitive problems, including poor concentration and language development, occurring in 69 cases.

Other problems occurred in between 40 and 50 per cent of cases, including poor social involvement by the child, physical health or disability problems, somatic problems, uncertain or confused identity, educational under–achievement and somatic problems. There was rather less difference in child problems between the three groups than might be suggested by the differences in parenting problems, and parent–child relationships. The few significant differences, however, were interesting. Child behavioural problems were significantly more frequent in the 'troubled and troublesome' group. Thus 85 per cent of this group (24/28) had this problem, 50 per cent severely, compared with 57 per cent (30/52) in the 'genuinely depressed' group and four fifths of 'stoics' (11/14) (Kruskal–Wallis test, p<0.05). Physical health or disability problems, on the other hand, were far more frequent amongst the 'stoics'. Over four fifths of 'stoics' (12/14) had children with a physical health or disability problem compared with under a half of the 'troubled and troublesome' group (13/28) and just over one third of the 'genuinely depressed' group (17/52) (Kruskal–Wallis test, p=0.001).

Health problems

Health problems were widespread also, present in over three quarters of cases and severe in over two fifths (Table 6.1). Unlike other problem areas, however, there were no significant differences in their frequency between the different groups. There was a marked degree of long term physical ill health or disability amongst the mothers themselves. Two fifths of women suffered ill health, and nearly one fifth (17/94) did so severely. These covered a wide range of problems from varicose conditions, disfiguring and debilitating illness, injury impairing mobility, angina, severe asthma and menstrual problems. This degree of ill health is remarkable, but reflects the severity of disadvantage to which these women were subject, a relation which has been widely recognised in literature in the sociology of health. Nevertheless, ill health and disability impaired further the mothers' capacity to care adequately for their children.

One fifth of women had close adult relatives with long term physical disability or ill health (18/94), seven of these were serious. Eight of the women (9 per cent) had close adult relatives with a mental health problem. These presented the women with an additional burden, in the requirement to care for them.

Key points

1 Families had a wide range of difficulties in the areas of social, relational, health, parenting and child problems. These problems were set against a backdrop of poverty and disadvantage which were reflected in their financial, housing and other social problems.

2 However, there were interesting variations between the three groups. These were groups with great differences in the nature of their problems. In general the 'troubled and troublesome' group had higher frequencies of problems than either the 'genuinely depressed' or 'stoical' groups. This was a graduated difference, with 'troubled and troublesome' women experiencing the most frequent problems, followed by the 'genuinely depressed' group, and least frequently, the 'stoics'.

3 It is in the link between their characteristics and problems that further insight into these groups may be gained. 'Troubled and troublesome' women were perceived by social workers as very 'needy', tending to be egocentric, self–absorbed, and at times aggressive. This chapter shows them also to have chaotic lives in a number of ways. Their social relationships were particularly problematic, with difficulties, often severe, in relations with both friends and family, and they were themselves subject to considerable abuse and violence. They were more frequently involved in close relationships with those whose criminal behaviour varied from relatively minor misdemeanours, such as theft, to major problems, such as violent behaviour. These women were frequently unable to sustain supportive and friendly relationships, and were often involved in seriously problematic relationships.

4 The parenting of 'troubled and troublesome' mothers was by far the worst of the three groups. This was especially true of the most basic of parenting tasks, physical care of children. It could extend to more abusive acts, such as physically aggressive acts or neglect which affected a child's health, such as allowing sores to develop. In other ways they displayed neglectful behaviour, in the limited provision of positive affection – an absence of caring or warmth, which could extend to downright hostility – limited involvement with their children, and a failure to provide the children with adequate guidance. This is consistent with the social workers' descriptions which suggested these women placed their own needs before those of the children, and were self–absorbed.

5 The 'genuinely depressed' group displayed the same problems, but in a less frequent or severe way, and their nature may, in the light of the previous chapter, be interpreted differently. These were women who were self–critical

and sometimes withdrawn, who wished to care adequately for their children but found themselves unable to do so. They wanted support to enable them to cope better, and attempted, not always successfully, to respond to social workers. However, their inability to respond meant there were sometimes severe parenting problems. In general, problems were more severe in this group than the 'stoics'.

6　The most frequent and severe problems of the 'genuinely depressed' group indicate they had similar difficulties to the 'troubled and troublesome' group but to a lesser extent. Financial difficulties often provided a background to their other problems. However, they also had marked relationship problems, with the extended family, with their partners, and with social isolation. This is consistent with their being withdrawn, and difficulties sustaining adequate relationships could feed into their sense of low self–esteem. This was similarly the case with parenting problems, the most frequent of which was in relation to the provision of guidance and criticism of the children. This indicates again their difficulties engaging with their children, and at times a low tolerance of them, for which they were nevertheless self–critical.

7　The 'stoics', on the other hand, were the least problematic across the majority of areas, confirming the social workers' perception of them as women able to cope in conditions of adversity. Their social and familial relationship problems were relatively small, they suffered no sex abuse or violence, and were not involved with those perpetrating criminal acts. Perhaps most significant were two observations: the 'stoics' had far fewer parenting problems, particularly compared with the 'troubled and troublesome' group, confirming their capacity to manage this most important set of tasks in adversity. However, with a few exceptions, their child problems were as extensive as the other groups, and child health and disability was more extensive than in the other groups. The social workers' involvement, in other words, was related more to child than parenting problems.

There was a wide range of problems present in the group as a whole, and in the women described by social workers with different mental health attributions. The next issue is the extent and ways social workers sought to respond to these problems.

7 Social work responses

The very wide range of problems and needs, and their severity, presented social workers with a considerable challenge. These were, on the whole, cases of extreme complexity, with multiple problems, which would be expected to provide a challenge to the skills of the social workers. While social workers could be focusing on one particular problem area, they might be doing so with a view to dealing with several problems. Another unavoidable feature of practice is the statutory nature of the social workers' involvement with some problems. Where, for example, parental behaviours were abusive, these were (at least in principle) a key element of practice.

Although social workers spent considerable time and energy working with the children, in 46 per cent of cases (44/94), they considered the mothers to be the primary focus for intervention, compared with 40 per cent where attention was primarily on the children. Working with the mother was, in many cases, perceived to be the key to assuring the welfare of the child. Whether or not the mother was the primary focus, however, the range of problems and needs was such that they provided a number of potential 'targets' for intervention. This chapter examines the differing ways in which social workers responded to these women's problems, and begins the process of providing some understanding as to why they would respond as they did.

Social, instrumental and health problems

Material, practical and financial needs were not only the most obvious, but also those needs for which mothers were most likely to ask for help. Social workers were frequently able to see the facts for themselves, in that mothers had no food in the cupboard, there was no money in the electricity meter, no carpets on the floor, or a new bed or refrigerator was needed. Social workers were constrained by budgetary limits, particularly the use of section 17 money (specifically for use to support families 'in need'). Nevertheless, nearly four fifths of these women had received either direct financial assistance, or practical help, support, advice and advocacy within the previous six months, or since allocation of the case, or since the previous review, whichever was the sooner. Of these 56 per cent (53/94) received direct financial support from social services and 73 per cent (69/94) received practical help, support or advice. There were no significant differences according to subgroup ('genuinely depressed', 'troubled and troublesome', and 'stoical'): around four fifths of all three groups received this help.

Section 17 money, in particular, could be used to help families over crisis periods, where they had insufficient money for food, heating or other fundamental needs. There were restrictions, for example, with limited funds or a concern the family would not use the money wisely, or for its intended purpose. Where the situation was not one of crisis, but the needs were considered basic, and they could not access social services funds, social workers were often prepared to write to various charities with the purpose of procuring the financial support necessary to obtain the items needed. This could be the case, for example, with washing machines, beds or refrigerators.

Housing problems and needs were generally equally obvious, in that mothers lived in housing which was inappropriate, cramped or in poor condition, or in poor environments involving, for example, health hazards, vandalism or the possibility of violence. In other cases, housing problems could be more a function of the difficulty the family was experiencing in fitting in with the neighbourhood. These problems were, of course, both housing and relationship problems at the same time. Social workers often took considerable time and effort trying to help move these mothers, or to sort out their various problems, such as housing arrears, or giving advice about how to deal with difficulties with neighbours. One social worker spent:

> ... a huge amount of time hassling people, especially the council to set up these meetings...we have got some extra points on medical grounds. But it's still not enough. She has got 105 points, for a house – needs 400.

Social work responses were not just about the direct relief of deprivation, but also involved the quality of life of these families. This related to the provision of 'extras' at special times of the year, or special support for the children or mothers. These took various forms, although the most common was procuring Christmas hampers, or holidays for the mothers and children in summer.

Social workers focused on material and practical issues, at times, to deal with more fundamental issues which in themselves were neither material or practical. This approach emphasises social workers' recognition of the interrelated nature of the problems in these multi-problem families. In one case, for example, the social worker secured extra money to help a mother's self-esteem. This mother had had a debilitating illness and a serious weight problem. The money was provided to buy new clothes which might make her feel better about herself and her body image. In another case, the social worker also sought to facilitate improved self-esteem by supporting childminding in order that the mother could go to work. Where social workers felt that the constant strain of material deprivation was affecting the women's psychological state and parenting capacity – indeed where quality of life issues were involved, as with supporting holidays or provision of hampers – they were in the happy situation of being able to justify their provisions directly in terms of the children, through, for example, widening their horizons, providing them with stimulation, or just giving them a break.

Focusing on material and practical needs could provide a useful way of building the mother's confidence and trust in the social worker. In these circumstances, although the social worker sought to alleviate these problems directly, there was some hope that this would facilitate good relations and subsequent intervention. This was the case with the following family. Commenting on why they responded to practical issues, the social worker said:

> I think it was a mix, really, you know, it was a mix because there was a need to do the practical things like the Home Office and solicitors and health authorities and housing and things like that and the DHSS. There was a need for that and really that was the family's main priority. They didn't really see that they were needing other intervention, where obviously there was a need for it.

The social worker had a clear agenda, which was about promoting the possibility of further intervention later. Indeed, in addition to the 'trust' issue, these problems could be sufficiently severe as to inhibit the woman's capacity to respond to other issues.

Housing and environmental problems could equally be linked with other areas of difficulty. One particularly strong link was with health problems. In one case, for example, the social worker sought to get extra 'points' through which a seriously ill mother could gain greater priority for rehousing from the third floor of a high rise block of flats. She also considered it unsuitable for a family with five young children, including three who were under five. Another example linked health with housing problems, but also had a major connection with child protection:

> My initial involvement was in '95 when [mum] had [a debilitating illness], we then facilitated a move after that, to be closer to her mum. Her mum moved into the new houses [nearby]. She then wanted [her daughter — mum] down here, 'cause the children were running, even the little ones were running, between [the two roads]. It was only a matter of a few hundred yards. But it is across the road. And the bigger ones would take the little ones. And [mum], at that time was mentally quite ill as well. At times she didn't really know where her children were, and when they all lived in [the old house] — one of the strategies that the children had learnt for themselves, even during the night — if [mum] was very ill during the night, the children would go across the court and get grandma. What they were doing when [mum] was ill and grandma had moved, was actually going down during the night to grandma's in [the new area]. So we facilitated a move with the Housing Association, for [mum] to have one of the new properties down [there].

This case not only illustrates the multi–problem nature of many of the familial situations, but also highlights the ways in which one problem – in this case housing – exacerbates other potential problems and needs within families.

Parenting support

Another area of high visibility, arising in this case out of the key status of these problems in childcare practice, related to parenting. Help in these areas was again carried out with a high frequency by social workers. They provided advice and guidance on childcare and parenting to nearly 70 per cent (66/94) of the mothers. Parenting skills work was carried out by others referred to by social workers, rather less frequently, in only 16 cases (17 per cent). In all but two of these latter cases, the social workers were also carrying out work on parenting and childcare advice. This, then, was predominantly an area of practice carried out directly by the social workers themselves, although the more sustained and detailed work occurred where, for example, family support workers were also involved. There were no significant differences between the three groups ('genuinely depressed', 'troubled and troublesome' and 'stoics') in either advice or parenting skills development. However, there was a tendency for 'troubled and troublesome' women to have greater parenting skill input: a quarter of them (7/28) received this help, compared with 15 per cent (8/52) of 'genuinely depressed' and one out of 14 'stoical' women.

There was, of course, an intimate relationship between parenting problems such as, for example, hostility to the child or poor attachment, and child problems themselves, such as emotional, behavioural, cognitive and somatic difficulties. There was also often a close connection between focusing on the parent and working with the child. As one social worker observed, 'If you work with the mum, you get through to the children'.

Some of the mothers were heavily implicated in the development of their family's problems, yet these problems nevertheless required some action, particularly where concerning the children. Many social workers were quick to appreciate this, and concentrated on the issue of parenting regardless of whether they attributed the fault in these cases to the mother. This was well put by one social worker, in relation to support she was providing for her parenting:

> To protect the child, my main concern was the child, but I was also concerned for her [the mother]. What I didn't want is for to be part of...a child being injured or killed, so I said this is money well spent, whether she deserves it or not, to protect the child. Nobody said anything to me, the services were administered and nobody questioned it. It was a good decision. Whether she deserved it or not, whether she fulfilled the criteria or not, that is another question.

The connection between mother and child problems was widely appreciated by social workers. There was a frequent and clear recognition that little progress could be made with the children unless work was done with their mother as parent. This was particularly the case where mothers were so overwhelmed by their own problems and needs and this itself had an impact on their parenting. In these cases, focusing on parenting was also designed to facilitate progress with the children. In one such case, the social worker commented, in relation to parenting:

> I think mum needed supervision. Mum wanted something for her as well. It was hard for mum to deal with her daughter's needs and her own needs. Us social workers, she always felt, that we were looking over her. Which it is. She is not our priority. Although I work with mum in order to make things a bit better, at home etc.

Much of this support revolved, in one way or another, around advice on parenting. This could be achieved through direct work by the social worker, or through the allocation of support workers, family aides or befrienders. However, these services were often provided in the light of the connection between the problems and needs of the families and the quality of their parenting. This was particularly relevant where there were wide ranging other problems, social or familial, which had an impact on their parenting, or where they were particularly socially isolated. There were frequently advantages in using others, such as family support workers, since it was easier for them to be presented as the 'human' side of social services, whereas the relationship with the social worker was often mediated by their authority role with child protection. Many women were more receptive to such support, and commented very positively on family aides and support workers.

However, at the same time, such help was restricted by the limitations in skills. Where practical parenting matters were concerned these workers could, at times, encourage considerable progress, and they could provide a listening ear enabling women to express their feelings. However, more sophisticated counselling and psychological help was far beyond these support workers, and their contribution to the resolution of these underlying problems was negligible. Although they could help to deal with the surface problems of parenting, they could hardly be expected to help resolve the deeper problems associated with parenting difficulties.

Some of this support involved parenting training for the mothers. This, again, could be achieved in a variety of ways, including direct work by the social workers themselves, use of family support workers, specialised courses, and even the use of mother and baby units. In one case, the use of external resources helped alleviate the pressure on the social worker herself:

> She is not the only one, I have got, and then she got to the stage where she was so dependent on me that I had to try and wean her off. Well, it helped a lot when I put her in the Mother and Baby unit. She just turned to the staff then!! [Laughs] She bothered them then. It gave me a breathing space. She still phoned me but at least she was at arm's length.

Some social workers' actions were more proactive, seeking to develop resources, and to provide solutions for groups of mothers with common problems. These solutions were developed initially by identifying particular problems in individual mothers, as in the following example:

> I mean, mum is quite needy in her own right...and when her children no longer need her, that is when the problems start...in fact a colleague and I are thinking of setting up a permanent support group that, umm, people like [her], in order that they can meet for X amount of time a week with other mums in similar positions to themselves. And actually just discuss these problems...because we've got quite a lot of mums like [this]...but it's not necessarily, they don't want to go off to counselling, they don't want to go here, there and everywhere, they quite rely on social services themselves.

As with the use of support workers, however, these groups were not designed to lead to some dynamic change in the women's underlying emotional problems, but rather provide a venue for offloading, and helping them negotiate the continuing experience of the problems.

The focus on parenting skills gives a rather instrumental picture of work undertaken with mothers to improve their parenting, and, to be sure, this more instrumental dimension of parenting was a major feature of practice. However, some of the work involved the relationships the mothers had with their children. Thus while work with parenting skills occurred, when referred by social workers to others, with 16 mothers (17 per cent), family therapy, also relevant for these relationships, was employed with 17 families (18 per cent). When family therapy was offered, the general idea was to help family members communicate better with each other. This combination of work had two, often closely connected, dimensions: the need for developing skills and inner resources of parenting, and a need for the family to change their dynamics in terms of communication and behaviour.

A distinction was made between families with older children and those whose children were younger. Where children were older, more work was done directly with them rather than the mothers. In general, however, although work was done with older children, the main responsibility was clearly laid on the parents.

Emotional and relationship problems

This area evoked a rather different response from social workers. In particular, the mothers' own emotional and adult relationship difficulties were far less a focus for social work intervention than either the more practical and material problems or their parenting difficulties. This did not mean that social workers never got involved in these issues – some social workers made particular efforts in this area

– but attempts were more sporadic. There were complex issues involved, but social workers needed to have the capacity to recognise the problems clearly, to believe they had the skills to deal with them, and to be prepared to make an effort with them.

Relationship problems often involved interpersonal conflict, and social workers made some attempt to address this issue with 26 women (28 per cent). Conflict was occasionally with neighbours, but more generally with relatives. Some attempt to deal with these issues, where they involved the mother, father or other relatives, occurred with 12 women, though, in general, social workers did not expend much effort on these relationships. This was true regardless of subgroup of 'genuinely depressed', 'troubled and troublesome' and 'stoical' women.

More generally social workers focused on problems in relationships with partners, which occurred with 19 women. Where mothers were not single, and often where socially isolated, they tended to have problems with their partners, in the form of relationship difficulties and/or domestic abuse or violence. Social workers did not, on the whole, offer much support or work with partners to help resolve the conflict: joint work was offered to only nine couples (of the 94) and work with partners alone occurred with four families. Rather, they sought from partners a commitment to carry out supportive tasks, regardless of the difficulties between them and the women. One social worker commented:

> I've sat down with him a couple of times and said, 'Look, you've got to present a united front to your children, because otherwise you're going to play their mother off all the time. It's you that's going to come out being the goodie guy and mummy as the baddie person'.

This limited attempt at positive improvement in relationships was to a considerable degree the result of the partner's unwillingness or inability to work with the social workers, and there was certainly evidence of hostility from some partners.

However, even where there were relationship problems with partners, they were not always hostile to social work involvement. Although problems could exist, some relationships could be at least reasonably stable, and where this was the case, partners were encouraged to support mothers with various areas of need. Social workers were involved with partners in this way with 30 families, and they focused on a range of support needs. Most frequently – in 23 families – this involved encouraging the partner to provide more support with childcare, a feature which had more to do with the inadequacies of the parenting responsibilities which the fathers or stepfathers were taking, than an uninhibited enthusiasm for the task.

The main element of the social workers' concentration on the emotional content of these relationships was evident in appeals to the partners, in 19 cases, to reduce the degree of interpersonal conflict. This, however, with the exception of the few cases of family or partner work, involved little more than an exhortation to change their ways:

> We tried to get [partner] himself into the work but he has refused. Mum won't get rid of him. I mean, unfortunately you can lead a horse to water, but you can't make it drink.

The limited capacity for positive emotional work by the partner is clear from the infrequency with which social workers sought to get partners to try to increase the mothers' self-esteem, for instance by reassuring them of their worth. This was an element of only nine cases, and most of these involved disabled children rather than child protection.

Problems with partners, and indeed other problems with children and those in their social networks, were often considered to arise from a lack of positive relationships. Mothers were frequently seen to be involved in negative, destructive and unsupportive relationships, and this was often attributed to the mother's character. Mothers who were involved in these types of relationships tended to be seen as overly needy with many unresolved issues of their own. These, as has been shown earlier, were often considered to be very deep rooted indeed, part of a self-destructive pattern with which mothers conducted their lives.

These deep seated, self-destructive patterns often resolved themselves, as far as the social worker could see, into emotional, psychological or mental health problems. Most social workers did not, however, work with these problems directly themselves. Where they could, social workers frequently referred these women elsewhere, to mental health services, family centres, and occasionally NEWPIN, or employed the services of a family support worker (this matter is discussed in more detail later). One social worker gave the following reason for not getting involved directly with the mother's emotional problems.

> Yes [mum needed more time than the family]. But then the family care officer did this work with her, and [the eldest daughter] quite extensively.

There were, however, problems of gaining access to limited resources, particularly in the case of mental health services, and other services generally did not possess the skills to do much more than provide a listening ear and generalised support. Any hope, therefore, of actually seeking to resolve these women's deep seated emotional problems was curtailed by the limited skills of those chosen to deal with them.

Sometimes, the social workers were prepared to work with these problems, and they reported undertaking esteem building activities with 35 of the 94 mothers. While a substantial proportion, this was still a minority, particularly in that over four fifths of women reported feeling a sense of failure, and two thirds experienced this severely. Indeed over 90 per cent (86/94) had strong feelings of self-blame, and over half felt these severely. Much of this work may be characterised as being more supportive than dynamic, attempting to help the women to negotiate their distress and lack of confidence, rather than dealing with the factors underlying the distress in a way which might help them ultimately resolve their depression. As with other areas, there were no marked differences between 'genuinely depressed', 'troubled and troublesome' and 'stoical' women.

This limited response of social workers to emotional problems is confirmed by the women themselves. Nearly two thirds (54/87) expressed a considerable need to talk about their private feelings. Of those expressing this need, only just over a third (20/54) felt they could confide in their social worker, and under a fifth (9/54) had actually confided in their social worker in the previous month. The need for positive feedback was also widely felt, with 54 per cent of women (47/87) expressing a need for such support. Of these, just over a third (17/47) considered they had received some positive feedback from their social worker in the previous month.

Where there was a convergence of social work skills with a problem that was amenable to resolution the opportunity did exist for considerable improvement in the woman's situation. It was, however, important to distinguish with which mothers practitioners could hope to work successfully. This was certainly the case with many of the mothers who were considered 'genuinely depressed', or even 'stoical', as opposed to those considered 'troubled and troublesome'. The need for sensitivity in selecting the appropriate case, and, indeed choosing the moment, is clearly evident in the observations of one social worker in relation to a mother who was periodically depressed:

> If somebody was to do a short focus piece of work with her, she certainly has the intelligence, the insight enough to hear what they were saying, and that. I think while she's not very ill, that would be valuable to her. Of course when she is ill then none of this matters, because she's ill.

This combination of recognition, skill and choosing the moment was often not evident in the practice of social workers, and even where one element was missing this could prevent action being taken. One social worker clearly recognised the distress of a depressed mother whose children had been accommodated and whom she wanted returned to her, but had no idea how to respond constructively to her emotional needs:

> I was concerned for her. I really was concerned. Because she was so flat. And I wondered whether she had, an underlying question mark, suicidal tendencies. But she wasn't, well she didn't, I don't know, other persons perceived what they feel could be done, I didn't think pick that up. What I felt was a lady who was depressed, she was either tearful, whose needs were around wanting her family, but I didn't know how to get back in.

While, however, social workers did identify emotional and relationship problems, and were also, in some cases, prepared to respond to them, these needs were far more likely to be neglected or marginalised than practical and material or parenting problems. While it was frequently clear to the social workers that emotional and relationship problems were present (except when women tried to hide the extent of their distress), their interpretation, in terms particularly of practice responses, was less clear. For example, while the lack of money could often elicit a response, whether or not it was considered to be the fault of parents, because the financial needs were such that the welfare of the child was threatened, social workers were often unable to make such clear connections between practice actions and intervention outcomes with emotional and relationship problems. The depth of the problems could discourage social workers, and it was uncertain whether the women's response would lead to any long term beneficial effects. In some cases, there appeared a danger that large amounts of resources could be thrown at a problem with little positive outcome.

Social workers gave several reasons for not working directly with the mothers' emotional and relationship problems. Frequently these related to their perceptions of the problem or need, areas with which they felt it was inappropriate for them to work, or questioned whether they had the skills to work in these areas. Their responses showed a number of variations around this theme: it was not in their remit to work with these problems; specialist help was needed; someone else could do it better; they felt unable to work with such deep seated emotional problems; if they offered a service the mother might expect something which the social worker felt they would be unable to sustain; or the emotional needs were so overwhelming that they got in the way of work with the children. The deliberate decision to avoid these problems is well illustrated by the following dialogue between researcher and social worker:

Social worker   Umm, no I have discussed with her about her situation [her mental health problems, and her relationships problems], in the absence of her husband.

Interviewer   Do you actually work with the mother herself in terms of her problems, apart from the relationship, her depression?

Social worker   No.

Interviewer   Could you tell me why that is?

Social Worker   Because her depression is not a concern to me. We look at the welfare of the children.

Another argument often deployed was the conflict between entering into a counselling relationship with the mother, and the other work they had to do with the mother, in particular their authority role, or work with the children. Entering into the more person–centred realm of counselling could divert attention away from their requirement that they should not respond exclusively to the mother, but that, in fact, the social worker frequently had to exert some control over the behavioural excesses of these women in order to ensure the welfare of the children. Although this general point applied to families with children of all ages, social workers were, on the whole, more inclined to focus on some of the mother's emotional needs where younger children (under five) were concerned than where the families had older children, particularly those in the teenage years.

Key points

1 The multi–problem nature of the women and their family's situation meant there was a considerable challenge to social work skills. Although the principal concern was with the children, the mother was the primary focus for intervention to a slightly greater degree than the children.

2 Material and practical problems were often the most obvious in a very deprived group and also the most likely to be those for which the women sought help. Social workers responded routinely, but in a discriminating manner, to financial problems. They spent considerable time on housing problems, although their influence in this area was limited.

3 Responding to material and practical problems was often seen by social workers as providing a way of building confidence and trust, thus improving relationships as well as solving problems. This was often also seen as a way of alleviating other problems indirectly such as reducing stress increasing the risk to children, or enhancing self–esteem.

4 Parenting problems provided another major focus for social work intervention. Much of the work was direct advice and guidance by the social worker. Less frequently, parenting skills development was undertaken by others, although this was likely to be more sustained and in depth. Work could be instrumental, but at times was also oriented at relationships with the child.

5 Generally, the work undertaken with the mother was really about helping the child. Social workers often felt that this was the best way of reducing the risk to, or ensuring the welfare of, the children. Frequently social workers considered there were advantages in using others, such as family support workers, since they were less obviously involved in the controlling aspects of intervention, and could present a more 'human' face of social services work.

6 A focus of work on the mother's emotional and relationship problems was much less frequent, as well as more sporadic, when compared with material/practical and parenting problems. When it did happen, the work was oriented towards emotional support and sustainment, rather than dynamic and therapeutic work.

7 When this work was undertaken, the most frequent emphasis was on relationships with partners, or in eliciting support from the partners (or ex–partners when appropriate). However, some partners were unwilling or unable to engage with the social worker. This is perhaps not surprising because mothers were often seen as being in negative, unsupportive or destructive relationships.

8 The emotional problems of the mothers were seen as more appropriately the preserve of other professionals, although they had limited access to outside

resources. Social workers did attempt to use social services resources, and on rare occasions NEWPIN, but these were not considered to have the skills to do more than provide support, rather than resolve any deep seated problems.

9 Despite the marked differences in number and types of problems between the three mental health attribute groups, no significant differences were found in the degree of emphasis, as between material, practical, parenting, emotional and relationship problems, given by social workers to each group. Social workers tended to emphasise parenting, material and practical responses regardless of these groupings.

In view of the extent of these women's emotional problems, and the extent to which they interrelated with other problems, the relative lack of attention paid to them by the social workers may be something of a surprise. These women were, after all, universally depressed, not an auspicious state for ensuring the welfare of the children or resolving their problems. In the next chapter we will seek to identify some of the factors which led social workers to focus to such a relatively limited extent on these problems.

8 The context for practice

The work conducted by the social workers was undertaken in an environment where there were strong structural and cultural influences on their practice. Social workers were not simply able to do what they wanted; their actions were scrutinised, and often directed, by a managerial hierarchy which is typical of social services. Much of the work involved protection of children, yet the way this was carried out, in relation to depressed mothers, bore the hallmark of these structural and cultural influences.

These elements could affect practice with the mother in a number of ways. Four central features were: the way in which priorities impacted on the capacity of the social worker to focus on the mother; the effects of a care management orientation, the sense with which social workers felt they had a legitimate focus on the mother; and the extent of their mental health knowledge and skills. While there were clear boundaries to their actions, the social workers nonetheless showed different orientations to their work which had profound consequences for their case by case practice.

Cases, bureaucracy and priorities

One of the key reasons why social workers did not focus on mothers' needs was the priority given to other areas of work related to a bureacratisation of practice. The effect of this, at one level, was to limit the amount of time available to work on cases, or individuals within families, who were not themselves given priority. It also had a more insidious effect, of creating a 'mindset' in which there was a constant awareness of those to whom priority would not be given, even where this was not required by work pressures on the social worker.

Child and family services were not seen fundamentally as resources for mothers, unless there was a clear issue of risk or need for the children, despite the teams being named 'Children *and* families', and despite the potential for deleterious consequences for children following upon parental problems, particularly maternal depression. There was an emphasis on children in general, and child protection in particular.

The effect of this was often felt through the 'watching and direction' role of managers. Resource constraints meant that once the child's needs were not considered sufficiently severe for intervention, there was pressure to close the case, largely regardless of the needs of the mother. Social workers clearly saw managers as combining a role of interpreting policy and of managing scarce resources. Once the child protection issue is settled, commented one social worker, 'care managers find some difficulty in justifying keeping up that level of support...and...the case is closed'. However, this could affect the day to day practice of social workers even where their involvement was not in question:

> I have a practice supervisor who scrutinises pretty hard what I do, and is very prone to say, we don't do family therapy, and you are not the mother's counsellor, you are the care manager for the child. Whether he does that to make me justify my existence — I have a feeling that it is not quite like that — but I find that I have to fight to stay with some of them.

One social worker for children with disabilities commented that she had fewer pressures on her than other team members, yet even she had difficulty finding time to focus on mothers' needs. She tended to ring mothers up for a chat instead of anything more constructive:

> I think if I had more of the critical disabilities than some of my colleagues [have], I don't think there would be quite as much support as I am able to give them. Having said that, when I am really hard pressed, like just before [I was away temporarily], I have the sort of relationship with her, it's awful to say, but just ringing her up and having a chat, and she says 'I understand'.

However, at times social workers routinely rationed their own time and resources in a way consistent with managerial expectations. One social worker, mildly exasperated by the amount of legal work involved in a case, commented:

> I mean there's a lot of work involved in it, and it is not just the one hour a week that you do with them. It's the thought that goes round it, it's the planning, it's the discussion afterwards, and...the discussion with one's supervisors... I just get sensitive, really sensitive, I think, because I get asked so many times.... I have barristers, practice supervisors, child protection officers, everyone asking me.... And I have to justify my actions, my involvement, all the time.

Other pressures could have an effect on the capacity of the social workers to attend to the mothers' needs. Social workers frequently mentioned administrative tasks, particularly recording, as taking them away from work with families, but did so 'off the record', outside the formal interview situation. This was a clear agency expectation, arising from a need for information and accountability. Nevertheless, many social workers had mixed feelings about it. Although it took them away from direct work, they recognised its importance for 'covering their back' should any questions arise about their conduct of practice.

The previous comment by the social worker drew attention to these 'surrounds' of case practice. Face to face work with families was only a small part of practice, and the other aspects had a very intrusive effect on the capacity to conduct such work. Other aspects, reflecting the legal context, managed environment, and procedural requirements, frequently took considerably more time than was available for undertaking direct practice with the families themselves, and particularly the mother. There was a definite concern expressed about this bureaucratisation of practice. One of the key concerns expressed by social workers was in relation to court work. The parents, in particular, some thought, would benefit from the time set free by reduced court work:

> The amount of time that you spend on court reports, you spend in court and writing placement care regulations — it's all very bureaucratic really. Very time consuming, and you think that if you spend the amount of time that you spend on paperwork in actually discussing with the parents their problems, and trying to get a better understanding and to get them better. To build up a better relationship. Then you would get to the bottom of trying to help the family with their problems, rather than just managing the case.

This combination of bureaucratisation and emphasis on child protection meant that social work was, according to some practitioners, and in some respects, going in the wrong direction. This social worker, musing on the conflictual consequences of the child protection process, which made it difficult to work constructively with the mother, commented:

> My higher risk cases, that I give big priority to…. Because I think that the nature of child protection is framed in that way. I don't think it is right, but I think it works that way…. It's the wrong prioritisation, the wrong split, from childcare to child protection, we should be more focused on family support than we are. But that is the way it is.

As child protection was given priority, all other areas of practice where the welfare of the child was a consideration were given less attention. For example, parents of disabled children, relative to those where child protection was an issue, were considered to be competent. While there was some recognition of the pressures frequently suffered by these families, provided the children were considered safe, they were less a cause for concern. This is evident from one social worker's comment, whose knowledge of the family appeared so poor that he seemed to be acquainting himself with the family for the first time. The mother here was severely depressed, yet his comments displayed no knowledge, nor concern, about this:

> I think this case is a medium to low level NSI [priority] really. And, from time to time she will phone me. She phones me about the housing, and then I decide to pay her a visit. So I looked up the file and find the file, did a visit, and read up on the family, and saw the boy had a club foot and that he was on the register. Look at why he was on the register.

The issue of intervention strategy with disability will be examined in more detail later, but this helps illustrate how resources, priorities and bureaucracy affected practice in a way which could disregard the often serious needs of the mother.

Care management

Agency function and practice had a considerable influence on the actions of social workers. In particular, this related to the extent to which social workers could be regarded, on the one hand, as predominantly managers of care, and on the other as more traditional psychosocial practitioners. The latter case saw the social worker working directly with the family and mother, while in the former, the tendency was to engage others for those tasks. Derived from the National Health Service and Community Care Act (1990), care management had two central characteristics: a division between the purchaser of services and those who provided them, and an emphasis on the practitioner as broker of resources rather than as psychosocial practitioner (Sheppard 1995). Both styles of intervention involved the mobilisation and use of resources aimed at ameliorating or resolving the family's problems. Differences lay on a continuum: on the extent to which more direct supportive work with the mother was undertaken by the social worker him– or herself.

Care management, however, exercised a considerable influence, both in the direct policies of agencies and in its indirect effects on expectations of social workers' practice. Thus, while managers' expectations varied, there was, in general, an environment where care management, rather than psychosocial practice, was the expected orientation to intervention. Social workers were very aware of managers' expectations, even where a rigid purchaser–provider division had not been implemented, of social workers to act predominantly as managers of care. This was noted earlier in this chapter in one social worker's comments, while another said, in a more positive way:

> We're very much expected to be care managers of the family, and if we go out of line we're quickly reminded of what we should do. The managers see to that. Not that it's too bad, 'cos it helps you focus on exactly what you should be doing and make sure the others are doing what you expect. That's really helpful, particularly with difficult cases like this one.

This was apparent to one social worker, a practitioner with many years' experience, who had observed a clear change of emphasis in recent years. She emphasised this point strongly:

> And I think there is another thing that is very very true nowadays — when we were doing this work up in London, we had very much more clinical discussion, much more case discussion. The supervision in those days was a reflective process, when you were looking at what the family is doing with you and what you are doing with the family. It is not like that either now. Nowadays...you are not reflecting where you are in relation to the work. So, I think that may be one of the reasons why I have tried to work with this family.

Her own efforts to work more directly with the mother were a consequence of her determination to hang on to the long–held ideals she had about appropriate social work practice. For those like this social worker, the degree of commitment to the mothers as individuals in their own right, rather than a more instrumental relationship with them based on their parent status, was evident. The more they were personally involved with the mothers, the better they were able to understand and respond to their problems. This was a position taken by one social worker, when commenting on a difficult case:

> Well, there's a lot of emerging problems, and I think the more you stayed in there, the more you found really.

A care managerial orientation could very much characterise the conduct of practice. This emerged in the way social workers described their practice, rather than direct statements that they were 'managers of care'. In the following case, the social worker's tendency towards managing care for the mother was also associated with her belief that she should focus on the child:

> I think that it is quite clear that mum has been going through massive emotional turmoil herself, apart from the physical demands imposed upon her, and at times, in the time I've been seeing her, she was just overwhelmed by the demands. And, so, while I am keeping my focus on the children, I am fully aware that she has these needs and issues, and I am hoping that they can be met and addressed somewhere along the line, by various people involved.

Although the mother's distress was considered to be the social worker's remit, this was only so in terms of the management of her care. Another social worker, who also saw her role as resource mobiliser, rather than direct carer or provider of care, sought help for more practical problems which she felt lay at the heart of the mother's psychological difficulties. When asked whether she had worked directly with the mother's main problems, she said:

> No, we have linked [mum] into a worker for herself, the family centre, and that is to help look at the financial management, which is an area which creates quite alot of stress for [mum], as there are considerable debts accrued in the family.

The care management environment meant that, for those social workers who wished to work more directly with the mother, this generally involved them in more work, over and above that carried out by those who were managers of care. Those social workers who did engage in this way, gave special attention to the needs of the mothers, mainly around their emotional problems, such as low self–esteem. They very much had to go 'the extra mile' and this could impose additional burdens on them, in an environment which was generally not set up for this kind of approach to practice. The result could be considerable strain through additional work: as one social worker put it, 'I feel I've done my best. I feel quite, it tires me out to be honest'. Another social worker commented on the way she tried to keep counselling on her own agenda, even when the circumstances were not auspicious:

> I do feel it is important that I focus on [the mother] as well as [daughter], but I don't always get much support in this. I'm told that if I want this or that done I should refer her elsewhere. It's this care management thing — you're expected to get other people to do the work. I still do it though, but I can't give it as much time as I want. It just gets too much, what with all the other stuff.

Where social workers tried to maintain a more traditional 'psychosocial orientation', this clearly placed them under more pressure. It is easy to see how, together with other responsibilities, this could lead to burnout in the longer term, or to a withdrawal from their more ambitious agenda, to become more care managerial in their approach.

 Although most social workers claimed they provided some degree of emotional support when working with mothers, those most focused on direct work as part of psychosocial practice generally made the strongest emotional commitment themselves to the mother. This commitment was clearly expressed by one social worker, who stated that 'I had more of an emotional, psychologically based relationship with mum'. It was frequently apparent in terms of the amount of commitment to the mother: 'And on the phone I speak to her every other day. She is quite reliant on me actually, come to think of it'.

Commitment to the mother could come out in a variety of ways, all related in some form to providing emotional support. One social worker sought to improve the mother's self-esteem by discussing the kinds of clothes which would make her look best. Another social worker spent a considerable amount of time directly working with the mother to understand more clearly her emotional needs, in particular, that she should speak out more clearly on her views of her own and her family's needs.

> I decided to go for this family conference.... It was very useful. It was quite emotional on a lot of counts. But it was very useful. It was the first time I feel that [mum] was able to say to these people, 'Look, this is how I feel, and this is why I feel like that'. And I don't want to feel like that. I want to be able to do this and be this. And it was good because they listened to her as well.... I was there to try and referee, if you like.

On a very few occasions this could involve social workers going out of their way to respond to and help mothers in very difficult social situations. One social worker commented on the mother feeling lonely and isolated:

> What would happen before is that she wouldn't say to me, oh, they are bullying me and they are threatening me.... I would go there and speak to them and say, look this really isn't on, and leave her alone.

Key focus

Another feature underlying practice was a particular orientation towards working with families. Social workers did not attend to particular members of the family solely on the basis of assessments of individual needs. In particular, whether or not the mother was given attention in her own right was not solely dependent on her needs, but was a result of the focus on the child. Social workers, and their managers, actively interpreted the Children Act, and one element had particular and fundamental significance: the 'paramountcy principle', that in all matters pertaining to working with families under the Act the welfare of the child should be paramount. There is nothing in this which implies that the social worker should focus only on the child. Indeed, there are key elements of the Act which indicate that the social worker should work with the family as a whole, and at times, the parent, in order to secure the welfare of the child. Nevertheless, many social workers misinterpreted the Act to indicate that they should concentrate on the child rather than the mother.

This, furthermore, was consistent with concerns arising from child abuse inquiry reports. One official document, summarising findings from a number of inquiries on this subject, expressed concern that 'the rights of parents...appear to take precedence over the rights of children' (Department of Health 1991b). The worry that the child might actually be placed at risk because there was too great a concern for the parents implies a conflict of interest (between the child and mother) which will be discussed later.

The dominant view was of the practitioner as 'social worker for the child'. This line was strongly presented by many social workers. One of them stated that 'mum has to understand I am the social worker for the child, I am looking at the child's interest', and another said 'She [mum] has to be secondary, 'cos she is not the client, [the daughter] is the client'. Another social worker commented that:

> The first thing was, we had to look at the needs of the child. I am [the son's] social worker. I am not anyone else's social worker. And sometimes I have to stop myself and say, I am [his] social worker, and therefore what are the implications for him...[mum's] needs are not addressed individually. They are seen in the context of where her needs could be supported to ensure the needs of the child are met.

This social worker made clear that the only point of focusing on the mother's needs at all was to service the needs of the child. As an individual in her own right, the mother was of no professional concern to the family social worker.

At least two ways of viewing this emerge. On the one hand, the social workers could be considered to be as good as their word; they were not directly concerned about the needs of the mother, whatever sympathy they felt for her. On the other hand, there could be an implicit conflict of interest thesis: that a focus on the interests of the mother, would at the very least divert the social worker from the needs of the children, and at worst would place the child at risk. This was, at times, entwined with the child protection responsibilities of the social worker. One social worker commented on the need to carry out child protection procedures:

> In a situation like this, we've got to look to the child first. Yes, I'm quite sure that the current situation care proceedings isn't helping her at all, but having said that, we've no choice under the legislation, we've got to look to the welfare of the child first.

This sense of not helping the mother was not confined to care proceedings, but was part of the general authority role of the social workers. One social worker drew attention to a mother who felt that she was constantly being monitored, and the deleterious effect it was having on her:

> I think mum needed supervision. Mum wanted something for her as well. It was hard for mum.... Us social workers, she always felt that we were looking over her. Which it is. She is not our priority.

Those who held the view that the mother was of interest only to the extent of contributing directly to alleviating the child's needs tended to make a distinction between the woman as an individual in her own right (a matter which was of little professional interest to them, however sympathetic they may be to her at the personal level), and as a mother. An obvious way this manifested itself was by concentrating on the mother's parenting needs, which would not necessarily deal with any of the underlying issues of her own needs contributing to the child's (and family's) problems. As one social worker said:

> I see the mother as the main, the single strong character, and she is the key to holding the family together, basically...with the high level of support she is receiving at the moment, she is doing quite a good job of coping.... If she was a single lady, I wouldn't be having anything to do with her.

A minority of social workers did not conform to this common view. Some social workers took a more systemic approach to family dynamics and family problems, although they rarely actually mentioned a 'systems theory' approach. These social workers, while recognising the child was the reason for their involvement, nonetheless found it difficult to work with the child without doing so firmly in the context of the family, in a way which demanded familial level intervention. They clearly regarded themselves truly as Child *and Family* social workers. This orientation emerges clearly from the account of one social worker:

> It has been vital to work with the whole family because they were so — how can I say it — if one thing is happening to one person, then it was affecting everyone else. So everyone needed to see what was going on...when [the child] got hit...he started to hit his [younger brother]. So it was like a knock–on effect, so you couldn't just work with [the parents] about that, you had to work with [the eldest son] and explain to him the effect that this would have on [his younger brother]. And to work with [the younger brother] to explain about the aggravating behaviour

For this social worker, the whole situation was so enmeshed they could not single out one individual, but had to look at family dynamics as a whole. This approach enabled the social worker to attend to the mother's own needs, and not simply as a parent, albeit as part of familial intervention. One social worker pointed to the 'therapeutic family work' she did, while, as part of this, she was undertaking 'one to one counselling...helping mum through some of the difficulties'. This was apparent with another case where, although the social worker was aware of the danger of giving too much attention to the mother, she nonetheless did not shy away from devoting considerable effort to securing her well-being. She focused, in a one-parent, one-child family, on

> ...both. I have deliberately focused on both. I think the temptation to be too focused on mum, but I haven't.... I have tried very much to look at the family's needs, and the family is [the daughter] and mum.

Some social workers took matters one stage further, and were actually prepared to work with the mother as an individual in her own right, because she had needs of her own. These social workers saw their role as being one of helping the mother even where they felt the children did not require any major work. This was the case for the following social worker:

> To all intents and purposes, he [the son] is actually functioning pretty well. So I tried to talk with [mum] about, that being more for her needs than for his needs. And that might actually be a positive thing for him.

In other cases, the work with the mother was seen as proactively heading off any future trouble with the family:

> I think that is the most important first step to make [working with mother]. Do things with mum before you can go any further, anyway. The way that I am doing that is to be a bit of a sounding board really. Where she can sit and bend my ear about anything that she wants. I believe that probably one of the most central problems that she has got is that she is isolated. If we can break that down and try to improve that, then I think things will probably improve all round.

However, this view had its costs. In an environment where child problems were seen as a prerequisite to social work involvement, a focus on the mother meant 'going the extra mile'. Indeed, where some team managers insisted on closing cases where child problems had been alleviated, and where they saw the social workers as managers of care rather than providers, there could be some personal cost in pursuing this approach. One social worker was prepared to take on the extra load:

> At the moment we could probably close it now, and there wouldn't be any problems at all. But I'm not sure that it is the right time for [the mother]. Just a few weeks more to see her through.

Professional approach

It is a paradox that a group of professionals who have such extensive contact with individuals with mental health problems should not be required to have any mental health knowledge or skills in the conduct of their practice. Social workers were actively engaged in situations which were frequently extremely complex. At times they were caught up between sympathy for the circumstances in which many mothers found themselves, and concerns about the risk to children.

As a whole, social workers showed limited ability to understand depression, and a reluctance to employ skills which were more dynamic and psychotherapeutically oriented. Some simply denied that this area was a part of the social worker's role. One social worker who was aware of the mother's mental health problems said, 'I think she has relapsed a bit [mental health]. She has gone back to the unit and has just come back again, but that is not really my remit'. Though partly an issue of their care management orientation, these social workers generally felt they had limited skills with mental health problems. Social workers in general felt they could provide a 'listening ear', that they could advise, and that they could begin to help these women to make decisions about their own lives, but little more. Social workers, in other words, were prepared to give emotional support (although even this was variable), but not more therapeutically oriented counselling. This, which we refer to in the book as dynamic, psychodynamic, or therapeutic work, covers approaches which go beyond being merely supportive and presenting a listening ear. It involves constructive attempts actually to tackle the woman's emotional difficulties, and can include, for example, therapeutic counselling, cognitive work, and other psychodynamic interventions.

Social workers' response to this was generally either avoidance, or referral elsewhere, to counsellors or mental health specialists. An example of the latter, with clear reference to limited skills, was provided by one social worker:

> And I think I have just realised that there could be an enormous amount that came out, if I actually tried to do the work myself. But I didn't, I stayed with the brief with referring her on specifically for that.... I actually did feel that she maybe could benefit from one to one very regular counselling over quite a period of time. So that she would actually be able to get something out of her system. But also being able to process it.... And my skills, I don't think they are up to this, even perhaps if I had time.

Another said, 'I mean, I could talk to her every week, and I'm sure I'd get absolutely nowhere, because she is beyond my skills, to actually work through the complexity of the issues that are her problems'. The fear here, as with many social workers, is that of opening a 'can of worms', of doing more harm than good, and of being swamped by the emotional content of the counselling.

For those who had less knowledge of mental health, and confidence in their skills, one of the key elements in their response was the extent to which the woman's behaviours or symptoms were construed as 'active' or 'passive', whether they were more inward–directed or externalised. The former would be characterised by features such as self–blame or low self–esteem, whereas the latter were most frequently present in terms of anger and aggression.

This aggression could present a serious threat to the children. Furthermore, some women were considered either overwhelmingly needy and self–regarding or malicious, or both, and these characteristics were considered by the social workers to be of more significance in some cases than the depression itself. In these cases, regardless of the origin of their problems, about which the social workers might have some sympathy, it was their destructive and dangerous effects which were their primary consideration.

Some social workers found that the anger and aggression directed towards them was unacceptable, and this made it more difficult to engage in direct work with the mother. One social worker was at pains to suggest that the aggression had not blinded her to other aspects of the mother's personality, but it presented a barrier to greater direct involvement:

> I don't dislike her, it's just that she's very accusative, umm and that, I mean she's been very abusive to most people in this office, which is culminating enough, saying this cannot continue. We are going to stop contact if you can't behave yourself...it's not, not acceptable.

Such women were, in some respects, their own 'worst enemies'. It is perhaps not surprising that social workers were reluctant to put up with such behaviour, involving a daily routine which constantly brought them into conflictual situations. The distinction between 'passive–internalised' and 'active–externalised' symptoms was clearly made by another social worker:

> Yes, I find it quite distressing, 'cos I don't think I'm paid enough to, to take this sort of abuse. I'm very happy to deal with distressed people, and I am very happy to facilitate contact, but I am not prepared to put up with that abuse, you know. And often, yeah, I do find it distressing because I then...have to think very carefully [not]...to spite her because she is upsetting me, do you see what I mean?

Social workers rarely made reference to the past life experiences of the women in a way which constructively engaged both with the women's current problems, and informed appropriate interventions. These are the kinds of approaches which have, for decades, characterised mental health social work, and which has placed at its heart the social history. The result was that many social workers were rooted in the 'here and now', or at least the recent past, in making sense of the mother's situation and familial circumstances, rather than taking account of long term factors, including child and adolescent experiences of the mother. This could seriously affect the extent to which they could develop an adequate framework around which to consider the mother and her problems, as was clearly stated by the following social worker, referring to the presenting circumstances:

> Well, I think you would develop the way you would work with any client in response to how they present to you or how they react in a given situation, so you would always adapt to how a client presents.

On other occasions the need for these kinds of skills was recognised, and the social worker had some belief in their ability to carry them out, but did not feel they were always the best people to do so:

> Children's family social workers have to play a lot of roles really. You have to be investigator and counsellor etc. Yes I do it. But there are many other people that could do it better.

A minority of social workers did have the skills, or at least the confidence, to work more dynamically with the mothers' depression, but they were usually those who had experience of working in mental health or therapeutic settings. One commented:

> Well, I suppose I just brought basic counselling skills to it really. I just sat down, I just wanted to show them that (a) I was going to be genuine about how I felt...and what I'd heard from them, and (b) I wanted them to know that I was prepared to listen to them and their thoughts and ideas about the situation.

When this happened, the social workers could be aware of the deep seated basis for the problems the women and their families were suffering. In this case, both mum and daughter had been sexually abused. The social worker recognised the need to connect the two and to work therapeutically:

> The links between with [the daughter] and [herself]...it may benefit her if she were able to address her experiences, so as to defuse, and likely separate them out, her experience of abuse and what happened to [the daughter].... I was trying to help them make connections rather than me sit down and say this, that and the other...mum would find that [abuse of daughter] very, very difficult to recognise because unconsciously it would be too unbearable for her to contemplate.

Where therapeutically oriented, social workers could confront problems which were not faced by less skilled practitioners, and which required them to make judgements based on their higher skill levels. In one case, the social worker's therapeutic response had brought out strong emotions towards her from the mother. In this case, the social worker was working with a lesbian mother and she feared the mother was 'crossing over that therapist line' in wanting more than a professional relationship:

> I was talking to her in a therapeutic way...[but she] was openly saying that I'm a lesbian.... I wasn't about to put myself in any, in those kind of [compromising] positions.

This social worker attempted both to keep some professional distance and yet retain her therapeutic orientation. When this did not work, she concluded that a change of practitioner might be required.

Key points

Practitioners worked in a context which had a clear influence on the conduct of practice. As bureau professionals, their actions were not simply limited by managerial control, but the expectations of practitioners and the control itself were, in turn, influenced by agency function and expectations. Hence, social workers were not able to act independently, without contextual influences. However, their practice also reflected the culture with which policy and procedural expectations were interpreted, most obviously in relation to the manner in which social workers sought to prioritise the child's interests, largely to the exclusion of others.

However, this also displays some theoretical naiveté. The main approach was to work with the mother as parent rather than as an individual in her own right. However, the woman's role as parent tended to be de-coupled from her 'self' and personal needs and interests. Hence, for example, social workers focused on parental coping while ignoring their needs as individuals. This behaviour at the very least is questionable, in view of the link between depression and childcare problems and the associated psychological attributes, such as low self-esteem and pessimism.

The woman and her needs as an individual therefore tended to be marginalised, and this could be understood in terms of a number of contextual factors:

1. The priority given to areas of practice other than the needs of the mother was related to the bureaucratic dimensions of practice. Bureaucracy both limited the time available for working with mothers and had the insidious effect of creating a mindset of marginalising the mother's own needs. As a result, social workers routinely rationed their own time and resources in a way consistent with the expectations of their managers.

2. Managers undertook a watching and directing role, and part of this was to manage scarce resources. They therefore enforced, as far as the social workers were concerned, the continuation of a set of priorities which tended to marginalise the mother's needs. Hence it was difficult to find time to focus on the mothers' needs, and there was pressure for cases to be closed once it was considered that the child's needs were met.

3. Administrative tasks had an impact on social workers' time, and hence their involvement with the mother. This was based on agency expectations arising from the need for information and accountability. Social workers tended to have mixed feelings about administration: while it took them away from their face to face practice, it also helped them 'cover their backs'. One key concern was about time-consuming court work, and arose in the context of child protection, and was given priority.

4. There was a greater emphasis on social workers as managers of care, rather than as psychosocial practitioners. Care management, both as agency policy, and as

an idea, influenced practice. Managers tended to reinforce this message, and many social workers were themselves committed to this orientation. When social workers wished to work more closely with the mother, they often had to 'go the extra mile' over and above their care management work.

5 The focus on the child was the key to social work practice, based on the principle that in all matters the welfare of the child should be paramount. This paramountcy principle did not prevent them working with the wider family, but the dominant view by practitioners was that they were the 'social worker for the child'. The only justification for focusing on the mother's needs was to enable them to respond better to the child's needs.

6 A clear distinction was made, in much of practice, between the mother as an individual and as parent. The focus on the mother's problems and needs as a parent was at times decontextualised from those as an individual in her own right. There was also a 'conflict of interest' thesis, that concentrating on the interest of the mother would detract from the needs of the children, possibly placing them at risk.

7 A minority of social workers did not conform to this view. A more systemic approach led them to focus on the whole family. Some took it a stage further, dealing with the mother as an individual in her own right, but this also involved 'going the extra mile'.

8 There was no requirement for any specialised mental health knowledge, which was paradoxical in view of the extent of mental health problems in this group. Some denied that dealing with mental health was part of their role; others were reluctant to deal with emotional issues fearing they would 'open a can of worms'. A minority did have the health and/or counselling experience which equipped them with the skills or confidence to work more dynamically with the mother's emotional problems.

9 Social workers rarely referred to past experiences of women in a way which engaged constructively with their current problems and informed appropriate interventions. Symptoms tended to be seen as 'active' (aggressive and externalised) or 'passive' (depressive and inward directed). Some social workers saw aggression as intolerable and possibly an indicator of risk to the child.

There were, then, a range of contextual factors influencing the marginalisation of the mothers, particularly their individual needs. Part of this involved a belief that others would be better suited to this intervention; an ethos influenced by care management, which involved seeking outside support. A key issue is raised here about the extent to which collaboration with mental health services merited this view. This is the subject of the next chapter.

9 Working with mental health agencies

The multifaceted nature of the situations of these women, in terms of conventional agency divisions, arises clearly from the combination of mental health problems, the mothers' underlying depression, and the parenting and childcare problems which led to their involvement with childcare and family services. Family services were, in effect, fragmented. In social services there was a division between childcare and adult services, and mental health workers were employed within the latter. There was also a division between childcare social services, and mainstream mental health services, which were a health service provision. Social workers, as managers of care, could be involved in co-ordinating resource use, in which a variety of agencies could provide services in different ways.

While all the women in this study suffered clinical depression, over half (51/97) suffered this severely. There was, however, a limited use of mainstream mental health services. Only 17 women were involved with some form of psychiatric support, whether from psychiatric workers in the health service, or mental health workers within adult social services, well under a fifth of the total depressed mothers. Of these, twelve were being seen by a psychiatrist, a further five were seen respectively by psychologists and community psychiatric nurses, and just three were seen by mental health social workers.

Where there was psychiatric involvement, social workers generally did not display a clear understanding of its nature. Of the 17 women receiving mental health intervention, the diagnosis was not known to the social worker in relation to eight of them. Where social workers were aware of the diagnosis, only three were considered to be depressed, though with limited knowledge, social workers may not have been reliable reporters. Overall, these data suggest a lack of involvement with the mental health services.

It was noted earlier that social workers were prepared to use their own service provision for what might be termed mental health purposes. This was particularly the case with family support workers or family centres, which could provide emotional and practical support. One additional facility which linked mental health and childcare issues was NEWPIN, a service designed specifically to help depressed mothers with childcare difficulties. This was part of the voluntary sector, rather than NHS or social service provision, and largely run by mothers for mothers. Although Borough had the services of two NEWPIN facilities, these, like mainstream mental health services, were used very little. They sought to provide a combination of emotional and practical support, such as a crèche, and in some respects were similar in these broad aims to the services provided in a more formal way by family centre and family support workers. However, only four women attended NEWPIN, all of whom were referred by social workers. This was perhaps surprising because they were part funded by Borough Social Services.

Falling into the gap

Social workers, as noted earlier, made reference to depression, and other mental health problems, but rarely viewed it *per se* as a mental health case. The language they used referred to issues such as low confidence, self–esteem, hopelessness and the like. As a result, their response was frequently to seek a range of support services, including family support workers and family centres, which largely reflected their psychosocial orientation to the problems, rather than a focus on depression and a mental health response.

The institutional division between mental health and childcare services was exacerbated by a growing distance between them. Just as childcare social workers have in recent years increasingly concentrated on the most serious of cases – those involving child protection – so mental health services have increasingly focused on the management of care of the seriously mentally ill. The result was that, while a family might be considered high risk in one area, that of childcare problems, they were not necessarily considered high risk in the other – mental health – even though they were clinically depressed. A priority case for children and families, in other words, would not merit priority if presented to another part of the same service because they would not fit with the eligibility criteria of that particular area. This could be the case even though there was a belief that involvement of mental health services might reduce the risk to the children.

This situation was understood by social workers, affecting their collaborative intent. In one case a social worker felt a woman had clear mental health problems, though she was uncertain as to their exact nature. The involvement of mental health services, she thought, could facilitate her working with the mother, but they were reluctant to become involved:

> I must admit I do find it difficult to work with her. And I actually think there needs to be some input from the mental health agencies. But umm, I've tried to make referrals to adult mental health team, but what they've said is that she's not severe enough in term of the sorts of criteria in which they work. They sort of did a rough assessment with me, and they were saying that [they couldn't take her on].

This was also the case with the main alternative, adult services within the social services department:

> I think she would benefit very much from having her own adult female
> worker, but she is not going to get that...because the mental health team
> are only dealing with severe cases. They are looking at sections and things. I
> know myself from duty, and I know if I went to them with this case they
> would laugh at me, and say sorry, top end only. All their cases are
> schizophrenic and manic depressives.

The division between services, then, created the rather bizarre position that
families with high priority were unable to gain access to services they needed
simply because of the artificial, organisational division of services. Where
psychosis was not involved, the problem associated with the mental disorder had
to be sufficiently severe, and perceived to be centrally related to the mental
disorder, to get through the threshold for service provision. Such was the case with
a depressed woman who attempted suicide:

> The adult mental health team was involved...I think she tried to gas herself,
> and she rang her sister, and told her and her sister contacted [the team] and
> they went straight to her house and they got her admitted to the hospital.

Even where some response was forthcoming, it was at times rather more limited
than the social worker hoped. A social worker was hoping to get long term help for
one woman, but was disappointed by the lukewarm response. She referred her to
the mental health social worker:

> The children went home with her that evening and...the Approved Social
> Worker...saw her, and referred her to psychiatric assessment, and it went
> from there actually...definitely not long term input.

Even where mental health services became involved, they could back out rather
more quickly than anticipated by the childcare social worker. The key here was
that the woman was expected to be 'in crisis' as well as having a difficult
character, for her to be allocated to a mental health worker:

> She becomes abusive, and we can't carry on the conversation...at the
> moment, because the EIS are saying that she is not in crisis, and she is
> stable as she is going to be, they are withdrawing. The mental health
> worker is now the worst person, and I am OK.

The woman, already a difficult client, took a dim view of their withdrawal. Where
they were prepared to be involved, the presence of a childcare social worker could
make a difference to attitudes. In one case, when a psychiatrist refused to take on a
woman, the adult social services team were prepared to step into the breach.
However, the fact she had a childcare social worker meant that the support
provided was likely to be limited, regardless of whether the social worker had the
skills to provide the necessary mental health support:

> Speedwell would do the assessment, but there is a psychiatrist there, made
> the diagnosis or whatever, that she wasn't mentally ill. OK so the
> psychiatrist then sent her back to me. And I tried to get the adult team

involved. They said that, we can actually do it, but you are doing a lot of the work.

Collaboration: initiating involvement of mental health services

The social workers themselves could be partly responsible for the limited involvement of psychiatric services. Collaboration was limited from the outset, not simply by the perceived inaccessibility of the services, but by the ways social workers made sense of the familial problems, which could lead to the minimisation of mental health issues. Although they could accept that women might be depressed, some were reluctant to see this depression in terms of psychiatric treatment. Beyond this, however, their construction of the women's problems did not always lead them in the direction of mental health intervention. To describe women in the ways which occurred, for example, with the 'troubled and troublesome' group, often left the social workers focusing on personality issues rather than a discrete mental health problem. Theirs was at times a compartment-alised view of characteristics, which did not coalesce to formulate some kind of mental health diagnosis, but rather entailed a judgement on the woman herself, and her reliability with childcare.

There was, then, a tendency for a gap to develop between a 'mental health discourse' which organised the information and assessments in terms of mental health concepts, and a 'childcare discourse', where mental health was generally peripheral, and in which issues of risk, parental competence and associated parental characteristics came to the fore. This gap provided a backcloth to social worker actions and was evident in the low number of women considered by the social workers to be depressed.

The denial of a mental health issue was particularly graphic, although not unusual, in the account of one social worker. This was despite the multiple layered mental health problems identified by the social worker herself:

> She has not had a mental health worker. As I said, I don't think it was a mental health problem. The depression was because of what was happening and then she turned to alcohol and made it worse...I don't know if the alcohol was a big issue, because she was not in charge of him [attention deficit disorder child] any more.

This woman was severely clinically depressed. However, for this social worker, because the psychiatric problems were explicable in terms of environmental issues, the involvement of mental health professionals was not appropriate.

One way the gap between childcare and mental health services emerged was in the expectations that clients rather than social workers take the lead in obtaining psychiatric help. One social worker stated that clients in general did not want involvement and as a result there was no point in making a referral. This lack of interest was itself seen as an indication that they did not really need psychiatric support, because if they did they would make more attempt to obtain it. They suggested that 'nine times out of ten, these people don't want to go. They don't feel they have got a problem'.

Collaboration could be further limited by social workers' reluctance to be proactive in attempting to involve mental health services. Rather than make the referral themselves, the social workers frequently sought to get women to make first contact with mental health services. There was an element, at times, of washing their hands of responsibility, as in one case where the social worker steadfastly maintained that the woman should deal with this herself: 'She would have to refer herself for mental health help, umm she could as an alcoholic, have a social worker for herself, but she won't'. Some social workers appeared not to consider the reasons why the women should be reluctant. Although these could be varied, one social worker, without registering it, provided a hint:

> She finds it very difficult [engaging with psychiatric services].... I think it's that element. I think she would be more likely to engage with Adult Services — she doesn't at the moment — but I think in treatment somewhere, she could come across and be more open with them.

The hint was clear that the stigma attached to involvement with psychiatric services was a disincentive.

However, where social workers were lukewarm in their encouragement, there was little help given to enable them to overcome this disincentive. The social workers were not in direct control of requests for specialist psychiatric involvement. One of the problems in seeking help from mainstream psychiatric services involved the referral route. In order that access could be obtained to specialist services, it was necessary to route the referral through the GP, who had a 'gatekeeping' role. However, the woman could decide not to take matters to the GP, or the GP could decide not to refer, or provide a service themselves. This led to referral to a GP as an end in itself for psychiatric support. GPs were, according to social workers, involved with 22 of these mothers. However, GPs' involvement, not based in the notion of an allocated case, as with social workers, could include very sporadic contact. There was no guarantee that the GP would seek to have consistent and planned involvement with any of the mothers referred.

In some cases, these referrals could involve a rather touching faith in the capacity of GPs to provide particular kinds of services. One woman, who was recognised as being in emotional turmoil, was referred to the GP for counselling. The social worker commented that 'we've attempted to work with mother, which involves advising her to seek counselling in her own right from her GP'. This faith shown by the social worker in the GP's ability to deliver some therapeutic service is not borne out by the literature (Goldberg and Huxley 1992), or the experience of most practitioners. It is, perhaps, a testament to their difficulty in finding appropriate support, that they sought to refer to the GP. In another case, the social worker was rather more realistic about the prospects for GP involvement:

> I did tell her...to consult the GP. I just felt she needed a proper assessment.... I feel that I have a depressed mother out in the community who may actually need more help than I can give her. And also I think the other thing, although I don't like medication. I do think some drugs around now...might just shift things round for her.

In this case, there was no indication that the GP would seek out specialist services. However, the social worker set some store in the possibility of appropriate medication being provided, rather that having any faith in the time or capability of GPs to carry out supportive therapy themselves. There was, on the whole, some distance from the GP, with little evidence of detailed collaboration. However, the GP did have the advantage of being relatively non–stigmatising compared with either social or specialist psychiatric services and hence GPs provided a service some women were prepared to attend even if it was of limited adequacy.

Using mental health services

Mental health services were the preferred destination for most women whose psychological problems appeared to the social worker to be beyond their expertise. Within this general therapeutic rubric, social workers were interested in a variety of service types. At times this was presented by social workers through the general term 'therapy'. In one case, it involved working with long term trauma:

> It was quite severe, the abuse that [mum] suffered. Mum has had a lot of therapy. She originally worked with a...clinical psychologist. He worked with mum alongside the children in the relationship.... Then she was referred to a family centre day project [for support], where mum would go in at 10 o'clock until 2.30 pm.

The notion of 'therapy' for this social worker, as with many others, was relatively undifferentiated, a general term to refer to some kind of psychodynamic work with the mother. The mother's problems were deep seated, arising from long term abuse in her childhood, which was perceived to affect her relationships with her own children. The provision of this generalised notion of therapy was variable. Sometimes it was infrequent and fairly cursory, and as a result could hardly be considered psychodynamic. In some cases, however, it could be quite intense and long term, as with one mother who had serious mental health problems and was the subject of extensive resource provision:

> She has an appointment most days of the week. Either with her GP or an individual session with her worker, or a group, and she goes to a mental health pop–in. I think five week days are covered by [mum] going to somewhere or other...and it's very important to her that she has the structures in her life.

More specific foci were mentioned, but not consistently. Management of anger, sometimes through detailed therapeutic work, was mentioned:

> I was hoping they could explore, in a safe environment, their own issues and feelings with each other. About [the daughter], the way she had been parented, and about [mum], about the way that [her daughter] had reacted to her. And if they could start talking about, you know, I am really angry with you, I hate you. Even if they got to the point of acknowledging that, and saying nothing else, it would be a way forward.

This case alludes to an important aspect of service use, particularly where the parents had an ambivalent attitude towards the child, combining both deep affection and strong feelings of anger. Mental health services could provide a setting where the authority role of the social worker was less immediate. Without the fear that this role could engender, the family could be more open, and explore their familial issues with more honesty, unencumbered by the persistent fear that saying the wrong thing could lead to the child being placed in care.

In other cases, there was a more limited aim, seeking specialist assessment or advice which could help case management. In this case, it was seen as part of the perceived efficient use of services:

> We wanted to keep things tight, and have a purpose in all the intervention that we were doing. So [it]…was a time limited assessment for the purpose of getting the social history on the parents. And how they were feeling about things.

A further dimension was the use of specialist drug or alcohol agencies. These were used in relation to nine of these women, although 19 of the mothers were considered to have some problems in this area. Despite being part of mental health services in a wide sense, these were different in that they did not generally contain a consultant who was head of the team. Referral through a medical route was not required. They could be focused on psychosocial aspects of cases, and be run by non–medical personnel. Alcohol problems, as was shown earlier, form a significant aspect of some cases. Many of those with alcohol problems were mothers in the most difficult 'troubled and troublesome' category, and some of these were involved in the more serious child protection cases. Mental health services could be engaged to support the general aims of the social services, as in one case where the children were in care. Here, in a worsening situation, the social worker persevered with mental health support in the hope that the work undertaken with the mother would reduce alcohol dependence and improve parenting capability:

> …to look at counselling with her alcohol abuse…to help her with her alcohol and to get the children back. Originally to keep the children based at home. And then to get the children back.

While the authority role was at the forefront of some work, mental health services could provide an escape, at least in part, from this role. One social worker commented on the efforts made to help a woman, where alongside their counsellor, alcohol services were sought for emotional support:

> I have tried to encourage her to attend places like AA (alcoholics anonymous), for her drinking. That often with peer group support, allows the opportunity for counselling and support. Not necessarily formal counselling, but informal.

While in some cases women were able to use mental health services constructively and supportively, one difficulty was the failure of some women to maintain their involvement having been referred, or agreeing to go in the first place. Women were described as 'resistant' because of a deep reluctance to use these services. One woman encouraged to have pharmacological intervention was viewed as 'fighting it, every way along the line...at the end of the day [I suppose] she's got to listen to her own instincts of what she wants'.

At times social workers regarded pharmacological intervention to be of considerable importance, and resistance severely damaging both to the woman herself, and her chances of coping adequately with her children:

> We have to find something consistent for her. So that she can stop hitting these dips. And actually start — the trouble with [mum] is she gets better, and then stops taking the anti–depressants. Things like that. It's no, no, no.

Another side of this problem of involving women is the fear of the emotional pain that a more therapeutic response could entail. For many of those with alcohol problems, avoidance could be the best way of preventing deep and difficult feelings from emerging. Thus, even where mental health services were involved, it was not always possible to provide extended and consistent support. Indeed, having begun using these services, involvement could break down through non–attendance. In some cases, social workers could be quite persistent, to little avail:

> She was referred there [to mental health team] twice. But they, mum stopped engaging. It gets to the stage whereby when things get quite difficult in counselling and therapy, she just withdraws...they were going as a family.

NEWPIN

NEWPIN presented, for Borough, a particular facility directly related to maternal depression and childcare. It was a voluntary service, funded by Borough, and lay outside mainstream mental health facilities. However, the overwhelming majority of users were not referred by social workers, an interesting commentary on the limited extent to which social workers were prepared to use this facility. Where it was used, NEWPIN was seen as part of a nexus of available psychosocial support agencies:

> I've done a lot of networking with other agencies. I've first of all, I've realised the family were isolated socially, is first of all, I referred mum to NEWPIN.

NEWPIN operated, as far as the social workers were concerned, in a manner similar to a family centre. At the heart of its contribution were attempts to improve parenting skills, a feature cited by the social workers for all four women. These were generally directed at the mother, but could involve the partner as well, as happened in one case: 'I hope the referral would involve the whole family and that he'd [partner] go along, so he learns the basics of parenting'.

In general, parenting advice was directed at the mother, and involved the link between the risk to the child and the inadequate parenting:

> The concern was mainly around the child's failure to thrive...[so] we have this referral. Certainly the child is beginning to put on weight. Here we had a mother who really didn't know how to care for the child.... I think now, all she needs is the one to one work about being a parent which NEWPIN can provide.

NEWPIN was used as an all purpose agency which could address the range of psychosocial problems experienced by these women. This case was typical of the four who used NEWPIN:

> Well NEWPIN helped her in terms of her, visiting NEWPIN for counselling, socialising with other women that were going through the same problem. Yeah, for domestic violence.... And parenting, also, like, they had a playgroup, for parents and their children could sort of socialise.... And through discussions and advice given, she'd spend more time with mum, her parents. Her mother, rather. Then she started to have links with her friends, that she didn't have links with before. So, they built up her confidence as well. They would visit. So, things like that, she started to grow that way.

Social workers might refer in the first instance for one or more of a range of reasons, such as parenting, social isolation, need for relief from children (crèche), advice, counselling, support, and developing friend relationships. Once referred they could have access to all these different services. In its emphasis on key issues specifically for depressed mothers, it was able to offer a more focused service than was generally available in the health service, and to some extent it was seen as more informal than the professionalised services of the NHS. In Borough therefore it was distinctive from NHS facilities. Nevertheless, NEWPIN resembled some models of family centres which would offer very similar services.

Collaboration: involvement with mental health services

Where mental health services were involved, social workers expressed mixed feelings about this. In some cases social workers felt they were able to collaborate constructively with mental health specialists, usually where the cases were regarded to be most serious. This was certainly true of the few families who came to childcare attention because of a pre-existing psychiatric disorder, as with three women diagnosed with psychotic disorders. The seriousness was presented in two ways: where the woman's mental health problem was itself regarded as severe, yet potentially workable, by both mental health and childcare services; and where both childcare and mental health services appreciated the need for support to help family functioning and parental coping (both of these could occur together). In these cases, mental health support was part of a wide variety of resources available. This was commented upon by one social worker:

> Yes, phenomenal cost. I would say the health services as well. The adult mental health team...part [social] and part health services. So I would say the health service pays the biggest chunk of the family. The GP is seeing her once a week, for example. It is costing agencies a lot of money.

Mental health services could help the childcare workers plan their intervention strategies by offering quite detailed information on the woman's mental health state. These could then vary according to the mental health state of the mother:

> It is often more useful for me to liaise with her mental health worker than perhaps it is directly with her [mum]. Who she knows very well, and who can give me a very good and current assessment of the situation — which then enables me to go and plan my strategies depending on how well mum is.

Involvement of mental health services could aid a more holistic approach to intervention, in which the family, rather than the children or mother *per se* could be seen as the focus for intervention. This again could involve the use of a wide range of resources:

> She has got so much going in and people constantly thinking of ways that we may be able to enhance the lives, not just of [mum] but her entire family. So I think she is probably getting the optimum. I don't know if there is anything more that we could provide.

At its best, collaboration with mental health services could fundamentally and positively alter childcare involvement. In this case, it was not so much about direct specialist help as the general counselling and advice which was provided:

> I think that the support that Adult Services has given her, in helping her understand the role of social services, and why the children have been removed, what role she can play now, has turned everything around for her, so that she feels more positive. Even to the point where she is seeking advice from social services about another child which she may conceive.

On other occasions, even where they were involved, specialist mental health services were not seen as very helpful. This was the case where they provided only limited support or were perceived to have only limited commitment to the mother. This could take the form of crisis intervention, followed by withdrawal when the immediate crisis was resolved. One social worker commented negatively that the crisis team had been involved 'because of her depression...talking support, therapy...but they are retreating'. The result was short term work with little long term follow–up, which could have supported the social worker with their own case management.

Specialist mental health services were also seen as unhelpful because the messages from mental health services were mixed. When this was the case, it was difficult for the social worker to make sense of the mother's condition in terms of their planning of childcare strategy. One social worker was perplexed by these changes:

> Mental health service diagnosis has changed now. They feel that, yes, she does suffer from depression, she is on medication, but can't maintain medication. But actually they think she is likely to have a personality disorder. That is why she is volatile, that is why she is aggressive...so at the time we were thinking this is [mum] with depression, but actually now this is [mum], this is what she has been like for 10 years.

For this social worker, this change had a significant bearing on the prognosis for childcare intervention, but it was unclear whether the diagnosis would change again, requiring a further change in direction.

A further problem was where limited information was passed from the mental health team to the social worker. In one case, the social worker herself referred, but was given little information about their assessment. Commenting on what had been decided, she said:

> I don't know really. All I know is that...the assessment was that she wasn't depressed enough to affect her housing, which is one of the reasons she said was causing her depression, so whatever the outcome of the psychiatric assessment was, it wasn't perceived as being that severe.

This social worker knew little, and what she did know did not help her intervention strategy much, which involved supporting the woman being rehoused. Of course, information provision goes both ways and where limited information is provided, social workers could themselves seek further information.

Key points

1   In view of the extensive and severe problems of depression suffered by these women, the involvement of mental health services was low, with sporadic support provided. This is a problem of fragmentation of services, with bizarre outcomes. While both mental heath and parenting problems were features of these women's lives, the services were separated and operated according to different criteria. The result was that cases with the greatest need sometimes did not receive a mental health service because that family's risks did not fit with the eligibility criteria of the mental health services.

2   This division was based on a focus in mental health services on particular psychotic conditions, from which, in general, these women did not suffer. One area which did elicit some response was severe alcohol problems and this reflected a different approach in some street-based direct referral agencies.

3   Access to mental health services was also limited by the gatekeeping role of the GP, which meant that it was out of social workers' hands whether or not a woman was referred on to specialist mental health services. Direct referral could be made to adult social services, but they too had eligibility criteria which made it unlikely that they would be allocated an adult worker.

4   Mental health involvement was limited by social workers' own orientation to these families. They frequently focused on facets relevant to parental functioning and risk rather than maternal mental disorder. They were more likely, therefore, to carry out their own 'rationing'.

5   The action orientation and eligibility threshold meant that conventional childcare services were used for support purposes which might otherwise be carried out by mental health specialists. This was the case with family centres and family support workers. NEWPIN was rarely involved, and generally used for similar purposes to the social service supports, particularly family centres.

6   When used, social workers generally saw mental health services in terms of therapeutic work that could have a dynamic effect on psychological functioning rather than simply emotional support. Specialist alcohol and drug agencies, although having a therapeutic role, would often be seen more as providers of emotional support and guidance.

7   Where mental health services were involved, collaboration between childcare and mental health services was best where the problems were serious and obviously interconnected. These tended to be part of an intensive service response involving various resources. Mental health services, social workers felt, could provide support through a more holistic approach to intervention. They were least helpful where fragmentation occurred through, for example, mixed diagnostic messages or limited support.

Part four

Social workers' intervention strategies

4

10 Child protection and child abuse

It is possible to identify three distinct groups, where the intervention strategy by the social worker differed markedly. These were the child protection–child abuse (CP–CA) group, the child protection–family support (CP–FS) group, and the disability group. In each of these groups, the ways the social workers understood the parents and conducted their intervention varied considerably. In this chapter, the focus will be on the child protection–child abuse group. For the purposes of this research this group was marked out by the social workers' own definition: that the family had at least one child on the child protection register, or their children were known to have been abused, or both. Altogether 53 families fell into this category.

These were, as a whole, the most problematic cases, in that they were assessed as presenting the greatest risk to the children. Thirty of the 53 families had children on the child protection register. Table 10.1 shows the differences between the three intervention groups in terms of the average severity of their problems:

Table 10.1 Problem score comparing the depressed women by intervention strategy

Problem area	Max* score	Intervention strategy			
		CP–CA	CP–FS	Disability	p
All problems	114	26.1	18.6	14.1	0.001
Social	27	4.4	4.2	2.5	0.07
Adult relationship	18	5.2	3.9	2.6	0.006
Adult health	21	2.5	2.1	1.9	0.5
Parenting	18	5.1	2.1	1.5	<0.0001
Child	30	8.9	6.3	5.6	0.009

Test Kruskal–Wallis

*Maximum score =highest possible score for each area

In this table, the basic position is that the higher the score, the more severe the problems. Overall, Table 10.1 shows the child protection–child abuse intervention strategy to be undertaken with families which had the most severe problems. This was followed by families subject to child protection–family support intervention, with the disability group having, relatively speaking, the least severe problems.

This may be explained in a little more detail. The table is based on the problem scores obtained from the Social Assessment Schedule, in which each problem is rated with a score of 0 for no problem, 1 for a problem present but not severe and 2 for a severe problem. It should be noted, therefore, that a score of 2 would mean a severe problem in any one problem area. Thus, for example, even in the disability group, mothers averaged nearly three severe problems in the domain of child problems, the CP–FS interventions averaged marginally more, and the CP–CA interventions higher still. Nevertheless, the table shows child protection families scored higher in all areas, and the difference was particularly marked, as would be expected, with parenting problems. Nearly two fifths of these women neglected their children's physical care (20/53), and for nearly a quarter (12/53) this was a severe problem. Nearly four fifths of children in this group were given inadequate guidance (41/53) and for a half (26/53), this was a severe problem. Just under a half of these mothers showed little interest in involving themselves with the child (24/53) and for over a quarter of these mothers (14/53), this was a severe problem.

There is, in turn, an important relationship between the social workers' mental health attributions and their intervention strategies. It should be noted, however, that this is a significant tendency rather than a universal relationship, as is evident in Table 10.2:

Table 10.2 Relationship between mental health attributions and intervention strategies

Mental health attributes	CP–CA	CP–FS	Disability	Total
Troubled and troublesome	22 (78%)	5 (18%)	1 (4%)	28 (100%)
Genuinely depressed	27 (52%)	21 (40%)	4 (8%)	52 (100%)
Stoics	4 (29%)	1 (7%	9 (64%)	14 (100%)

Correlation (Pearson) 0.24   p=0.02

Chi–squared test: CP–CA versus other cases:

X^2=10.43   df 2   p=0.005

The findings of this table may be summarised fairly simply. A large majority of the 'troubled and troublesome' group was subject to a child protection–child abuse intervention strategy. About half the 'genuinely depressed' experienced child protection–child abuse intervention, while most of the rest were subject to child protection–family support intervention. Two thirds of the 'stoics' were in the disability group. There was, then, a clear link between mental health attribution and intervention strategy.

At the heart of the relationship between mental health attributions and intervention strategy was, in this case, the issue of risk. The fact that the majority of women in this group had children on the child protection register, and that in all other cases, social workers considered that children had been abused, made risk a central feature of their intervention. The features of parenting just identified serve to confirm this. Key elements of social workers' intervention strategy, such as the use of authority and control, followed from concerns about the danger to the child.

However, this further links with mental health attribution. It is perhaps no surprise to see 'troubled and troublesome' women encountering the CP–CA intervention strategy, since it was noted earlier that this group had significantly more severe parenting problems than other groups. There was, furthermore, a central issue of character. Some of the key defining characteristics of the 'troubled and troublesome' group made these women, from the social workers' point of view, considerably more likely than others to be a danger to their children.

Where mothers were seen to be overwhelmingly needy, and found it difficult to place their children's needs ahead of their own – or even to ignore their needs – social workers were far more likely to express concern over the child's welfare and safety. Hence the construction of the woman's depression became a key factor in the ways social workers in turn constructed the cases. A mother whose depression, if recognised by the social worker, took the form of high levels of self-absorption, or periods of aggression and rages, represented a greater threat to the child's safety than one with less aggression and self-absorption. This is clearly evident in the quantitative data. Social workers considered nearly half the women in the child protection–child abuse group to express hostility and criticism towards their children, and for over a third (19/53) this was a severe problem.

The focus of social workers' concerns and an underlying feature of their intervention strategy was risk to the child. The mental health attributions of the social workers, then, were significant in their link to action: women were defined in the way they were, because social workers were always aware of their responsibilities (as they understood them) and the possible range of actions they might have to undertake. Their definitions were action–oriented.

Authority

At the heart of social workers' actions was their preparedness to use the authority invested in them by the Children Act to protect and promote the welfare of the children. This was not always stated explicity, and, indeed, where mothers sought to co–operate with social workers, it would be a background factor subsumed under the immediate need to develop and maintain a good relationship. However, there was frequently a need to make it more overt, and where this happened, it pervaded all aspects of the mother–social worker relationship.

The use of authority meant social workers tended to pay less heed to parental preference. Where a child was at risk, it became necessary to be very clear about this risk, and the possible consequences if matters did not improve. The emphasis on the paramountcy of the child's welfare, and possible conflicts of interest between mother and child, emerged most clearly as factors underlying this intervention strategy.

This is what happened in one case where the social worker was concerned about the potential for abuse to be perpetrated by the mother's partner. Here the mother was forced to choose between partner and child:

> There was a lot of involvement. The social services team did case reports and everything like that because the children were at risk...and there was a lot of monitoring, and we said to her that the children were at risk and that they would be taken into care if it went much further. And that, she ended the relationship, that was her way of getting out.

In a very similar case, the mother's life situation was substantially affected by a similar injunction:

> She was saying that she did not want [her son] removed. And that she feels her partner could change his behaviour.... What we were saying was, well, the partner should move out of the house. And the partner wouldn't move out of the house.

The threat from the partner meant that the social workers were unequivocal that the mothers needed to make a choice which could, for them, entail considerable emotional conflict. In this case the result, unsurprisingly, is that the child was placed in care, and social services would not allow the child to return anywhere where her partner was living. In the end the mother moved out and went to live in her own father's flat, whereupon her child was able to live with her again. This illustration is typical of some of the clearest examples of authority use, and illustrates the extent to which mothers' lives could be turned upside down by the requirements of the social workers.

The routine actions most closely associated with the authority role were those of assessment and monitoring. This was carried out in 85 per cent (n=45) of CP–CA cases, a proportion which goes up to 92 per cent when outside assessments are included. Most fundamental to this was the assessment of risk. Although a feature of child protection cases in general, these assessments were particularly important at times when registration on the child protection register was being considered. This was particularly clear in cases where comprehensive assessments were carried out. This was the case with the following example:

> The evidence that we had [at the conference was] that we had a couple who really weren't functioning as parents and partners, there was very little reward going on for anybody – but there were certain worries about who really wanted what...we pulled all the information together. So, in about eight weeks we worked with family, we had it in mind that [two children] were probably the two we were most concerned about. There was a lack of understanding of general roles: who does what, who allocates that role...and what actually goes on. Dynamics which we didn't really have any understanding of...so we did, and it turned out to be a really good...piece of work for us, but it was just so interesting to get the family together.

The key to the social workers' involvement was not here so much the presence of depression, as their concern with the degree of risk. In this respect, this was not untypical of child protection cases. While the presence of depression might, in principle, provide a focus for their assessment, it was not generally significant for the assessment of risk (although in some cases it did play an important part). Risk assessment was on the whole carried out in terms of other concepts, such as adequate parenting, parental relationships and familial functioning. In this case, little reference was made to depression as a critical factor in the situation. In fact, this was a case which fitted the 'troubled and troublesome' category, so depression as a feature tended to be considered lower down the pecking order than key facets of the mother's (and partner's) personalities.

The monitoring role was also one which generally owed less to an awareness of depression, than to the importance of keeping an eye on the situation. Again the emphasis tended to be on examining those overt behavioural or personality characteristics which placed the children at risk, rather than upon the depression of the mother. The result in one case was that little was done to help resolve the mother's problems by providing more psychodynamic, or even emotionally supportive actions, and depression did not emerge as a major dimension:

> [At] the case conference, we agreed that only one of the boys should be on the register. And instead of an intervention, social services would have more of an information gathering role. [It was a] monitoring role...I would have some intervention, although my visit wouldn't be weekly. They would be two or three weekly.

This case, where child protection was an issue, was the exception rather than the rule, in that something considerably beyond monitoring would usually take place.

However, practice strategies frequently used monitoring as part of interventions where considerable familial support was being provided. These strategies could entail recognition of the mother's own mental state, and the support was designed to enable her to function better as a parent, as well as providing her with the kind of listening ear which might help her negotiate her depression better. This dual focus of monitoring and support were frequently central facets of the family support worker's role:

> The family support worker was visiting every morning...at the beginning of the work we rated [mum's] likelihood of harming [her son] under three categories...the neglect, the poor routine, being 'mental' with [him]. So, going mental, the lack of routine and the lack of appropriate expectations...we could demonstrate in the case conference that things had improved.

Monitoring helped them identify improvements. The use of the term 'mental', although rather unedifying, made explicit reference both to the psychological state of the mother as well as that aspect of depression which was specifically associated with her tendency to lapse into uncontrolled rages.

Support

Although the issue of risk and the associated use of the authority role pervaded all aspects of practice in this group, this did not exclude supportive actions by social workers. Indeed, such actions were widespread, reflecting the Department of Health's (1991a) strong injunction for social services to consider that generally the best place for a child is with his or her parents. The fact that only 12 families had children who were compulsorily in care illustrates the extent to which the social workers were committed to the natural family as the appropriate context for the child's upbringing, even in circumstances of risk. Additionally, 11 mothers had children who were accommodated, and in some cases it will have been a 'Hobson's choice': if not voluntary, the care would have been compulsory. This, however, was not always the case, and some were accommodated as a means of supporting the mother. A majority of families, furthermore, had children who were living with them despite the risk.

Although support was important to many families, it could be particularly relevant for depressed mothers. The depression could reduce the mother's capacity to respond, through, for example, a lack of confidence, or psychomotor retardation: a kind of overwhelming apathy and difficulty in responding to life situations, particularly in the face of the demands of their extremely problematic circumstances. This provides part of the reason for the significant degree of supportive resources which were provided in many cases.

In order to support these families, social workers used a wide range of resources which were also greater in number than these provided with either the CP–FS or disability interventions. This is evident from the data provided by the Social Assessment Schedule. Social workers averaged 16.1 interviews with the CP–CA interventions, compared with 11.4 and 4.2 respectively for the CP–FS and disability interventions. The number of types of social worker actions undertaken directly by the social worker was 9.2 for CP–CA cases, compared with 7.3 for CP–FS and 3.9 for the disability cases. The average number of types of resources used, as defined by the Social Assessment Schedule was 3 for the CP–CA intervention, 2 for the CP–FS intervention and 1 for the disability intervention.

In some cases resources could be expended, to a considerable degree, in support for the mother. In the following example, the social worker regarded the mother as being 'genuinely depressed' rather than 'troubled and troublesome' and this had an effect on the intervention strategy:

> She [adult mental health worker] sees mum twice a week. On a one to one. And once a week in a women's group. When times are ordinary that is the case except for me...the GP is seeing her once a week.... All those other things are in place. When life is normal. That would be stepped up if she was in crisis. And it would increase from my point of view. Enormous [amount of support]...it is costing a lot of money...and I think it is probably essential to her for family functioning.

This case involved, interestingly, therapeutic work with the mother herself. However, even in this exceptional case, although the mother was the focus for the therapeutic help, the reasoning behind this was presented in terms of family functioning (for which it was considered essential) rather than the needs of the mother herself. It remained the case that these services were being provided in terms of the degree of risk presented to the children.

Although some social workers were more oriented toward managing care, they all tended to provide support to some extent themselves. This direct support could take a variety of forms, whether emotional or practical. Where mental health issues were involved, direct work in CP–CA intervention tended, like other cases, to be emotionally supportive rather than psychologically therapeutic. This was evident in the ways social workers presented elements of their direct work, one stating, for example that 'I am there really to build up her self-esteem' while another commented that 'yes, well, we have tried to empower her to do things for herself'. Such esteem support occurred with 25 mothers (47 per cent). While esteem building was clearly a laudable and relevant aim for these mothers suffering depression, there was little reference to anything other than exhortation and encouragement as a means by which they would be able to build up this esteem.

This emphasis placed on support rather than more dynamic approaches meant that the emotional support provided, in principle, a kind of maintenance function for the women (Davies 1984) similar to that provided by more practical support measures, rather than attempting to make more deep seated change. Such was the case with, for example, financial support, such as section 17 money (which was provided for nearly two thirds of these mothers (34/53) or some kind of external funding:

> We looked at trying to help her with financial problems with herself with her childcare, with her practical problems and we applied from a charity for a new washing machine and got a new washing machine. Practical things to try and get her on a more sound financial footing.

Support could take the form of advice, which, not including direct advice on childcare, occurred in over three quarters of these cases, such as the following where the social worker sought to get the mother to obtain additional help. In this case, where the social worker recognised the mother as being depressed, her lack of sleep was affecting her capacity to care adequately for her children:

> She's not sleeping she should go to the GP to get tablets. And she's fighting it every way along the line. I say to her, at the end of the day she's got to listen to her own instincts of what she wants...the way I see it now, is that we can't offer any more to her.

Despite the social worker's humanitarian concern for the woman, however, their concern was mediated by their interest in her children's well-being.

The functional similarity which could occur between emotional and practical support is clear in the following example, where there was a link between the practical actions of financial support and the emotional consequences of lifting self–esteem:

> Because mum was having a lot of trouble in parenting, I then, very unusually, got my team manager to pay for childminding, so that mum could go out to work. I felt that if we increased mum's self–esteem and confidence it would enable her when she was with [daughter] to parent her better. It was no good leaving mum with [daughter] for a long period of time, she didn't get on with her.

Use of accommodation and other respite care also came into this category of support for families in a way which would reduce the risk to the child. However, there was also considerable concern to prevent the family becoming separated. As with CP–FS and disability cases, respite care was seen as a way of keeping families together by giving family members 'time out' from each other. These actions could thus be seen as directly supporting the mother's needs, yet the degree of significance of this arose only because of the risk to the children, as was the case with the following woman who was recognised as being depressed:

> It has been really difficult because the clinical diagnosis of mum was that she was suffering from depression, and so we were accommodating them. We didn't go down the child protection route, which we could have done in view of the injuries. We decided to be supportive. So the aim was, perhaps mum needed a month to recover, and it was going to be very short term accommodation. That she was depressed, this is why the children were treated as they were. She needed time and space without the children to get better and then we would take the children back.

This respite, then, was not simply designed to provide the mother with a breathing space, but ultimately to contribute to a significant improvement in her capacity to care for the children. The same end result occurred with shorter term respite:

> We actually developed a strategy whereby mum would actually let her go and spend the odd overnight, other weekend with one of her school friends, because she needed that time out overnight, and a way of recharging the batteries.

There were various kinds of support, from child minding, to use of nurseries, support for holidays, as well as use of short term accommodation to help the families over periods of difficulty. Relief care of children was provided for 28 per cent of mothers (15/53) in addition to the 11 mothers who had children accommodated. All of these approaches ought to ensure the maintenance of the children at home, in the long run, by separating them in the short term, even if it were only for a few hours.

Where the social workers tried to operate through the provision of support in CP–CA cases, social workers' experience of the mother's depression influenced the ways they conducted cases in general. Where the mothers were seriously needy, and fell broadly into the 'troubled and troublesome' category, social workers generally struggled to control their degree of input, frequently feeling they were being 'sucked in' to providing very large amounts of support which they had neither the time nor the emotional energy for, or alternatively, feeling alienated by the degree of aggression manifested by the parents towards them. In these cases, the capacity to set boundaries was a key aspect of their conduct of intervention:

> So what we have done, we have set boundaries or limits. But within that, I hope that we have tried to help [mum] to feel personally supported.... For example, helping her move.... Too, if she said she was going to live with somebody, for example, we would check those people out and we have explained to her, that we want to make sure that everything is OK for her. If she has done silly things, we haven't criticised her, we have just been there.

This capacity to set limits was not always possible, and where this was the case, as we shall see, social workers sought to withdraw to some degree from direct involvement with the mother.

Non–compliance: managing risk through contol

Authority could be exercised at the same time as an emphasis on support provision. Authority could be more overtly invoked through measures for control, particularly where supportive actions were seen not to work. The key to this was the issue of compliance. Where risk was the issue, social workers' general expectation was that the mothers would need to respond in terms of the social worker's frame of reference, rather than their own. Such compliance was less likely amongst women in the 'troubled and troublesome' group, where, because of the mother's extreme neediness or aggression, the social workers found it difficult to engage them constructively. Where the social worker considered there was a risk of significant harm to a child, and the mother disagreed, rather than providing a point of debate, the disagreement was more likely to be seen by the social worker as an indicator of increased risk to the child.

The issue of compliance, then, was significant in the distinction between predominantly supportive actions, and those characterised more by control. In one case, all the efforts of social services came to little in the face of the mother's own limited coping capacity. Her overwhelming neediness, her inability to respond, meant that the social worker was unable to feel that risk to the children could be managed through the use of supports:

> We have tried. I am sure there are so many other things that we could have tried, if we had infinite resources.... We tried to put her back into Trevy House, when she rehabbed...but then, having said that, could she live in Trevy House indefinitely?...it just became so complicated. Maybe if you could have someone living with her as a supporter, a befriender

[but]...sometimes we have had to say to her, that is tough, the children's needs have to come first.

Non-compliance occurred not simply through inability, but also through refusal to respond. Where the social workers saw the women's problems as the key to reducing the risk to the child, a failure, in their eyes, properly to address this issue was viewed very negatively. This was the case with one woman with alcohol problems. The social worker, while sympathising with the woman's own problems, was left with little option but to take more controlling actions:

> We tried to look at other AA sort of things. Then we introduced her to [someone] from the SMAT team, substance abuse, alcohol and drug adult workers.... And they put in...counselling and support work for her. She had been offered a retreat. Which she refused to take. We looked at CLOUDS, a detox.... But she refused.

In other cases, mothers actively resisted the social workers' attempts to reduce risk. Resistance became particularly significant where it touched upon their parenting role; that is, where women were perceived as not prepared to take actions which could lead to improvements to substandard parenting. This was the case with two parents:

> She left him there [at assessment centre].... We can have parents who have a lot to learn, but they want to learn.... It was that issue for me, I think, the lack of commitment.

> We've talked. I mean, she said I'm not that kind of person [to receive parenting skills training]...I am sure if I'd said that to her initially, she'd have laughed at me in my face and said, you know, what do you think you are suggesting, a load of rubbish.

Some went further, and their resistance took the form of aggression and threats. Where this was allied to high risk situations, and a failure to respond to the social worker's agenda, social workers felt the need to invoke their powers to control the situation. This could be extreme: one social worker had, in a previous post, been so threatened that she had changed her name by deed poll and moved office completely. Another social worker commented on the way she had to use authority more because the mother's aggression made it impossible to work in any kind of partnership, and the child was considered at risk (by, in part, her aggression):

> I had her in...she, she then, you see, becomes abusive personally, so then she personally threatens my children, my family. She does the same to my senior, and that's the time you say 'enough is enough' — you can't take any more of that.

It may be that anger, at least in some mothers, is not surprising, in view of the threat they felt from social work intervention, and as an aspect of their depression. Where, however, it was also aimed at the child, this both undermined partnership, and increased risk to the child at the same time.

Coming into care

The use of accommodation could, as we have seen, be undertaken as a means for supporting families, even where the issues of risk and child protection were present. However, care could also represent a breakdown of confidence in the mother's capacity to care for the children. This did not necessarily mean abandoning hope of change and improvement, although there were times when such situations were regarded, in this respect, as hopeless cases.

At times, reception into care was an issue of severe difficulty in coping, which meant that the risk to the children remained high. This problem in coping is one associated with depression, but was particularly manifest in cases where mothers' needs were the greatest. Sometimes, their support needs, or the resources required, were so great that leaving the children with the mother became unsustainable. One such case occurred where an attempt to rehabilitate a boy with his mother backfired. She still did not want him home:

> But we said 'Let's try it and let us set up something whereby if you need respite, we can take him', or in fact what we set up was alternative respite every other weekend...that just freaked mum out. She did not want a new carer for [her son], which was fair enough. She was concerned about him...she is quite able...to think about his emotional welfare in some ways.... In the end, she said 'No, I am not having any respite. I will keep him at home'...just after Christmas it was, in the January, via the night duty he came to me [abandoned] again.

This was a mother whose mental state left her extremely fragile, experiencing great difficulty in focusing on the care of her son. When respite was not used, she simply could not cope, and showed this in the end by abandoning her son. Likewise another mother felt that she could not cope, and sought some respite care through which she could 'recharge her batteries':

> [Mum] realised that she was having difficulties, actually asked us for respite. Unfortunately, respite is an extremely difficult commodity. We haven't got many foster carers who provide respite.... I had just about found somebody who was able and willing to have her, when things got to the extent that she couldn't cope any longer. And we took her into full time care.

The unfortunate situation here was that a combination of limited resources, and the resultant slow response to the mother's needs for respite care, together with the social worker's reluctance to accommodate the child, actually made matters worse, to the point where the child had to be accommodated on a longer term, rather than respite, basis.

These cases, where accommodation by the local authority was primarily an issue of non-coping by a mother who in other respects was seen as co-operative with social services, were the exception rather than the rule. However, there was another, rather more significant group, where the non-compliance of the mother clashed with the authority social workers were able to wield when the case became one of child protection. Non-compliance was particularly likely amongst 'troubled and troublesome' mothers, because of their preoccupation with their own needs, often to the detriment of the children's, and at times, their emotional disregard for the children's well-being. The result was that social workers' concerns grew about the degree of risk to the children.

In one case, after a string of failures by social workers to get the mother to comply both in relation to her own parenting needs, and her need for alcohol detoxification, the social workers accommodated the children. Although accommodation was voluntary, it would ironically have been compulsory had she not complied. The children were taken in late, and rather hurriedly:

> Not until October, November time. That was when we put in all the packages of support, the rehab, the detoxing of her. She was on Librium for a while under the GP.... It was the very last resort that they were taken into care. They were accommodated voluntarily to start with. I say that, but basically it wasn't voluntary. She was told that [otherwise] we would EPO [Emergency Protection Order] the children.

Non-compliance could arise from a complete failure to appreciate the extent of childcare problems, a lack of insight. This was the case where despite the social worker's continual attempts to improve what appears transparently to be inadequate parenting, neglect placed the child at considerable risk:

> I can recall many a visit when [her son] just didn't get a look in really... there was concern about his lack of development and...as he got older, his gap in development has got bigger and more easily recognised...there was very little insight into the needs of [him as] a baby...the midwife was chasing around just a few days after he was born, for basics like nappies and clothing and bottles and stuff...he then came into care because the duty officer went down following a referral from the health visitor...[the child] was admitted to hospital because he was malnourished and concerns about his emotional — he was a very deprived child...he was developmentally delayed and there was bits of behaviour as well in care.

Despite lengthy monitoring, the actions, in the end, were taken very suddenly by the duty officer.

Some women failed to engage with the social worker at all. Where a breakdown in partnership occurred, alongside a concern that children were at considerable risk, this made reception into care rather more likely:

> She [daughter] was removed...we tried to work in partnership with the mother. When the child is on the 'at risk' register, there is an agreement. We have to do tasks, and one of them was going in there...mum kept on avoiding this, moving the day closer. When we did phone her, she wasn't in, or they didn't phone me. That still remained the same.

Without any contact, it was impossible for the social worker either to monitor the situation, or to engage the mother in changes which would reduce the risk. This group of 'troubled and troublesome' mothers were also more likely to experience problems when the child was in care. Although in general social workers felt they tried to maintain the contact between mother and children, this did not always happen. Social workers felt that many needy or aggressive mothers who fell into the 'troubled and troublesome' category projected the problem on to social services:

> Whatever is arranged is not good enough. She [mum] wants to see [her daughter] weekly, but...we haven't got the staff to do the supervised contact. The fact is that the daughter does not want to see her more than once a month...in [mum's] eyes it's social services that are preventing her from seeing [her daughter], and that [mum] has this fantasy that [her daughter] is going to go back and live with her when she is 16.

This case carries all the elements of neediness, including projection and fantasy which for the social worker meant that she had the kinds of characteristics which would place her in the 'troubled and troublesome' category. Indeed, the woman's idea that the daughter would live with her later, was, according to the social worker, clearly a matter of the mother being blinded to the reality of the situation by her own needs for her child's return. In the event, the relationship between mother and social services made it more and more difficult for contact to occur, and the distance between the social worker and the mother gradually increased.

In other cases the mothers expected the social worker to agree with them, and when this did not happen, the relationships with both the social worker and the child in care were soured. With their view of the situation rejected, the mother could be distanced from the child, and the social worker from the mother:

> I've found my relationship with [mum] has completely broken down. And this is because I believe that she was expecting me to be completely on her side, and as soon as I wasn't she became really hostile. I think [the doctor's] assessment is absolutely perfect, because she is now making allegations about all kinds of people harassing her, like, for example, you were one of my spies, for example the foster carer is making decisions. It's very difficult to communicate with her.

In such circumstances, there is a clear danger of a drift occurring in which social worker, child and mother become increasingly separate.

Key points

1 Intervention strategies threw up three distinct groups: CP–CA, CP–FS and disability. The severity of problems was significantly greater in CP–CA interventions than CP–FS, which were greater than disability. CP–CA strategy was

marked out by children being on the child protection register, or, according to the social worker, known to have been abused. Severe parenting problems were noted in CP–CA interventions.

2 There was a relationship between mental health attributions and intervention strategy, with 'troubled and troublesome' women tending to receive CP–CA interventions. These women's character attributes made them appear more 'risky'. The link between mental health attributes and intervention strategy was, according to social workers, the presence of serious risk and danger.

3 Authority was at the heart of CP–CA interventions. Social workers therefore paid less heed to mothers' preferences, especially where views conflicted. Social workers emphasised the paramountcy of children's welfare. Assessment and monitoring were key features of CP–CA, and assessment of risk was fundamental. However they rarely focused centrally on depression, although it could sometimes be an aspect. Monitoring enabled social workers to identify change and improvement.

4 Support provision was a major feature of CP–CA interventions, designed to help keep the family together. Support was particularly relevant because of the serious effects of depression. CP–CA intervention had a higher intensity of intervention and resource use than other strategies.

5 Direct support was provided by all social workers. When focusing on depression this consisted mainly of emotional support. Practical support could also help with self–esteem. Accommodation and respite care could give parents and children 'time out' from each other. However, social workers struggled to control their input with particularly needy mothers.

6 Authority was more overtly used with non–compliant mothers. Mothers' failure to respond within the social worker's frame of reference was seen as a major contributor to risk. Lack of compliance could shift actions from a supportive to controlling form, and could occur through the mother's inability to respond, active resistance to the social worker, aggression or threats.

7 Children could be placed in care could as a result of a breakdown in confidence in the mother's parenting capacity. The mother's needs could be so great that leaving the child with her became unsustainable. Care also became an option when mothers failed to comply. Non–compliance could be a result, according to social workers, of lack of insight, failure to engage the social worker, or distancing through disagreement.

11 Child protection and family support

A second group of families were those where social work practice was designed to support parents in their childcare responsibilities without reference to legislation empowering social workers to protect the children. There were 27 mothers in this group. These were families where the children were neither on the child protection register, nor did the social workers consider that actions sufficiently serious to be termed abuse had been perpetrated on them by the mother. They were also, however, cases where social workers were not involved by virtue of children's disability or special needs, a group which is considered separately. These cases were generally marked out by the fact that social workers felt the mothers genuinely cared for their children, and were motivated to resolve the problems they had with childcare. Nevertheless, they had significant parenting and childcare problems (see Table 10.1) and the support was designed to protect the child from further deterioration.

Many of these women, although not having problem-free childhoods, did not suffer such serious past abusive experiences in childhood and adolescence as the women with CP-CA interventions. These families also display the connection between social workers' mental health attribution and intervention strategy. Over three quarters of women in this group (21/27) were considered 'genuinely depressed', under a fifth (5/27) were considered 'troubled and troublesome' and one other was a 'stoic'.

This link is an important feature in intervention. 'Genuinely depressed' women were viewed in a considerably more positive light by social workers than 'troubled and troublesome' women. Their depression was a major dimension of the ways social workers understood them, and they tended to be viewed sympathetically, to a considerable degree, as a victims of past or present circumstances. They were also viewed as caring for their children, very often manifesting feelings of guilt about their own parenting behaviour and worried about its effect on their children. Alongside this, and of considerable significance, was the fact that they were considered clients who were co-operative with social workers in the aims and objectives, as well as methods to achieve them. Whether or not they were able to improve or sustain such improvement, there was an effort for change.

While risk to the child remained an issue (hence these were child protection cases), the element of active danger was less because the 'character' issue of the women bestowed a more 'protective' than 'vulnerability' dimension on the situation.

While social workers tended to view the characteristics of 'troubled and troublesome' women as potentially dangerous because of their self-regarding, needy focus, the caring and co-operative dimensions of 'genuinely depressed' women left social workers with a sense that the women themselves were less of an actively dangerous element in the situation.

This contrast is important to make, but should not be exaggerated. First, of course, a considerable minority of these women were from the 'troubled and troublesome' group. Second, these characteristics may be considered along a continuum, and women with the degree of personal, psychological and social troubles which they possessed could, at times, slip into a more actively dangerous situation. Nevertheless, the contrast helps link with intervention strategy, for although risk was still an underlying concern in relation to the mother, parental competence rather than dangerousness was much more to the fore. Parenting was viewed in terms of encouraging parents to cope. Much of the focus of social work intervention, therefore, was designed to support the mother to this end. This more positive approach to intervention was facilitated by the perception of the mother as co-operative, and hence that mothers and social workers were working together more effectively than was frequently the case with CP-CA mothers. Mothers were perceived as concerned about the child's welfare, so that this could become a common goal.

Thus, while parenting was a problem, it was significantly less than in CP-CA interventions. The most frequently identified difficulty was inadequacy in the provision of guidance which occurred with marginally over half (15/27) of these cases, and was a severe problem for a quarter (7) of these mothers. Other problems were less frequent: hostility towards, or criticism of, the child occurred in nine of the 27 cases (a third), and was a severe problem for two mothers. A lack of involvement with the child was a problem for six of the 27 mothers, and severe for only one, exactly the same figures occurring for unrealistic expectations by the mother of the child.

Direct work

Although the general trend was for social workers to limit the amount of direct work with mothers in relation to their own problems, with CP–FS intervention social workers had a greater tendency to consider themselves social workers for the mother and child rather than the child alone. Their focus, though, was on the mother as parent. Social workers made comments such as, 'I would say I did more support for mum than I did for her [daughter]', or 'supportive work is what I call it, Is what I do with mum more than anything'.

Some of this help was primarily practical. Financial support, generally use of section 17 money, was provided in marginally over half (14) the cases, and this could be used to bail out families with short term difficulties, or for more sustained support, like helping with nursery fees or helping mothers to maintain contact with children who were accommodated. Practical information and advice was provided for 19 mothers, 70 per cent of cases, and this included activities such as advice on welfare rights, means for procuring household equipment and helping mothers complete forms to apply for new housing or welfare benefits.

Emotional support

The key term describing social work intervention with this group was 'support'. Social workers described themselves as conducting emotional support with two thirds of mothers (18) and esteem support in over three fifths of mothers (17). This support orientation was also considerably facilitated by the absence of child protection procedures. This allowed a very different, less intrusive, focus from that where social workers felt they had to keep pushing and pressuring child protection features on the mothers:

> Yeah. Supportive work is what I call it …on the phone I speak to her [mum] every other day. She is quite reliant on me, come to think of it…the hours that we spend talking is probably pretty helpful for her. She certainly does not hold back, she is quite open with me.

This approach was also possible because these women were generally not perceived as overly needy, having demands to which social workers could not respond. Indeed, where they became demanding this was something to which social workers felt they could set boundaries:

> They [mum and son] would become anxious, and so would start phoning and making demands. It was starting to irritate…. We have now got a pattern of visiting…same day, every week, same time. So they know when I am coming, and if I can't get there I let them know the day before.

When direct work was undertaken with the mother, it excluded the use of psychodynamic work, which was typical of social work intervention as a whole. In one of the cases where the mother had suffered severe childhood emotional trauma, the social worker was concerned to obtain appropriate external support. In the following example, the mother had been sexually abused by her own father, and was raped in adulthood, as a result of which she had a son. The woman had an eating disorder, and the social worker felt the problem was better dealt with by an experienced practitioner:

> Well, I am conscious that I do not have the training in the area…I have been quite conscious that I have almost got into more of a counselling role with her and I realise that there are other people who are there to do that, and I haven't wanted to cause any distress by going too deeply into it.

It is interesting that the adult consequences of the kinds of trauma frequently dealt with by social workers, such as sex abuse, were something with which the social worker felt uncomfortable, consciously pulling back.

Emotional support: talking through mothers' concerns

At the centre of this support work was the client–worker relationship, through which social workers were able to talk through the mothers' problems. These generally involved a range of concerns as wide as those considered important by the mother or social worker. The mothers were frequently quite responsive and spontaneous:

> [We discussed] mostly anything that she wanted to talk about, [her son] and wanted to talk about her husband. And she wanted to talk about when [her daughter] was a young child, and she wanted to talk about what she'd heard [her daughter] was getting up to at school, and anything and everything really.

Another commented similarly that she was 'giving her time in answering her queries and discussing her options with her'. There were a number of themes which emerged in this emotionally supportive work, one of which was around relationships. This involved the relationship with the social worker:

> Until I can build up a really trusting relationship with mum, she is not going to take any notice of me. And I don't want to jeopardise everything.

It involved also relationships with others, particularly the partner, as in one case where they were 'talking about relationships, encouraging her to look into other areas that she can go into' and another case, where they were:

> ...help[ing] them to identify problems that were happening in their relationship...they might be able to reach some compromise...about where they are in their relationship...I have sat down and counselled them a couple of times.

Assessment and advice was a routine facet of this support mode. Assessment was conducted by social workers with 22 mothers (81 per cent). However, social workers saw this assessment as part of, and contributing towards, the emotional and other support they were giving, enabling them to monitor and evaluate the case regularly. One social worker referring to emotional support, said:

> I haven't done any specific work with [mum].... I wanted to understand why, you know, her side of things, and do an assessment — perhaps trying to understand [better].

Likewise, explanation and advice were significant dimensions of this work, and could entail implicit personal support:

> I was giving her the opportunity to talk it all through, and giving her the opportunity to get the right answers to questions that covered the legal stuff and the social stuff...how the court worked...anything she wanted to ask about how she could handle things better.

The idea of 'talking it all through' clearly implied a more supportive orientation than merely providing technical information. Other areas involved a strong psychological dimension. Building confidence was a frequent reference point, as many of the mothers were considered to have low self-esteem. This occurred with eight (30 per cent) women. In one case, the social worker sought to counteract the effect of an overbearing mother:

> Support was provided, allowing her to be confident to speak for herself, and not allow her mother to speak for herself all the time. That was the main thing I was sometimes asking [grand]mum that we wanted to see [mum] alone, inviting [mum] to come to the office.... It was saying to her that, look, you know, speak for yourself.

In slightly over half the cases (14/27) the social worker sought to build a relationship which would enable the mother to talk about her feelings and emotional turmoil, in this case relating to loss:

> Well, I started with mum really...her grief about the fact that her daughter had upped and disappeared when she thought they had a...good relationship. Even though she described that as best friends, rather than mother and daughter, and started to wonder about that, you know.

Another way this psychological dimension was tackled was in the less attractive area of dealing with aggressive emotions, reflecting the mothers' own emotional turmoil. With this group, it was possible to retain a more constructive relationship because the underlying demands were not as great as with many of the child protection cases enabling them also better to cope with periodically expressed anger. There was not the same all-pervasive aggression or overwhelming neediness, which made it difficult to set boundaries:

> I was visiting every week, and during that time, they were quite long sessions actually, because you tended to be about half an hour...before you got into doing any work. As it takes that long for mum to wind down. She is always wound up when you go in there. She is always angry about something, or someone has done something wrong. So you have to get all that out of the way before you can start doing any work.

Conducting direct support: parenting and coping

The other main area of direct work with mother was in relation to her parenting. Information and advice on childcare was widespread, and provided in 20 of the 27 cases (74 per cent). This work was supportive, in the sense that the parenting advice was designed to enhance her capacity to care for the children, and reduce the likelihood of deterioration which might make more draconian intervention necessary. It could be required where the woman underestimated the degree of concern with which the social worker regarded the situation:

> [We were] helping her to see our concerns as well...she doesn't feel concerned. Her focus of concern is on her ex-partner. She feels that he is the one who is making all of the anonymous referrals, and if he doesn't he gets people on the estate to do that.... So she just feels that if she can talk him out, all the other problems will go away.

The social workers sought not simply to give direct advice, or to inform the mother about particular concerns, but also to encourage a reflective approach to parenting, one which could be applied to one area and transferred to others. This was the case with the following example:

> I would go to [mum] and I would say to her, you know, give her advice about something i.e. I don't know how to deal with the partner the, so to speak. To think about her relationship and the effects on her and the effect on her child.

However, this was not a one way process. The social workers were concerned to understand the women's own perspectives as a basis for conducting intervention, and in view of the absence of the highest risk child protection issues, the capacity of these women to determine the direction of their children's care. In one case, the social worker was preparing the ground for a child to be returned home, having been accommodated voluntarily:

> Well I did see mum in her own right...very important. Because if you're trying to do the best for a child, you have to take account of the family situation. If the child is to go home successfully, you have to take on board issues for her as a woman and her as a parent.

Much of the work in this area included directly discussing strategies for coping with childcare responsibilities, and offering mothers a variety of options as alternatives to current coping behaviours:

> Yes, helping her, you know, offering her different coping strategies of trying to resume her relationship with her daughter.... I just felt that if [the daughter] was going to return home, the mum was going to make quite a lot of the running really. And that...she was also going to be the one, you know, maintains the relationship at home...she needed to...sort things out, and looking at how to handle things in the future. And, you know, more open discussion and explanations.

Some of this involved rehearsal, that is, working with mothers to enable them to develop strategies designed to improve their relationship with their children:

> Trying to talk it through with [mum] to get her to express what she wants. And to support her and to maybe give her strategies to trying to achieve

that. Just a confidence in being able to ask [her daughter] if she will come down and spend some time with her. I think that was a major hurdle, for [mum] to say, this is what I would like.

In other cases, these responses could occur in periods of stress, in which coping advice would be allied to a supportive emotional response:

I work with her in a positive way...for example, I ended up seeing her yesterday 'cos she phoned me in quite a state, because of [problems with the children]. And talking through, and that was an issue between [the daughter] and her mum, and not one that [her son] should have interfered with.

Social workers' management of care

An apparent paradox of CP–FS intervention was the lower level of resources used to support mothers relative to CP–CA intervention, reflecting both the severity of the problem and the degree of priority given to these cases. This would have implications where there was a scarcity of financial resources to provide services. The issue of scarce resources is evident from comments by one social worker, referring to the frequency of home support for the mother with her children:

It was two sessions two days a week. But it was down to one for the past couple of months because of other priorities.... She [mum] has got to make some fundamental decisions about what she wants from her life.

Social workers were constantly aware of these constraints and the consequent need to justify their use of family support. Difficulties could arise with managers who were always looking for ways to reduce expenditure or redirect resources to more needy or risky cases. One social worker drew attention to this:

That is something that is being questioned at the moment actually by my team manager, who is wondering about the family support worker going in twice a week, because this is not a child protection case.... I feel that it should be continued particularly at the moment and I have written a report to my team manager and my practice supervisor, saying that, you know, it should not be pulled back at this time...because [mum] has really gone downhill again since leaving hospital.

The remarkable feature of this example is that withdrawal of support was even being considered, in view of the mother's deteriorating condition, indicating the very high thresholds for receipt of services. In these cases social workers acknowledged that some women could be their own worst enemies:

She is showing that she is a good parent, and that she is coping and she does not want to feel, even inside, that she is not coping...[but] because the manager's view is: why is a family support worker going in twice a week after all this time?.... She did then open up a bit about being sick all the time and not being able to think about anything else when she gets like that.

Although resources were limited, three broad, often interrelated, resource areas can be identified in the social workers' management of care for this group: relief care of children; a range of activities undertaken by family support workers; and psychodynamic and psychological or emotional support work.

Relief care

The most widely used resource for supporting mothers was relief care of children. This occurred with just over two fifths (11) of families. This involved both relief of parents from the responsibilities of childcare, and time out for children who would benefit from respite from the problems presented by mothers' difficulties in coping. This was most evident with the use of accommodation, where the capacity of parents to care for the children had temporarily broken down as a result of, for example, illness or problems coping. Six of these mothers had children accommodated at the time of the research. Overall, accommodation was used as a means for supporting the integrity of the family, rather than as an alternative to family care. In some circumstances it was a periodic response to repeat difficulties, which helped the family remain intact, including monitoring links while the child was accommodated:

> I would say it happens when the need arises, and the need is greater around this time when the son needs to be accommodated...and the communication that needs to take place while he is in foster care, and things like contact.

In other cases accommodation was provided with hospitalisation for physical illness, or mental illness. When it occurred, the intention was for the child to return to the parent after hospitalisation. However, it was not always straightforward, particularly where there was a mental health problem, because discharge from hospital did not always mean mothers were able adequately to care for their children. In one such case, although the child did return to his mother, social services were not sure that this would be maintained:

> From social services point of view...there had been a planning meeting held, and I know [we were]...quite concerned about the long term welfare of [son], whether or not we should be considering planning long term away from his mother's care.

In the event their fears were not realised, but occasionally, family support cases did teeter on the brink of becoming full blown child protection cases.

Accommodation was not always a matter of brief respite, as originally intended, such as in the following case, where the mother had been imprisoned for shoplifting:

> He [son] went into foster care, and it was supposed to be short term, and he was due to return to her, but she couldn't have him back...I think because she found his behaviour too difficult, too much for her.

The son displayed violent and unpredictable behaviour, including taking knives into school, and he was referred for child psychiatric support, and although his mother did not rule out a return in the long run this was not something which could occur in the immediate future. In these circumstances, the social worker sought to maintain the closest contact between mother and son, while working in a way which did not exclude his ultimate return home.

Relief care could be provided without the child leaving home for extended periods, often involving 'time out' on a day by day or week by week basis. It could include child minders, nursery care or mother and toddler groups:

> We have set up the child minding.... I managed to get funding...it got quite an arduous task, because initially I gave them the list and wanted them to take responsibility in finding the minders.... Finding a minder that would bring their children up the way they wanted...use discipline the way they wanted it used. All those sort of things. They found that quite difficult.

The use of mother and toddler groups enabled women to socialise with others while keeping an eye on the children in an informal setting. Nurseries could become part of a differential response which varied in the degree of support provided according to the gravity of the situation. One social worker described a support mix of this sort:

> Social services have provided support for [mum], funding for [her son] to go to nursery , and providing foster homes for [him] during hospitalisations, when he needs to be accommodated.

Family support workers

This was one of the key areas of help for mothers, a role that could also be provided by family support workers sharing responsibility for care of the children on a regular basis within the mother's own home. Their remit was largely to carry out support work with the mothers and families under the direction of the social worker. The support they gave was a combination of the practical, such as with home management, and the emotional, supporting the mother herself, which however did not stray into the therapeutic. The importance of emotional support is evident from the following quote:

> In fact it is not even her [family support worker's] primary aim to clear up. I have said to her...even if she left every day and the house was in the same state, I wouldn't mind. It is more about raising [mum's] self–esteem and giving her the opportunity to do something, by having someone else there...she is there for mum to talk to, more or less.

This focus on emotional problems could be very specific, as in one case of a mother who suffered severe anxiety about the care of her children:

> What happened was on a daily basis...there was a family support worker who would arrive about 8.35 a.m. to sit with [mum] to enable [mum] not to

have the panic attack while her partner took the two boys to school...that happened every morning and every afternoon.

The family support worker also provided practical help, although even when this was a key element of her role, it was always considered in the context of her relationship with the mother, for example:

> I have now got half home care, half befriending, so it is someone that goes in twice a week for one and a half hours and helps out with cleaning and the house work, as well as being someone that [mum] can chat to and talk about parenting and things like that. And also to take her out if she wants to go out.

This essentially practical role was also complemented by one which focused on parenting. In the following case, the social worker sought to create a constructive debate about childcare between family support worker and mother:

> Hopefully, she gives her [mum] an opportunity to talk to someone about parenting and about [her daughter]. And someone to knock backwards and forwards ideas about what is going on.... If she is able to talk to someone about that, not like in a counselling sense, but in a chatty sense. Then you hear someone else's views, and there is a kind of role model thing in there.

Family support workers were often seen as more informal than social workers, more like chatting about things with a friend. This could be a considerable advantage in attempting to engage the mothers in intervention.

The approachableness of the family support worker could help in other respects: the role of one in particular was:

> ...to befriend mum and to help with any problems. For instance when [her son] had tantrums...the family support worker would help and give advice to mum.

The less formal, less authoritative role adopted by family support workers enabled them to provide advice on childcare and parent responses which was likely to be heeded, in this case and others.

Psychodynamic, psychological and emotional support

The management of care also involved interventions which focused specifically on psychodynamic and psychological or emotional support work. Parental education, or psychodynamic intervention, occurred in six (22 per cent) of the cases. This was largely specialist, often involving mental health issues. Psychodynamic counselling, as opposed to emotional support, tended, as a whole, to occur elsewhere. In one case, specialist counselling was provided for an individual with an eating disorder, while in another, family therapy was provided:

...the Bloomfield Centre who are involved, therapists there.... It's like a child guidance clinic, family therapy type of thing.

In a further case the psychodynamic needs of the mother were related to a woman–centred perspective, in which the social worker perceptively linked the mother's experiences to her parenting and childcare:

One of the things I recently talked to her about was some counselling maybe, for her as a woman. In terms of her own experience, and what means she brings to her parenting role. She has got quite a dynamic way of looking at things. But I think that's so obvious with her, that she is really so needy herself.

In another case, the counselling was provided by Relate to a couple:

I think that it is important for them to have some space to explore her expectations of wife, mother, and him. And look at what happened in the marriage and how, what has worked and what hasn't worked, and what might be useful for the future, if they are to parent their children in a way that doesn't involve crisis intervention by the police or ourselves.

In this case, as in so many others, the referral to Relate occurred because the social worker both felt their primary focus was the child, and that they did not have time to undertake this work. The fact that the worker acknowledges that this work could be crucial to keeping the children with the family makes their idea that this work could not be given priority a rather odd one.

A final major area was in the use of support groups which occurred with 8 (30 per cent) of the mothers. These were widely used, but were primarily a facility for reducing isolation and helping with socialising. Support groups generally took place in a family centre setting, as with the following example of a drop–in facility:

[Mum] has been offered input at the family centre at Leander House, which offers an open drop–in type of facility, for mums and their children. And also group sessions.

This facility could be offered elsewhere, and in Borough they had a NEWPIN. In the following case, the support group was mixed with other support services:

Through NEWPIN she started to have links with friends that didn't happen before. So they built up her confidence as well...NEWPIN helped in terms of her visiting NEWPIN for counselling, socialising with other women that were going through the same problem...for domestic violence.

Key points

1 CP–FS families were those with child and parenting problems, without their children being on the child protection register or suspected victims of abuse. The aim was to facilitate the mother's coping through support. The social workers generally felt that the mothers both cared for their children, and were motivated to resolve their childcare problems. These facets underlay both direct and indirect intervention strategies, and distinguished this from other intervention strategies.

2 Direct work was an important feature of this intervention: practitioners had a greater tendency than usual to see themselves as social workers for the mother as well as the child, although more as a parent than individual in her own right. Some of this was support practical including section 17 financial help, material and practical advice.

3 Social workers also provided emotional support, facilitated by the absence of child protection procedures. Mothers were also less frequently seen as overly needy, and social workers felt able to set boundaries to their practice. However, it tended to be supportive rather than dynamic.

4 Assessment and advice were routine facets of intervention, contributing towards emotional and other support. This enabled them to monitor and evaluate the situation. Where aggressive behaviours were manifested, social workers coped better because they occurred within more constructive mother–social worker relationships.

5 Parental coping was a major focus for direct intervention. This included information and advice on childcare, widely provided by the social workers. Social workers at times sought to encourage a more reflective approach to parenting, and to understand the women's perspectives as a basis for conducting intervention. They also concentrated on strategies to improve relationships with children.

6 Management of care was another major dimension of practice. Overall, there were fewer resources used when compared with CP–CA cases, reflecting priorities and lower average levels of problems in the CP–FS group. Indeed the pressure on resources was such that they could be withdrawn even when problems still existed.

7 Relief care of children was an important dimension of resource use. This provided relief for parents and time out for children. Accommodation was one means with which social workers attempted to support the integrity of the family. This could be a periodic response to recurring problems, or a crisis response. Other help could be provided while the child remained at home, through child minders, nurseries and mother and toddler groups.

8 Family support workers could help mothers, partly through regular sharing of responsibility for the childcare. They could also help develop mothers' parenting

skills, as well as providing practical support. One advantage of family support workers was that they were thought more informal and approachable than social workers.

9 Emotional and psychodynamic help could be provided by outside agencies. Psychodynamic help from outside was considered more appropriate, rather than attempting to provide it themselves. Amongst agencies used were a diverse group of mental health agencies, NEWPIN and Relate.

12 Families with disabled children

Parents with disabled children form the third clear intervention group. There were 15 such cases. In one case the social worker had not seen the mother. These were families with whom social workers were involved, not because of some inadequacy in parenting, which was a particular feature of child protection cases, but because their children's disabilities were such that they were considered to be 'in need', both in terms of the support requirements of the children, and the demands these disabilities placed on the parents. These cases were, therefore, marked out by the view that parents were generally considered to be competent, but that they were placed under unusual pressure by their children's disabilities. The response of social services was based on the extent to which the parents, and the mothers in particular, were able to cope with these pressures.

This group included a range of child disabilities. This broadly covered those with life threatening illnesses, chronic long term physical illness or disability, and those with learning disability. At times, these children required extensive medical support which could include numerous and painful operations. The problems included sickle cell disease, hippisonaemia, liver disease, epilepsy, club foot, aphasia, brain tumour, and hydrocephalus. Learning disability included problems arising from brain damage at birth, autism, including Asperger's syndrome, and attention deficit hyperactivity disorder (ADHD).

While there were differing levels of disability, these children (and their families) faced long term and chronic conditions which were generally unlikely to improve, and could deteriorate with age. The most severe could exert considerable strain upon the parents, including emotional stress, with the need for continuous observation, and the possibility of relapse and deterioration. Mothers often had to contend not only with the pressures of caring, but with their own feelings of guilt and inadequacy in the face of their children's disability. There was a relentless quality to their situation, with chronic problems, and responsibility for care which stretched into the future.

This was clear from the length of intervention, which averaged 36 months, markedly longer than the time for intervention of the family support group. In most problem areas, these families were rated as having fewer problems than either child protection or family support cases (see Table 9.1). However, the kinds of child problems characteristic of this group differed from the CP–CA, or indeed the CP–FS, group: the most frequent in the disability group were child cognitive difficulties and physical health/disability problems.

Learning and physical disabilities were largely the reasons for social work involvement with these families and were practically the defining characteristics of this group. Thus 11 mothers had children with cognitive difficulties, eight of these severe, and nine had children with long term physical health or disability problems, six of these severe. All families had one or the other. Other problems most frequently associated with these disabilities were: nine mothers with children with behavioural difficulties, seven with poor social involvement and six mothers who had, respectively, children with somatic problems and school behavioural problems.

The competence of parents was reflected in the relatively low number of parenting problems despite the adversity of having children with disability. This meant that the degree of risk to the children, despite the range and severity of their problems was, relative to the other groups, rather low. Thus, none of these women had problems with attachment and bonding, or with their physical care of their children. The most widespread parenting problem was the provision of guidance, which occurred with eight of these families, and this would perhaps present a particular difficulty with disabled children. Apart from this only three mothers had problems, respectively, with criticism of the child, and involvement with the child. Parents were viewed as a protective rather than risk factor for the children.

Resources and crises

The key to understanding the intervention strategies of social workers in these cases, was the relatively small amount of attention given to them, mostly because parents were seen as competent. They were, for this reason, systematically given lower priority than child protection cases. They were seen to need, on the whole, rather less support than either of the other two groups, to a point which at times involved practically ignoring them, and social workers tended to respond only where crisis occurred.

These families had the least support provided by social services, whether in the form of social work time, or in terms of resources mobilised on their behalf. The average number of interviews undertaken by social workers (4.1) was just over a third the average number for family support cases, and a quarter of child protection cases. The range of social worker actions undertaken, as classified by the Social Assessment Schedule, averaged 3.9 for the disability group, compared with 7.3 for the family support group and 9.2 for the child protection group. The number of types of other resources used, again using the Social Assessment Schedule classification, averaged 1, compared with marginally under 2 for the family support group, and 3 for the child protection group.

There was some variation in social workers' responses. One social worker showed considerable interest and concern for the mothers in families she supervised, and made an effort to contact them on a regular basis. When she was away, she ensured that all the mothers knew they could contact another social worker, and informed colleagues of those most likely to need support. Such proactive work was, however, the exception. Even though most social workers said these mothers were welcome to contact them, most did not contact mothers unless there was a query or crisis. Placing the onus on the mothers in this way could leave them feeling awkward about the expectations with the social worker, and reluctant to contact them even where problems emerged.

In almost every area of intervention and support, these families received the least help. The exceptions were respite care for children, provided for two thirds of families (10), although sometimes it was little in amount, and practical help, provided for just over half these mothers (8), neither of which exceeded the amount provided to other client groups. Indeed four families had not seen their social worker at all over the preceding six months, and at times, the social workers were only dimly aware of the families and their difficulties. The shortage of resources, and the priority given to other cases, was also evident in the amount of time social workers felt they were able to devote to these families. One social worker's response was not untypical:

> I would probably not have the time to be [there] in all reality. I mean I am quite happy to go and visit her, but if I felt she was expressing a big problem, then I would refer her on, tell her to go to see her GP or get a mental health worker.... If she was just wanting to talk to me about feeling down and whatever, I would probably do that occasionally, but not on a regular basis.... [Anyway] it depends on whether they want you to be there. I would not have thought that [mum] would want you to be there.

This social worker clearly felt the need to ration herself as a resource, even to the point where she would only conditionally respond to a crisis. Her resolution of serious problems was to get the woman to seek alternative help in the rather pious (in view of its limited availability) hope that support would be forthcoming. Her final comment – that the woman probably did not really want help – seems to be a *post hoc* justification for the limited response she was prepared to make.

Others were more responsive. However, unsurprisingly, many of these cases were characterised by periods during which little or no support was provided, interspersed by crisis responses to support parents where care of the children simply became too much. One social worker commented:

> I think for her, certainly, [it]...is important that there is somewhere that she can go, and if necessary in an emergency situation, where she finds herself so stretched that she needs to clear the decks a bit and stand back.... She will phone me up and invite me round to have a chat and a cup of tea, and let off a lot of steam...I provide her with a kind of safety valve.

Another social worker made a direct link between the woman's depression and their own crisis response:

> I think that is the main reason the depression comes in, she feels guilty. She rings me up sometimes, and says she is feeling bad, and could I come over to see her, so I do, and ask her what is wrong, and I am there as a listener, and she will tell me...it is mainly just talking through things, talking through her problems.

This response, while helpful in bad times, is hardly designed as a means for resolving the ongoing depression suffered by the woman. However, there was, at times, a misplaced justification for the minimalist response in terms of encouraging empowerment. Whether women under the day to day pressures of their children's disability would feel empowered or unsupported by the following social worker's attitude is an issue which will be discussed later:

> You have to let people try to get on and to run their lives in their own way. To empower them so as to make sense to them, rather than you go in and do this that and the other for them, making them feel hopeless and helpless. Obviously, there are times when you have to go in and do things, when it is absolutely necessary, when they can't do things for themselves.

Stoics

Many of those women who were 'stoical', a feature which we have discussed in previous chapters, fell into this group. Nine of these 15 women were described in a way which placed them in this group. A further four were 'genuinely depressed', only one was 'troubled and troublesome', and in the other case, the social worker had not seen the woman sufficiently. These 'stoics' were mothers who tended not to ask much for themselves, though many fought doggedly for the needs of their children. Theirs was competent 'parenting in adversity'. Their attitude, together with limited available resources, enabled a culture to develop in which women were praised for their self-reliance, while some social workers justified their non-involvement on the basis of the women's strength of character. Evidence for this, from the social workers' point of view, was provided by the women's failure to request help (hence they could manage).

Social workers felt most of these mothers focused strongly on their children, and went to extraordinary efforts to care for them. One social worker commented:

> She focuses a lot of her feelings into supporting [her son], so that is where a lot of her energies are directed...she is a very, very determined woman, to the point where some people find her quite difficult because she can be a bit obsessive, or seem a bit obsessive...in some ways because she is so focused.

Their determination to take responsibility themselves, which was a feature of many of these mothers, and an element of their stoicism, seems to have had a detrimental effect, in that some social workers seem to have ignored the possibility that the needs of the woman herself, for support with childcare, and emotional support, may have been greater than apparent to them. Some social workers would wait until women had reached a state of despair before they responded, and regard such a response as appropriate:

> Yes, well, she is not a person who rings social services and says I need this and I need that. Things have to be really bad, she must be in bed, then she will ring social services. People like that are very proud and self-reliant, so you have to respect it.

Another commented:

> No, there was nothing I could detect that would make me quite concerned about — like I have to get over there now because she might do something. I think she is probably a little stressed and needs a little support.

Minimisation of the difficulties faced by these mothers provided a justification for minimising social work involvement. Others approvingly drew attention to the women's resourcefulness, their ability to manage in adversity. This was a positive comment on the woman's character, and in one case it arose because she did what she could to avoid seeking social services support, in particular through the use of her family:

> It doesn't affect the family as much because what happens is, she is a very strong person, she is a very strong person, and if...she can't take care of [her son], her husband normally comes and takes care of him.

This was all very well, but such approval could be a poor substitute for support which would frequently have been welcomed as a means of lightening their responsibilities in situations of adversity. Some of the women, social workers were prepared to concede, were very reluctant to ask for help, even when circumstances became difficult:

> Well, the work I have done is basically to see if everything is OK. To see if she needs help...But all we are doing is supporting. We cannot give help if she doesn't ask for it.

Even where support was needed, some social workers were reluctant to respond. As with many other cases, including family support and child protection, the focus on the child could draw attention away from the mother:

> It is a difficult balancing act. It's so easy to get drawn into awful traumatic unresolved experiences of parents, and forget that there is a child there and that child needs attention.

This may be an appropriate response where there are major child protection concerns, and the mother tends to put her own needs before those of the child. It is a rather different matter where the mother is the primary caregiver, and is in principle competent as a parent, but where her capacity to care may be undermined if her own distress is not confronted. This attitude can actually contribute to the emergence and exaggeration of stress within the family for both mother and children.

Direct work

The view that the social worker was there for the child sat uneasily with the fact that social workers were not involved because of the threat posed to the child by parents and that the child's best interests could best be served by supporting parents in their difficult tasks. A conflict of interest thesis, between mother and child, was not an appropriate basis for the tendency to define the objectives of involvement exclusively in terms of the child's interests.

The emphasis on the child's interest, in these cases, tended to be represented in terms of providing support to parents in order to help them cope better with the child. Thus where social workers attempted to concentrate on the mothers' needs it was a double edged strategy: by focusing on mothers' needs they were most likely to serve the child's interests. While the mother's needs became a priority, this was only to the extent that it helped with the child's needs. This view was well expressed by two social workers:

> Basically how best to support mum in doing the best that she can to support [her son]...her needs are not directly addressed individually. They are seen in the context of where her needs could be supported to ensure the needs of the child are met.

> My main concern was the child but I was also concerned for her...this is money well spent ...to protect the child. Nobody said anything to me, the services were administered, and nobody questioned it...whether she deserved it or not, whether she fulfilled the criteria or not, that is another question.

The issue of desert emerged, with the implicit questioning of the mother's right to such help in terms solely of her own needs. Although most cases showed social workers' interest in mothers' needs was a secondary product of their interest in the child's welfare, social workers could express concern for the mother in her own right. This sympathetic social worker was aware of the determined independence of one mother, yet concerned for her as an individual:

> Obviously on reflection this woman is under enormous stress. The fact is she presents as someone who is constantly saying, 'I'm fine. I'm OK, I'm coping really well, I'm getting support from my sister' .... Even when I ask her...'How are you coping with things?' Not just her son, but generally. The response would be 'I'm OK, it has been difficult, but I'm coming through it'.

This social worker focused not simply on the mother's coping with childcare, but how well she managed with her life generally, and thus expressed a more general interest in her well–being. This was equally apparent in another case:

> It struck me that maybe.... I need to sit her down to talk about it, because her father died [abroad]...and I think she hasn't had time to let it go, to grieve properly. There are a lot of issues about her father, and property out there that hasn't been sorted.

Social workers broadly carried out two kinds of direct tasks. The first was to provide emotional support, although as an active strategy this was pursued in only five of the cases. One social worker drew attention to the need to be a sounding board for women who were under fairly constant pressure as parents with disabled children:

> What I felt she needed more than anything was a person that she could phone up, scream at if necessary, which is what she has done with me on a few occasions down the phone or whatever, and let off steam, and still have this person saying 'Fine, so what can we do with this, how do we deal with this'? And to be alongside then to explain, and, it's a kind of emotional holding thing, that there is one person at least that they can trust who isn't going to scream at them or let them down.

The other main direct work undertaken was the provision of information and advice, which in various forms was provided in two thirds (10) of cases. This included such advice designed to facilitate the women's capacity to make important decisions, and advice about childcare. Advice could be given to enable the women to sort out problems for themselves, an approach consistent with social workers' notion of encouraging women to take responsibility for their lives. One way of doing this was to encourage them to seek support elsewhere:

> Yes, I provided her with some telephone numbers and names, of groups and individual support. I suggested individual support as a first step, and then going on to a group, if she felt strong enough to do that.

This approach had the advantage of not adding to the workload of the social workers themselves: the women took responsibility for seeking additional support, and the additional support was not provided by the social worker or social services.

Social workers also displayed a concern for the families to obtain specialist information to help them understand and manage their children's disabilities. One social worker suggested this had particular importance where families had disabled children:

> This is quite an important issue in a case like this...when things come up, for instance there was a seminar at the postgraduate centre at Derriford...specifically in relation to Asperger's Syndrome with professionals all over the country coming down, giving lectures and so on.

And I gave the information to her, as I thought she might like to go along, and she did.

Indirect work

Where social workers did take action they generally saw themselves as managers of care. One commented that:

> The major issue I see with children like [this child], there are so many professionals involved, that the parents can often be swamped, and often need someone who can come along and help co-ordinate some of that.

In this they could be involved as an intermediary between professionals, or between agencies who could provide practical and material help, such as appropriate beds, mattresses for bed sores, and, very occasionally, financial support. These, however, were not generally families who suffered the same degree of material and financial deprivation as CP-CA or CP-FS cases. In a few cases social workers also sought outside help for counselling, particularly when pressures were building up, or when there was some traumatic event which overlay the routine problems of caring for a disabled child:

> She clearly needed direct counselling...it was a particular period when the effects on her son were building up, and concerns of whether he will survive the surgery. And I decided...that it was ludicrous to imagine that I could do anything...in terms of psychological counselling...and there were people out there, that were there to do that job.

This reluctance to undertake direct counselling was not untypical of many social workers. However, referral to an agency did not guarantee a service, and this approach could actually lead to no service at all.

Respite care, including help in the home, was the major feature of the support provided for these families. Two thirds of families with disabled children received some form of relief care with their children, although this could be limited. Respite was largely to enable the parents to cope better with the demands of childcare. This was evident from one social worker's comments about the particular circumstances of a single mother:

> It is important that [the child's] mum has to take on the responsibility that any parent has to take on, any single parent with a child of that age, and a child of that age would place great demands on a parent.... And yet...recognising the special circumstances that she finds herself in, and supporting them appropriately   always looking at what is respite.

Respite was, when provided, generally regarded to be of fundamental importance for the parents. Without it they could have even greater psychological problems, and may be unable to cope with the demands of childcare. The long term implications of a failure to provide respite when it was required could be serious. One social worker was very upbeat about the effects of respite care:

> Mum's psychological well being was being affected by it, and also in the last two weeks [of respite] things have started picking up and coming together. And there have been lots of good news on the respite side of alleviating the carer.... It means that mum and dad have more time to themselves. Sleep patterns are improving.

Another social worker commented similarly:

> So they can have time together and have some sleep probably, go out — why does anyone like to have respite from their children?.... When you have a child with a disability, it isn't easy to get someone to come in and baby sit ...they can't do that, so [respite care helps] the normal things that people do if they get a baby sitter — or sleep!

Respite care, as far as these social workers were concerned, enabled a process of greater normalisation, as parents were more able to behave in ways similar to other parents who were not weighed down by the additional responsibilities of caring for a disabled child. Yet, although the parents' needs were a clear focus for respite, the child still took a major focus:

> In an assessment...the impact of the parents' upon the children would be considered, and if the parents were struggling to cope, and requested a break, we would consider that. We wouldn't just be responding to the parents' needs — we would be assessing the impact upon the child...and looking from a child's perspective.

The issue of limited resources was always present in this group, and it affected the provision of support. As one social worker commented, 'Well the resources are very limited, so that does have a part to play in it'. Theirs was very much the role of manager of care:

> In that role [organising respite], it is a form of deal. We are the purchasers and I have the say about what gets brought in, if you like. And Withy Barn is a providing service of respite conditions...if I consider that it is necessary to increase the amount of respite...I have it put alongside the priorities of other cases that need extra respite too...I put my case.

Respite, then, was often a matter of finite resources with potentially expensive demand for services. Therefore, even where respite was provided, social workers were often not able to do all that was requested by mothers. How much care could be provided was a central concern:

> That is the question that I always ask in my mind and to listen carefully to what the carer is saying...and I feel we have got the balance about right. Mum would like more, and at times we try to be flexible and respond to that.

The respite itself took various forms, and in principle, on a case by case basis, was tailored to the needs of the individuals and their families. However, social workers were often able to provide rather less than they would have liked because of limited resources.

In some cases, respite was actually provided in the family's own home on a fairly regular basis. It was routinised, with the expectation of regular number of hours' relief on a long term basis. The combination of receiving help in their own home, and the consistency of the support was a particular attraction of this approach:

> I would at one point have said to her, 'What would be the most practical help to you in order to cope with meeting the needs of the [two children]?' That is how home care came about. And that is how the specified hours and times have come about in home care. Because that was what was most practical help for her.... Other types of respite resources have been offered, but this was the most helpful, and the one thing she has continued to use.

A widely used alternative was to link with another family who would in principle be able to provide support in an everyday family situation:

> The 'family link'? Well basically that provides mum with an opportunity to have some space each week when she can go and do something which is just her own thing. I think that it probably helps her keep some kind of hold on her sanity when things sometimes just feel totally out of control.

In the case of younger children (aged under five) when mainstream services were not available because of age, social workers were nonetheless able to help them get access to services available for the population as a whole. The social workers could be very positive about the use of these mainstream services for disabled children. One stated:

> Well, if the parents are going to have the energy and time to respond to [their disabled daughter] needs...it doesn't help if they are fraught with a toddler.... And I think they certainly have benefited.

These were the main routine sort of respite care. However, children could also spend breaks in residential care, or some form of holiday support could be provided. These had the disadvantage that they were not used as routinely as some other forms of respite care, but nonetheless provided support for relatively extended periods of time. The following social worker considered the concerns of the parent with this provision, and yet recognised the quality of the support:

> She needed somehow to make sure [her son] was being perfectly cared for, and being autistic he needed to be somewhere that would continue to give continued security, continued routines that he was locked into, and with people he would feel secure and comfortable with...she enlisted me to actually help find an appropriate place for [him] to be.... I made suggestions about places where she could contact, and she just spent hours on the telephone...exploring ideas

This, again, is an example of the social worker providing support, yet in a way which enables parents to take considerable responsibility for finding their own resources.

Key points

While the CP–CA emphasis was largely on the degree of danger or risk to the child, and the CP–FS intervention focused more on parental competence and providing support, interventions with families with disabled children tended to involve neither of these. Where women found it difficult to cope, it was not generally seen as because of their poor parental competence, but because of the pressure placed on them by caring for a child with disabilities. For most of these families, the issue was one of quality of life, both of the child and the parents. While the quality of life issue could be a painful one, as is clear from the depression suffered by these mothers, it was not one which attracted a great deal of resources. Parental incompetence and dangerousness, which could both give rise to risky situations for the child, were given far greater priority. Resource provision therefore tended to be low, except in those cases where the situation appeared sufficiently serious as to affect the capacity of mothers to cope. Crisis or support actions were designed to prevent risky situations developing, and the family's (particularly the mother's) capacity to care for the children breaking down. There were a number of features associated with this overall trend:

1 Parents with children with disabilities were the smallest group. Social workers were involved because of the special needs of the children, rather than to protect children. The children had a wide range of disabilities and illnesses. The competence of parents was indicated by the relatively low level of parenting problems, despite the adversity of having a disabled child.

2 The length of intervention was generally quite long, but limited resources were provided. There were fewer child problems than either of the child protection groups (though the difference from CP–FS was small). There was also a difference in the type of problems, with cognitive and physical ill health and disability problems characterising families with this intervention.

3 The key to understanding this intervention is the low priority generally given to these families and the consequent limited resources provided. This was partly because the parents were seen fundamentally as competent. Hence these interventions were less intensive, and at times very little was done for the families. In almost every area of intervention these families received the lowest amount of support when compared with the other two groups. Sometimes, the social workers did not see these families for six months or longer. There were often periods when little or nothing was done, interspersed by crisis responses.

4 Most women in this group were 'stoics'. Social workers felt that the majority focused strongly on their children, and went to extraordinary efforts to care for them. These women were seen as determined to take responsibility themselves.

Some social workers tended to minimise the degree of the women's difficulties, while others drew attention approvingly to their resourcefulness. However, there was also sometimes an inappropriate focus on the child rather than the needs of the mother caring for the child.

5 Direct work, where social workers concentrated on mothers' needs, was designed to help them cope better with the child i.e. it was a secondary response to the child's welfare needs. Generally two types of direct work tasks were undertaken: providing emotional support, by being a 'sounding board', and providing information and advice, mainly to facilitate their childcare.

6 Generally supportive action involved indirect work through the management of care. Respite care was the major feature, and was of fundamental importance to parents. However, the amount of respite available was affected by finite resources, with particularly expensive demands for services.

Part five

Receiving intervention: women's experiences

5

13 Child protection and child abuse

Intervention was not necessarily experienced in the same way as it was intended. Some of the methodological issues arising from this have already been discussed in Chapter 2. One obvious yet important difference is that the roles of the individuals – social worker as practitioner or service provider and mother as service user or client – were different. It would, therefore, be wrong to assume that the women always experienced the intervention in the ways expected by social workers. The kinds of contextual factors, also discussed in Chapter 2, provide a setting against which the women's accounts may be understood. The women could, for example, be using different frames of reference to understand the actions of the social worker and, for practice and policy purposes, it is important to gain some understanding of these (Rees and Wallace 1982; Fisher 1983; Barnes and Wistow 1992).

The child protection and child abuse group were distinguished by a combination of the perpetration of child abuse and use of child protection measures. They were, from the social workers' point of view, the most serious cases, which were defined by the sense that the children were 'at risk'. This issue of risk meant that there was a very strong focus on the child's well-being and that, in view of legislation-based responsibilities, the issue of the authority of the social worker, and social services, came to the forefront. Social workers were expected to take actions to protect the child despite different views and perspectives being held by the parents. There was, in other words, a strong element of control in work with families in this group.

This was a group with strongly held opinions. Women expressed their views about an area which was of vital interest to them, combining the issues of their own behaviour in childcare, the control which social services could exert over the child, and often their own perception of themselves. Involvement in the child protection process could induce a profound feeling of failure. Women's accounts revealed that the issue of control was at the centre of their experiences, exerting a powerful influence over questions of partnership, their fears for their children, their sense of victimisation and injustice, and the generation and maintenance of their depression. These themes provide the next focus for attention.

Partnership

Although official documentation emphasises that social workers should aspire to partnership, even in the most difficult circumstances (Department of Health 1995a) issues of partnership and of social workers' character gave way to control as the central feature of women's experience of social work intervention where child abuse was the concern. Theirs was not a perception of partnership, in any meaningful sense, but of powerful professionals able to control the agenda, and exert their will on the situation. This did not always mean that the women felt uninvolved in the decision–making process, but, where child protection was involved, to a considerable degree this was, as noted earlier, an issue of compliance. Women were involved in a high degree of conflict with the social workers. Over four fifths (43/53) stated they disagreed with the social worker some, most or all of the time, and nearly three quarters (39/53) indicated that they were angry with the social worker some, most or all of the time.

In this group, therefore, the sense of exclusion identified in some of the child protection–family support group was allied to considerable conflict. This arose, as examined in Chapter 14, in a context where child protection procedures were invoked, where women at times contested the validity of social worker actions, and where they felt entrapped by the power and authority of the social workers. As with the disability group, where the issue of resources tended to overwhelm other considerations when women made judgements about social workers, so this dimension of the power and authority of social workers, together with the women's responses, tended to overwhelm other considerations.

Some women felt able to work in partnership with social workers, and where this happened, there tended to be less conflict and disagreement, and the women and social workers tended to agree on the way forward. This involved recognising the risks to the children and being prepared to work with social workers to reduce the risk. Women who complied with social work expectations were those who could, according to the social workers, move forward, or at least agree with what was required. Marginally over a third of women (19/53) felt the social worker always kept them informed on what was happening, including their own actions, and a similar number (18/53) considered the social worker always discussed important issues with them before decisions were made.

Where women felt able to talk approvingly of their social worker, it was where their relationship was not overwhelmed by the conflict engendered by the issues of child protection, and the women's responses to them. Women commented on how social workers were helpful in various ways which enabled them to be involved in the decision–making processes of intervention. According to mothers, social workers variously supported them in front of their children, were always prepared to give helpful advice, enabled them to say what they really thought, and helped them to get a counsellor. One woman felt helped by the social worker who took into account her difficulties when attending review meetings (a problem identified by a number of women):

> I'm not very good at big meetings with lots of people. I just go into floods of tears. It's a bit better now 'cos they've stopped it and they're writing to me about reviews and things. It hurts me, but I'm better off not going, 'cos to be honest I just can't cope with it.

Some of the women also recognised the qualities and skills of the social workers, and this helped them to work in partnership, but, again, these were circumstances which were not overwhelmed by the conflict engendered by the issues of child protection. Where this happened, the women found social workers to be warm, empathic or listening, and felt that they could understand their feelings. One woman talked approvingly of the social worker in this way:

> As soon as I mentioned about, if I didn't have the kids I'd kill myself, and, she said, you know, do I really feel that bad, and feel that depressed sometimes, and that. And when I said about maybe going to see the doctor, she was saying that was a good idea. And maybe he'll think about something other than pills, you know, to help you sleep.

Where conflict occurred, however, it was difficult to find positive comments about the social workers. Some of this may have been related to the skills, and attitudes, of some social workers. As has been seen there were areas such as skills in mental health, for which social workers were not well prepared. There is also a fine line between the sensitive use of authority, often in difficult circumstances, and its use without any reference to the way the women might have felt. Some women felt that the social worker was callous and heartless, with an officious and bureaucratic approach.

The difficulties presented by the social workers' child protection responsibilities, and the antagonism generated by their authority role, as well as the aggression of some of the women, placed them at extreme disadvantage in attempting to work in partnership. Social workers were frequently the subject of extremely disparaging remarks, and there is little doubt that some women would have divested themselves of them given the opportunity. Indeed, there were circumstances where, no matter how supportive and skilful the social worker attempted to be, they were unable to get beyond the aggression and antagonism of some women. One woman described attending case reviews:

> It's like looking at the enemy. And I would rather not even sit in the same room as those people. There isn't anything they say that I want to hear. If they're going to make decisions, they are going to make them anyway.

There was a range of criticisms of social workers, all of which seriously undermined the possibilities of partnership. Women felt that social workers did not listen to them, or were not prepared to listen unless their views coincided with their own. They felt social workers were constantly harassing or nagging them, and that they did not try to see matters from the women's point of view. They felt a relentlessness about social workers, an unswerving focus on what they felt to be important. Some women expressed a lack of trust, which was implicit in many of the accounts, even when not directly mentioned:

> I was at a meeting and she was saying about, she was talking about my daughter. Well, I wasn't very happy…. I just wish they hadn't unloaded everything on me. I just couldn't take it and I couldn't trust them enough to turn around and talk to them about it.

In other respects, women made similar complaints. One involved the focus on the children, which had stronger 'edge' to it because of their separation or the threat of it:

> A couple of times I have had meetings with her and a certain amount of her felt that I was depressed, feeling down because of what had been going on. But in other way it wasn't me she was worried about, it was [daughter].

Others expressed concern that the technical language used made it difficult for them to understand what was going on, and thus to make any contribution to meetings and decisions. The process itself could have a profound impact on the women's self–image, and damage their capacity and motivation to work in partnership. In effect they would no longer have any 'effort for partnership'. For one woman matters had reached this point because of

> …mainly the issues surrounding my son. And the court cases I am going through. I am having people telling me that I am a child abuser, because I cannot cope with my son. So that makes me emotionally abusing him, because I cannot cope with him and put him in care. I feel like I have given up. I don't see the point.

Others felt an explosive anger which equally got in the way of partnership. This could come out in the 'set pieces' of conferences or reviews, or in the more routine contact with the mother:

> When a review comes along…they are picking up everything I am saying, they are writing it down…I am thinking 'thank you very much, you are using that against me now'…they basically piss me off. When I get angry and upset, everything that I am feeling just comes out.

> I don't like [social worker]. Every time that I have seen her, I takes the mickey out of her weight and that. She is so fat. If I go to a meeting, I says to her, you'll just fit through the door, or something. I tries to upset her, then she will know how I feel when she upsets me by taking my kids away.

While some women disliked the social worker, or felt disinclined to open up to them, some of the women were wary even of talking to social workers about their feelings, because they were afraid of the consequences. One commented that:

I was too scared to say how I really felt. I thought if I told them that I'm feeling really depressed and miserable, the first thing they're going to do, say, 'Well, if you're feeling that bad, you can't look after those children, you know'.

Entrapment — women with children at home

Amongst this group the women expressed a pervasive fear of entrapment: of being in a situation where they felt they had little power or influence to control the direction of events. This was in many respects not unrealistic since it was a subjective representation of their objective circumstances. Once women were involved in child protection processes, the social services imperative to protect their children, together with the legally enforced procedures in which they found themselves embroiled, took away their sense of security that it was their responsibility to bring up their children. They could suddenly find themselves on a 'rollercoaster' of unfamiliar procedures which could, even where the child was not registered, entail continued intervention which the women found threatening, and could go on indefinitely. This had a profound and shocking effect. The sense of bewilderment and trauma associated with social services involvement was expressed eloquently by two women (although in the first case her child was not subsequently registered):

> Then she said, 'Well we are going to have to call a meeting with the NSPCC — I am going to have to call them in because I feel that [daughter] is at risk'. It was like — I can't believe this is happening. Where is it all going to stop? How am I going to stop it? I can't stop anything. It was like everything was out of my control.... I spoke to my husband and told him everything that had happened, and he said, 'Well, what are we going to do?' And I said, 'I don't know. I don't know what we can do'.

> It was like one of those stories that you see these programmes on the television about social services being involved and children being taken away, and I can sit and relate to that, because it is literally taken out of your hands.... You have no control over this. It was just snowballing, one thing after another, and you felt you couldn't stop anything, and I felt that I couldn't do anything. Nothing I could say or do anything.

Many women — those whose children had not been received into care — expressed a pervasive fear of losing their children. Many women felt the social worker was not interested in retaining their children at home, and interpreted the social worker's actions as entirely hostile. It is apparent from some of the women's accounts, however, that the social workers were attempting to tread a difficult path, in which there was a conflict between the need to protect the child from harm and their desire to keep the child at home. This was a message whose subtlety was lost on the mother. How could social services, on the one hand, wish to keep mother and child together, while at the same time threatening to remove the child? The message mothers picked up was the threatening one, that the child could be removed if the situation did not improve, rather than the supportive one, that they would try to help them to care more adequately for their children. This was clear from one woman's comments, which showed the social worker's attempt both to support and protect, yet the mother only heard the threat:

> I don't want someone to threaten to take my kids away from me, just because I won't do what they want, I want support.... We had a conversation once...'I know that you don't like social workers. I know you wish that we were off your back, but unless you do what I tell you to do, and what I want you to do, you ain't going to get that. All you'll end up doing is losing your kids'. And I said to her, 'Why do you threaten me with my kids?' She said, 'I'm not threatening you with your kids'. I says, 'You are...you're telling me that if I don't do what you say, or do what you want, or do anything you ask me to do, you say that you are going to take my kids'. She says, 'I'm trying to keep your kids with you'. I said, 'You're not. You've got the evidence to take my kids. I'm telling you 'cos you look like the kind of wicked bitch that would do that kind of thing'.

This had a Kafkaesque quality. It clearly illustrates the way in which the inter-action between social worker and mother could degenerate into abuse, based on the mistrust which develops in child protection, even where, in this case, the woman accepted that social services had the evidence to remove the children. While the woman felt trapped, this must have been an extremely unpleasant experience for the social worker, whose message of support was lost amidst the threat felt by the woman. Indeed, the support message appeared to the woman to be uttered in 'bad faith', actually undermining further any trust in the social worker.

Many women reflected bitterly and angrily on this power, which dominated their thoughts about their relationships with the social workers. They expressed their anger fiercely and explosively, directing it at the social worker, as in the comments of the woman who referred to her social worker as a 'wicked bitch'. Others considered their pretensions to help to be 'extremely funny', accused them of being 'hypocrites', and wished they would simply 'piss off'. Most women were unable even to recognise that social workers were prepared to support them in the care of their children, as long as they were able to provide sufficient quality of care, and the supporting and enabling role, frequently referred to in social worker accounts, was lacking in very nearly all the women's accounts. Those few which made reference to it stood out by being exceptions, and even these were over-whelmed by their fear of social workers' power:

> I am always afraid of the social services taking my kids away from me, and he turned round and said, 'No, we are here to keep families together, not to take your kids away from you'.... Every social worker I have had said that. But I still have that fear'.

This pervasive fear could develop into something akin to paranoia, when, as in one extreme example, a woman asserted that 'they take the children away just to go on holiday', and that 'they get a hundred pounds bonus for doing it'. She was convinced that her social worker would receive £500 for taking her children into care.

Victims, lost causes and women unfairly blamed

The experiences women had of social services were influenced considerably by their perceptions of the justice with which they were being treated. This involved judgements, not just of the social worker's behaviour, but of their own actions. When negative, these perceptions could generate resentments, but they could also be quite partial, with women emphasising particular aspects of their situation, while ignoring or marginalising others.

Victims

These women were largely involved with social services because of serious concerns, right from the start, about risks to their children. This meant that most women were confronted by a combination of two factors: the power and authority of social services, linked to concerns that their care for their children was seriously inadequate. This helped initiate a feeling of embattlement, where social services could be seen as 'the enemy'. The processes, even where necessary, could contribute significantly to the development of conflict. This was particularly problematic where an Emergency Protection Order was deemed necessary. One woman expressed considerable indignation at such action:

> They brought the duty social worker around, the police and someone else. I left them outside...for a full hour. And they said, if I don't open the door they are going to break it down. And I said, 'Go ahead'...they took [son] to hospital, and that was it.... The cut on the head. Dropped on the radiator. I only took him to the doctor 'cos I didn't see it was that serious. So I just left it. So, therefore, they thought it was serious. It was awful.

It is possible to sympathise with the 'awfulness' of the situation. However, the woman, even in retrospect, failed to understand the seriousness of the issue. The referral had been initiated by a concerned doctor, yet her perception was of social services acting in a draconian fashion in collaboration with the police, on an injury which, to her, was nothing much out of the ordinary. This made her feel like a victim herself, rather than an inadequate parent.

This feeling of being victimised was often clearly based on a failure to recognise the seriousness of the situation, even in retrospect, and the part the woman played in it. This was true where there were potentially serious injuries to the children, as in the above case, and other examples included circumstances where an underage girl was a prostitute, a matter about which the mother expressed little concern, and a range of ways in which children were neglected. In part, some of this may have reflected different cultural expectations about legitimate childcare practice, particularly with regard to discipline, although this could not be said of potentially serious injuries of the sort leading to the above emergency protection order.

Lost causes

There were, however, occasions where the women clearly distorted their situations. This was less likely to be a simple matter of culture, and more to do with the woman herself. In these cases, the woman appeared to have little idea about the minimum reasonable expectations for childcare. These were most obvious with women who suffered problems with alcohol. One woman left her young children on their own in the house, while she went out, drinking with her partner. She recognised that she had:

> ...neglected them. All right, yeah, I did go out and do that. But it weren't till 7 or 8 pm in the evening. 'Cos I always had them in bed. I used to drink more during the day than in the evenings. Most of the evenings I was home with them anyway. They didn't see that.... Me and my social worker [subsequently] had a big argument. I said all that she wanted to do was to take the kids away. Never mind how I feel. Never mind how [partner] feels. They went into care.

The children, furthermore, had cigarette burns on their bodies. Apparently, it was all right to leave them at home on their own, only for some of the time, in order that she could continue drinking. She was unrepentant and unable to accept her responsibility for the children being received into care. This, and other cases like it, were marked by the woman's focus on her own distress, rather than the needs of the child, a characteristic already identified by social workers in the 'troubled and troublesome' group. The woman's self-interest did not give the social worker confidence that she had any insight into her own actions, and the way concerns about childcare arose directly from those actions. In this case, the children were received into care, and permanency planning was undertaken on the basis that they would not be returned home.

The social workers' actions indicated that, like some others, this situation was perceived as a 'lost cause'. This was less the fact that the children were in care, nor that the woman had placed her own needs ahead of the children's, both of which could in principle be, subject to change. Rather it was her failure to recognise her part in the childcare risks, even while recognising that they had been neglected, coupled with her antagonism towards the social worker, which meant that much of their interaction was characterised by conflict. Where social workers felt that (a) the prospects of improvement and change were remote and that (b) they found it difficult to work constructively with the woman, such cases tended to be considered 'lost causes'. Once placed in this category, it appears to have been difficult for women to break out of it.

In relation to this case, however, there could be little doubt about the severity of the woman's distress at the loss of her children. This woman broke down several times in the course of the interview, and her pain at the loss of her children was mixed with the pain of her own experiences. She had been raped when she was 18, subjected to severe physical and sexual abuse in childhood, suffered domestic violence in adulthood, and had severe alcohol problems. She had been reluctant to bring this background to social services' attention (the alcohol problems notwith-standing), yet she was given counselling support when they became aware of these problems. However, on the basis of information from the interviews, she was not the only woman who refrained from discussing her experiences of childhood and adult abuse with social services.

The result, in this and other cases, was that the woman lost contact with her children, and, full of antagonism towards social services, she was no longer in contact with them either. Her own needs and failure to respond had played a considerable part in this. The case is interesting in that while it would have been unwise for the children to be returned home, the woman's experiences of social services merely added to a catalogue of devastating life experiences. Where the rights of the child and the responsibilities of parents are strongly emphasised, there can be little room for a sympathetic response to the woman's own distress.

When women often felt victimised, this could be because they simply denied that they had done anything wrong, and that no abuse had been committed. The tenacity with which such women held on to their views that it was social services rather than they who were at fault could prove a corrective to the more enthusiastic of labelling theorists, where it was expected that the individual would take on the deviant identity, in this case, that of child abuser. However, even when they were prepared to accept that abuse had taken place, these women tended to criticise social services for a lack of proportionality in their actions.

Women unfairly blamed

Many women felt that they were being blamed unfairly for what had happened to their children. One woman was considered by social services to be unable to care adequately for her children. She was puzzled by their negative perceptions of her as parent, because she claimed she did not hit her children. Her mistake was to see the primary problem as that of physical abuse of the children, rather than persistent and severe neglect, despite attempts by social workers to explain this. Indeed, they had pointed out that her children's placement needed to be considered long term:

> I mean, that's what they're trying to do, put all the blame on to me. They're only trying to do their job, yeah...they look at me like I beat my kids up. And I have never done anything like that. I mean I got depressed because I was in a two bedroom flat. But I got this [larger] place now.... I don't see why they can't let me have them back.

Her distress and sense of having been wrongly blamed fuelled a strong feeling that the children should be returned to her. Another woman considered that social services had failed to appreciate the problems she was having with her child, when suggesting that he had been neglected:

> He wouldn't feed. He was constantly sick. I gave him a bottle, he would throw it back up again.... Every time I took him to the doctor they said to me, 'No, there is nothing wrong with the child'. And I knew there was.... He is doing it because he was premature, and he can't take the milk down. So obviously he was underweight because he kept being sick. And I got the blame for it from social services.

The women's perception of being blamed by social services was widespread, and did little to help them believe that they could transcend their problems. In some respects blame was a difficult thing to avoid. In most cases the women were indeed responsible for, or contributed to, the considerable risk to the child, and they needed to recognise this in order to develop better parental competence. The social workers themselves may not have sought to use the term 'blame', but recognised the importance of mothers being able to take responsibility for developing better and safer standards of parenting. Nevertheless, blame is a feeling frequently expressed by the women, and this had a potentially pernicious effect, in that it could reduce their self–esteem, and disable them where they might have been prepared to attempt to work on their problems.

Another concern expressed by some women was a feeling of being harassed by the social workers. In one case there were fears that the woman's daughter was being sexually abused by another member of her family, possibly the father. Like many other mothers, she found these allegations difficult to believe, and could not acknowledge that anything had happened. This in turn made the social worker's actions difficult to understand:

> She [social worker] came to the house. She hounded my husband several times. She would turn up at the most outrageous times. If [daughter] had a problem at school she would phone up and the next thing she would come out. My husband had been just finishing work. Now at the end of the day, he would come home and he was knackered... he goes out and he comes home he is sweaty and tired.

The woman's sense of harassment is understandable, on her assumption that there were no grounds for thinking her husband had abused her daughter. However, the social worker who had such suspicions felt she was acting wisely. She was attempting to monitor a difficult case, in which it was important that the parents did not know when she was visiting, to avoid the possibility that they were prepared for her. Her behaviour reflected her desire to ensure that she saw the family as it actually functioned, not as they wished to show her. Differences in perspective and a failure on the mother's part to accept the possibility of sex abuse, meant that monitoring behaviour which made sense within the practice of social work was perceived by the mother as harassment.

Guilt by association

Women felt victimised when they recognised that the children had been abused but were not the perpetrator. This could fuel a whole set of feelings of injustice, in which, on the one hand, they could experience a sense of despair, and on the other they could become antagonistic towards social workers and social services. Some mothers were convinced that it was their partners' behaviour which was primarily responsible for the loss of their children into care. One recurring issue was that of sex abuse perpetrated by the partner, in which some women, even where they accepted their partner was an abuser, felt that it was not their fault. One woman was distressed to find that social services were considering removing her children:

> ... because [partner] had a conviction. They wanted my children away from me, because they thought he was dangerous to be around the children. I felt a bit humiliated. They were coming out with all these things, like, why is [son] doing this, why are you doing that? And they sat here and said to me, there must be a reason behind the things that he is doing...after the conference I stayed behind, and [social worker] basically told me, if you hadn't been with [him] you wouldn't have lost your children.

She blamed her partner, but also blamed social services for not being totally honest about his status as a schedule 1 offender (although, since it went through court proceedings, her claim that this was not an issue seems a little surprising). She was angry at the situation, which she felt was not of her making, but was also badly affected by it: 'I had no self-esteem, no confidence at the time'. Eventually she was allowed to have her children back, but the experience left an indelible mark on her. Others, too, felt they were being punished for partners' misdemeanours:

> I had trouble with my husband again...and the social worker said to me, 'If your husband comes back, we are taking the children away'... I didn't want to see him...[but] he was pestering the kids...and he did it so much, he done it when my social worker turned up, and he said, 'Right. I am taking the kids away because you can't keep your husband away'. So I lost my husband — I don't care about that anyway — and I lost my kids at the same time. I feel that they were punishing me for what my husband had done. He was nasty to them, he was abusive to them, he used to be cruel, and lock them up, especially the eldest one.

Although the woman understood the reasons for social services' actions, this was a case where an innocent woman had been unable to protect her children against the abuse perpetrator. While she recognised this, she did not know quite what else she could have done, considered that social services had been insufficiently supportive, and felt that she had had to suffer the consequences. One woman's comments summed up the feelings of many: 'See, I am the one who is suffering, and he has got away with it'.

Some women were prepared to take responsibility, even where the abusive acts had been committed by others. When this happened, the possibility of developing a constructive relationship with the social worker increased markedly, because taking responsibility was seen as the first step to positive development and change. This was the case with one woman, who accepted that her drug addiction had led to serious neglect of her young children, clouded her judgement, and led to them being placed in some danger when being looked after for extended periods by a man who had practically disregarded them:

> His [son's] behaviour was really bad... and I know he would go off the rails, but because I wasn't here, and someone else was looking after him, which was why this all happened, I was unaware of what was happening back here. If I could turn the clocks back I wouldn't have left him here... I was getting drugs off [partner]. He was controlling me, and giving me some days and not others, and I was going up and down too much and I couldn't cope.

This woman was concerned to convince the social workers that she had become more responsible, and that she wanted to make improvements in her life. She wanted to make clear that 'the others [children] went on the [child protection] register because of the 'baby sitter' not because of me... I haven't done anything personally', and she wanted to avoid her youngest baby going on the register. As with other cases of this sort, the social workers were concerned that this intent should turn into real action, and that she demonstrate a reliable capacity to care adequately for the children.

One of the key difficulties for some women was their tendency to become persistently involved with violent and abusive partners. This presented various problems. Obviously the violence against the mother was intolerable (though some were prepared to tolerate it), but social services considered that witnessing this violence was potentially damaging for the children themselves. In addition, partners who were violent to the mothers could also be violent towards the children. In over half the cases (28/53) where abuse of the children occurred, this went alongside violence and abuse towards their mother. Nevertheless, some mothers found it difficult to make non–violent relationships and these were frequently those who had experienced abuse and neglect when they themselves were children. One woman commented for many:

> All my life, all I have had is violence...I always tried to hush, hush everything. I hate violence...it really upsets me. [I was] very, very confused. I wanted to finish with him. I knew that I had to finish with him, but I couldn't. I didn't know how to. And if I did kick him out, he would just come crawling back again. I just couldn't get over him.

Her partner, who was violent towards the children as well as the mother, stayed around, but the children were received into care. These women were clear about the link between partner violence or abuse and placement on the Child Protection Register, like this woman who commented that, 'They put my child on the At Risk register, and as each child was born, each child went on the register. This was because my first husband was beating me up'.

An important reason for registering children on the Child Protection Register was where the mother found it hard to believe the allegations made against her partner, even though these could come from her own children. Where such allegations were made, social workers became deeply concerned, both because of the allegations, and the consequences of the mother failing to take them seriously. This was generally regarded as a significant pointer to their preparedness to protect the child, and also indicated the disbelieving and negative reception the child was likely to get within the family:

> When they came to see me, they, she turned around and said that [daughter] had been in school and said that she was suggesting something [abusive] by my partner…I just couldn't believe it. I didn't want to believe it…. Then a second allegation was made and I didn't believe that for the simple reason that the girl was staying with me for the night with [daughter] and he was supposed to have gone into the bedroom to get them up the next morning for school and he is supposed to have touched her breasts and things. That was out of order, because he never went into the bedroom.

This woman's confidence was misplaced, as she subsequently discovered, and she did then react to protect her daughter. She nevertheless felt that she had not been the problem, and that she was suffering because of the behaviour of her partner. However, not all the women whose children disclosed abuse, particularly sex abuse, were prepared to believe these allegations. This was the case with one woman, whose denial of her daughter's disclosure made her aggressive towards the social worker:

> He has just got it in for me and [partner], for some reason…. If I had any thoughts that [partner] had done those things to [daughter] I would not be with him now…[social worker] won't listen to what I have got to say. He doesn't want to know about anything. All his main concern is that me and [partner] aren't together any more. He wants to split me and him up…it's not true. I know in my heart he is not guilty, because I know he would not do such a thing.

Where mothers were not prepared to act, they ran the risk of separation from their children, and this particular mother interpreted the social worker's primary motivation to be to separate her from her partner. However, for some of these women who relied on their partners, their own needs made it difficult to separate, and they could even, as with another case, believe that the partner would change his ways, making it possible to keep the children and the partner at home.

However, some women, while recognising that they were not themselves to blame for abuse perpetrated on their children, did take responsibility because of their own choice of partner. One woman, who had been involved with a man who was both a heavy drinker and violent, and who had been subjected to persistent abuse herself for some time, reflected on the consequences of remaining with this man. For her, this had had a profound effect because of the damage he had done both to her and the children:

> It affects me now really. I don't know, in a way I feel guilty myself. I have destroyed their life as well. Because I got involved with him [breaks down, very tearful].

Until social services had got involved, she had been so embroiled in this violent relationship that she had not stopped to think clearly about its consequences for the children. She now had to live with those consequences, and experienced a profound sense of guilt by association. Where this happened, women tended to internalise responsibility, and did not express anger at social services, in contrast to others who felt that they were suffering because of their partner's actions, but could not accept any responsibility.

Care and contact

Long term care presented problems of contact and relationships with children. Although contact was maintained between most of the mothers and their children in care, when they had not been the subject of adoption, there was a minority of women whose contact was restricted in a way they found unacceptable and unjustifiable, and others whose contact had simply ceased. In some of these latter cases, there had been a degradation of contact: it had gradually reduced and finally ceased through neglect. This could indicate a non-commital attitude on the part of some self-regarding mothers, whose indifference towards the child was reflected in their later lack of contact. For a few women, however, the child's placement in care was the physical representation of their own failure as parents, and could be accompanied by feelings of guilt. Particularly where their lives had been characterised by abuse, the pain of attempting to see the child could be covered up by an emerging lack of interest. One woman whose alcohol problems were associated with long term abuse showed exactly this trait. She had practically lost contact with her children, who were in long term care, yet became distressed when talking to the researcher about it. 'I don't get like this every day', she said, 'It's only when we start talking about it properly'. She had come to a personal accommodation about the loss of her children, but it could still distress her.

The limitations placed on contact could be a cause of profound sadness. One woman, whose contact was once every four weeks, summed up the feelings of many when she commented that the restrictions made it difficult to maintain or develop a relationship:

> I can't get close to them 'cos I don't see them often enough to get close...it does bother me. I have asked for extra contact. Whether I get it or no I don't

> know....I think it has more of an effect on them than it does on me. They
> can't relate to me because of it...the kids are always pleased to see me
> whenever I see them. It must seem to them forever that they haven't seen
> me...[It makes me feel] sad. They get a cab home, and you can see them
> waving from the back of the cab. It's upsetting for them.

Of course, matters were not generally a simple issue of a dutiful mother deprived of contact with children because they were in care. In some cases, social workers felt there was a need actively to restrict contact because of its deleterious effect. One woman's contact with her children was reduced from once every six weeks to three monthly. In a situation familiar to many social workers, they made the decision to restrict contact because after visits the daughter was likely to misbehave and become disruptive. They attributed this to the behaviour and statements of the mother when they were together, in particular encouraging her to return home, where, in the social workers' view, she would not be provided with adequate care.

The mother's view of this was rather different. She claimed that her daughter did indeed want to come home, and that this desire was independent of anything she said. Her visits simply served to act as a catalyst for these feelings:

> It depends on how her behaviour is. If she is very hyper and causing a lot of
> trouble, then they stop her visit, and she has to calm down. They put her in
> a respite place, which doesn't do her no good really, 'cos all she wants to do
> is come home.... She says, 'Let's run away'. I say, 'You can't do that'. I say,
> 'You will be back here again, or maybe in a worse place'. The very first time
> they allowed a visit, she hid in the wardrobe. She didn't want to go with the
> family aide that came with her.

For this woman, it was the placement of the child away from home which was the problem, rather than the contact she had while she was in care.

Supervised contact was a bone of contention for some women. They felt it was 'unnatural' and often affected by rules and regulations. They were uncomfortable with another individual sitting in the room, and often felt the restrictions made it difficult to relate to their child normally. Of course, contact was supervised by social workers because they were concerned about what could happen where it was left unsupervised, but women made little reference to this:

> The actual supervised contact has been going on for three years now...
> upset to say the least. I have to sit in the room with someone else to visit
> my children. I don't feel comfortable with it 'cos you can't act as you
> normally would do...an hour and a half isn't long. In that time you can't
> really find out much, or do much. And they just sit you in a little room with
> a few toys, and that's it.

In this case, the children, sexually abused by the woman's partner, were placed with their grandparents, and the woman made allegations of sex abuse by the grandfather. She was also considered by the social worker to be personally disorganised and dysfunctional, and there was no prospect of the children returning to her. The children, aged four and five, had been with their grandparents most of their lives, and both mother and social worker admitted there was a poisonous atmosphere between mother and grandparents. She commented:

> I am not allowed to ask them how they feel about being where they are, and all that kind of thing. They say it confuses their minds, because they reckon they are settled in the placement that they are in…that is their home, and I should not interfere with that part of their life.

Nevertheless, she made an important point, which resonated with many others:

> 'I don't think they understand that, at the end of the day, I am their mother'.

Producing depression

It is not always easy to identify, from these accounts, the extent to which social work intervention actually engendered depression. As has been seen, both resources and individual practice could have an impact on women's morale, particularly in the context of pre–existing depression. It would be rather surprising if depression was not associated with the child protection processes, which left women feeling out of control of crucial aspects of their lives, as a result of which they felt victimised, blamed and guilty.

Thus, when social workers focused specifically on child protection processes, there is some evidence that their intervention induced feelings of depression and desperation, and may even have initiated depression. Some of the trauma suffered by these women was mind boggling in its severity. The persistent fear of losing their children could place a severe burden on them psychologically. One woman expressed this clearly. Her fear made her both anxious and depressed: 'How can I put it? If my kids got taken off me, I wouldn't be here. I would have no reason for staying alive because all I am living for is my kids. My kids are my pride and joy'. While the fear of losing children was ever–present, the specifics of intervention took a considerable toll on some women. One woman came to the stunned realisation that her partner was an abuser, and this was related to the fear of losing her children:

> All of a sudden, out of the blue, I got a letter from social services. We want to come and visit you. I said, 'What's all this about?' They said that there had been an allegation, and we want to check it out because of your husband's previous conviction. Indecent assault and malicious wounding which comes under sexual assault. I got depressed about it for months. Basically they told me, unless he moves out of the property, I had a chance of losing them. That was the final straw for me. I could take no more.

This woman intimated the context of multiple problems upon which the shocks of intervention were built. Another woman's estranged husband was the subject of an allegation of sex abuse by her daughter, who was showing serious behaviour problems at school. The social worker insisted she go to live with the mother, for whom the prospect was too much:

> I had split up from my husband, and I am living in a home — bare necessities is all I'd got...I was hanging on to my job for grim death, and having all these problems with my daughter...a close relative had got a terminal illness. So I've got all that on my head as well...I broke down crying. She said, 'I am really sorry, but I can't see any other way out of this. Either your daughter comes and lives with you, or she will have to come into some kind of care'...my daughter is going into fostering! I just didn't know what to do.

The experience of ongoing intervention could also take its toll with women describing themselves as feeling guilty and watched when social workers insisted that they undergo assessment, either by themselves or through some centre. Indeed, the comments of social workers could produce such feelings as 'I was upset... she made me feel guilty, saying that I couldn't cope, and that I needed a lot of help'. Intervention, with its implications for parenting capability, tended to make women feel inadequate as mothers, and this could cause depression.

Reception into care — perhaps the clearest statement of parental inadequacy — was a focal point for depression. One woman, who had photographs of all her children in the room, commented on the persistent depressing effect of her children being in care:

> Yes, I miss them a lot... I still get pretty depressed that I can't have my children with me...I am trying to have another baby with my new husband... and I am always worrying that I can't keep this one... I do get depressed. It's when you don't see them growing up. The last time I saw them was when they were just babies and more than likely when I see them again they will be adults.

Another woman described the feeling of allowing the children to be taken into care as 'Horrible, indescribable — I feel like running away with them all, so they couldn't find us, but I can't do that.... It is horrendous. The kids are all I've got'. She said she 'felt guilty all the time, all the time'. Another with learning difficulties reacted very badly when her children were taken into care, and her description is particularly poignant and harrowing. She missed her children desperately, even though she was transparently incapable of caring for them adequately:

> I used to like talking to the photos. Very upset at not having the children with me... I was hurting myself all the time, hitting myself with hammer and that... all they said was that I wasn't going to be able to have my kids back. But they got told that I was hurting myself.... One of my neighbours was concerned about me.... They [social worker] said that I was being silly, and that I shouldn't hurt myself. They didn't understand nothing about how I felt.

Women reacted in a variety of adverse ways to the child protection process, all of which had seriously deleterious effects on their psychological well-being. Some of them expressed suicidal ideas which they attributed to social work involvement. Although not all women were as clear as these about the link between this process and their feelings of depression, many women talked of the guilt, upset and distress which they felt as a result of their contact with social services. There can be little doubt that, for at least some of these women, social work intervention had a profoundly depressing effect.

Key points

These cases were characterised by abuse and child protection, and at times there appeared a self-absorption which placed children in definite second place to their mothers' needs. The women's relationships with their children were characterised by a variable combination of love, ambivalence and a concern for themselves which played a part in engendering a complicated, and at times, difficult, relationship with the social worker. This could lead them on an emotional rollercoaster of anger and negative self-images when confronted with child protection processes.

1   The possibility of partnership was most profoundly influenced by the degree of conflict engendered by the control dimension of child protection work. Where mothers and social workers were able to reach some kind of agreement, mothers could make positive comments about social workers and engage with them in a constructive way. However, because of their power in these situations, agreement was generally only possible primarily on social services' own terms.

2   Where conflict was present – as in the majority of cases – there was little opportunity for partnership. Women refused to accept the legitimacy of the social workers' position, and relationships were characterised by lack of trust, antagonism, and explosive anger.

3   Women felt little power or influence over the direction of events. This sense of being 'out of control' stemmed right from early child protection procedures, and in this respect reflects experiences many of these women had of their lives in general.

4   Most significantly, even where women had their children at home, they had a pervasive fear of losing them. They were afraid that being honest with social workers – for example about their depression – would mean they could lose their children. This prevented social workers from gaining a fuller understanding of their situation. It also meant mothers were at times unable to hear the message of support, that social workers wanted to keep the family together, and were only aware of the threat. Interactions could then degenerate into abuse on the part of the women, which could cloud social workers' perceptions and assessments of them.

5   Many women saw themselves as victims, because they felt they had been wrongly accused, or that the social workers' actions had not been proportionate to their misdemeanours. Their tendency to blame social services could reflect cultural differences in expectations of childcare, or distortions in their understanding of what had really occurred. Either way, this could contribute to social workers' perceptions of the women as 'lost causes', where women seemed not to take appropriate responsibility and there was little prospect of change and improvement.

6   Women had strong feelings of being blamed for childcare problems. Regardless of whether it was their responsibility, this sense of blame could be undermining, and affect their capacity to engage more constructively in resolving problems. At times mothers felt harassed by social workers, particularly where they denied any wrongdoing or did not understand their monitoring role.

7   Women felt distressed and angry when they were not the perpetrators of abuse, yet seemed to be blamed, for example, when the child remained on the child protection register after the abuser had left the scene, or the woman did not believe the abuse allegations. This again could make women aggressive towards social workers.

8   Some women felt that the conditions for contact, where children were in care, were unfair and wrong. This was the case where contact was infrequent or supervised. The sense that they were still the child's mother was very important to them.

9   There is evidence that child protection processes could induce or exacerbate depression and that this depression could devastate and blight women's lives. This is a complex issue, since many of the women were already depressed, but these processes could make things considerably worse. The depression often occurred within a life of abuse, and women felt blamed, victimised and out of control in relation to their children. It is therefore not surprising that child protection processes could contribute to depression.

14 Child protection and family support

The CP–FS, as noted earlier, was involved with social services primarily because of the issue of parenting competence. Although there were some elements of risk in the situation, the circumstances were not considered sufficiently severe for the children either to be on the child protection register, or to be currently abused. This did not mean that there were not considerable problems, particularly with parenting, but social workers clearly behaved in a way indicating that supporting these parents was the way forward.

This did not mean that the circumstances were devoid of the authority dimension of practice, at least from the mothers' point of view. Indeed, these were dynamic situations, where a greater degree of risk to the children might emerge in the future. Inevitably, the social workers could not simply divest themselves of their agency responsibility, which could include more strongly authority–based actions, should the situation deteriorate. Nevertheless, much of the current concern revolved around the level of care for the children, and the extent to which the parents were out of control of them.

An interesting feature of this group was that they did not present their responses with as great a passion as either the disability or child abuse groups. This may be in part because of their situation, in which their parental performance was a key issue, yet there was a less overt authority dimension to social work involvement. It may also be related to the nature of their depressed state, as social workers perceived them. Many of these women were in the 'genuinely depressed' rather than 'stoical' or 'troubled and troublesome' groups, and their responses may have been muted by the effects of the depression. Most of these mothers were not seen by social workers as 'bad' parents, with egocentric, sometimes overwhelming personal demands and needs, as was the case with many of the 'troubled and troublesome' mothers.

Partnership: inclusion and exclusion in the intervention process

One of the key issues for many of these women was the extent to which they were involved in the actions and decisions which were taken with their children. Where social workers were involved primarily to help, rather than control them (the latter being more characteristic of the child protection–child abuse group), their participation was important not just in practical terms, since this could enable them to improve their parenting performance. It was also important in symbolic terms, since this reflected their continued responsibility for their children, unencumbered by as great a possibility of authority–based actions as was the case with the child protection–child abuse group.

One significant feature of this, however, was the mothers' *capacity* to participate in decision making or actions to resolve problems, including enabling them to become more involved and successful in the care of their children. However, these women were depressed, and depression itself can provide a barrier to participating in this enabling process. Those with low self–esteem, who feel helpless and hopeless, are not in the best position to resolve difficult problems.

The women themselves were aware of the difficulties they had engaging with the social workers' actions. This is evident from quantitative data on partnership from the first screening interview. Having the energy to be involved, even in discussions, was a problem for two fifths of the women. Six (of 27) women generally found it hard to summon the energy to say much at meetings and conferences, and a further six managed to get their views over with difficulty. Over a third had motivational problems: nine of the women felt that, in the face of obstacles to their involvement in decision making, they would either feel discouraged, or make little effort to overcome the obstacles. Confidence was the biggest problem: three fifths (16/27) of the women stated that, when making decisions with the social worker about dealing with the family's problems, they were frequently or sometimes unsure of themselves. Only two fifths proclaimed themselves to be generally confident. While these feelings no doubt reflected the sense of failure which many of these women felt about their parenting, and the relatively powerful position occupied by the social workers, they also reflected the self–doubt and lack of confidence which would make it difficult to engage fully in the intervention process.

A few women were prepared to state in their accounts that their depression affected their ability to engage in the intervention process. It is quite plausible, in these circumstances, that these women were characterised by some degree of timidity, and they presented their views sporadically and in a somewhat diffident manner. Lacking clarity, or without being sufficiently emphatic, it may have been difficult for the social workers to hear what the women were saying, even where they sought to engage women in the decision–making process. Certainly, while the women felt the social workers were responsible for providing insufficient information and consultation, social workers generally felt they did both extensively, but identified a sizeable minority whom they felt actively avoided discussing important matters with them. It is easy to see how some social workers might be wrongly gauging the information needs of the women particularly in the degree of detail required.

On this evidence, there was a considerable breakdown in certain key elements of partnership, based on differing perceptions of what was required by social workers and mothers. This is consistent with an explanation that there was a lack of sensitivity on the part of the social workers to the psychologically disabling effects of the depression. The absence of confidence and self–esteem could stand in the way of a productive open relationship, in which women felt able to communicate their ideas to social workers, and to exact the information they required. The breakdown in communication, in other words, emerges from both social worker and mother not giving each other the information they needed. However where they lacked the necessary knowledge and understanding of depression, and had limited skills in this area, social workers were at a disadvantage in attempting to understand or work with these women constructively.

This breakdown in partnership could be exacerbated by the latent issue of authority and control, the fear of the social worker's power to remove the children. It is therefore not surprising that some women reacted angrily to what they saw as exclusion from the decision making process. When women were unaware that their diffidence got in the way of their inclusion in the intervention process, it is easy to see how they would project the fault on to the social worker, and become angry.

Information

Information provision was an important dimension of women's opportunity to be involved with the intervention process. There were considerable concerns expressed by women in this area. Only seven (of 27) of the women felt the social worker kept them informed on what was happening during intervention, including their own actions. A further 13 felt that not all relevant information was provided and seven considered that social workers frequently did not keep them informed on what was happening during intervention. This, however, differed greatly from the social workers' views of their actions. Social workers considered themselves to be open and informative, and made a considerable effort to keep the women abreast of developments, including their own actions, in 20 cases. It was never the case that they 'frequently did not give the mother information on what was happening'. The differences were marked: only four of the women whom the social worker felt they had kept fully informed agreed with them about this.

In part this could be related to social workers' perceptions of the degree to which the women were actually seeking to discuss major issues with them. Some women, the social workers felt, were actively avoiding such involvement, and only 12 generally welcomed the chance to discuss important matters with them. A further eight, according to the social workers, sometimes welcomed this opportunity, and the rest actively avoided it. This raises the question: what were the women seeking which they felt the social workers were not providing?

Where women spoke positively about information provision, it was when they saw the social worker as helpful or supportive. One woman commented of her social worker that 'She was good. She would come down and just talk to you, and try and get you to'. Another caused a very favourable reaction when she reviewed the case management and provided information on what had happened, including admission of error. Referring to her as 'brilliant' (an uncharacteristically enthusiastic endorsement in this group), she said:

> She came here eating humble pie, and said I don't know what to say. I have looked through all the files and not one of the social workers you have had have done any checks on the family that they had placed [daughter] with… all I can do, she said, is apologise…they all thought the one before had done it.

Most, however, commented on information in its absence or inadequacy. This was an important part of their sense of exclusion from the processes of social work involvement, and set limits on the influence they felt able to exert. There were various dimensions to this. Women felt they were not considered important or competent enough to be told, and consequently felt discounted. It affected their sense of power over the situation – indeed, some women, even though there was no overt authority role involved, for example by the child being on the child protection register, felt profoundly powerless. One asked, 'How am I supposed to know what is going on if I'm not important?'. A particular focus could be the review meeting, where the mothers could be formally involved. They felt that social workers were secretive and had little trust in them, as exemplified by this woman whose daughter needed accommodation:

> I don't like going to meetings and find out there are surprises. I like to know what is going on and what has been said…so I says, what are they not telling me, what are they trying to hide?… When the placement was planned she said that was eight weeks, and then it was three months, and I said, 'No! you said eight weeks and eight weeks is all you've got her for. If she is not back in eight weeks then there will be a fight and I mean it'. But this is not the first time that I feel I have been stabbed in the back, and to me there is no trust. They say they will tell you everything, and that I have got parental rights, but yes, I am feeling left out.

The sensitivity of this woman is understandable in view of her daughter's accommodation, yet others commented on the limited information given in relation to various issues, whether specific, such as dropping support for nursery fees, or general, in terms of overall plans for intervention. Like this woman, considerable resentment was generated when they felt excluded in this way.

Consultation

Another feature of exclusion was where the woman felt she was unable to make a contribution to decision making and intervention through expressing her own ideas and opinions. Many of the women were not fully satisfied with the degree of consultation which took place. Only 10 (of the 27) women felt that social workers always discussed important decisions with them. A further 10 felt the social worker discussed some, but not all of these issues, and seven considered most or all important issues were not discussed at all. As with the provision of information, social workers had a far more positive view about the extent to which they consulted with these women. They felt they always discussed important decisions with 18 of the women, and that only in the case of one woman did they not discuss most or all decisions. Of those 18 women with whom the social workers felt they fully consulted, only six of the women agreed, and five felt most or all important issues were not discussed with them in advance.

As with information, where the women felt properly consulted, they reacted favourably to the social worker:

> She was good, and she herself said to me, what do you think about [your daughter]? And I said quite seriously, I think she needs some sort of help, not necessarily psychiatric, but some kind of help...if someone told her black was white, she believes it. She is very very naive, and very young for her years, and she acts young for her years...and [social worker] herself turned round and said that she is very, very juvenile. She was more in tune with me, she lived in the real world. I could speak to her on a one to one basis and she would understand.

The additional dimension of agreement was also important. Clearly, consultation was one thing, but consultation and agreement was another. Where women felt they had been consulted, they invariably also found the social worker agreed with them, so that their definition of consultation, or having their opinion sought, seems generally to have been related to that opinion being validated. Where this was not the case, their views could be different.Some felt that social workers were simply going through the motions, seeking their views, yet not ascribing any significance to them. One woman in this situation had no idea whether her views played any part in the conduct of intervention. In retrospect her comments seemed to have exerted little influence on the plans and actions of the social worker:

> I think I am being listened to. Whether it is being taken notice of, I don't know. They will listen to me, yeah. I mean to me, it is the impression I get now after everything that has gone on. Yes, they listen to me, but I don't know if they have taken any notice.

This woman made a similar point about specific issues. Her daughter was accommodated and decisions were made without consulting her. She reported the social worker as saying:

> 'By the way, we have stopped [daughter's] school meals, because it is more convenient for the foster carers and so on'. Yeah, that would have been fine, but I wasn't even consulted. Now the problems we had when [daughter] was supposed to come home. The school rang here once — now why did they ring just once in the first place. Had they been having problems with [her] all afternoon, or why did they ring back again 10 minutes later?

There was, of course, a relationship between meaningful consultation and information provision; where women were not given material information, they were limited in the extent to which they could express views. Occasionally, however, mothers accepted that they may have contributed to their not being consulted, and not been as involved as they might have liked in developments. This was an obvious corollary of the data presented earlier, where a high proportion of the women mentioned difficulties summoning the energy, motivation and confidence to participate. One woman, reflecting on the part she had played in developing the intervention strategy, wondered whether she had been involved as much as she might, although the authority role did not help:

> No, not really, but then I am not very good at, very good at putting my views forward. I tend to think, what is it they want to hear? And so on. I worry that, I think it is the same with all kinds of authority figures — making sure you don't push the line.

Child issues

Where women's views were marginalised this disturbed them considerably. Some mothers felt their social workers made little effort to seek out their opinions at all, so that their expression came unsolicited. This was a particular bone of contention where their children were involved. These women had a strong sense that although social services were involved, and although they might accept there were problems with their parenting, these were still *their* children, and they had a right to some kind of involvement through consultation and provision of information. Where the social worker talked to the child, and rarely or never to the mother, this could have serious consequences for morale, one woman commenting that she felt 'guilty, very guilty. To think they would come, and discuss everything with her and not me. So I felt awful'.

This was particularly significant where mothers felt they had an important contribution to make, such as in relation to their children's personality or behaviour. These women understandably felt they knew their children best, and that in planning, the social workers should take this into account. This was important not simply because they felt it was the reality, but because their self-esteem was tied up with knowing their children better than others. They might not be 'cutting it' as a mother, but at least they understood their children. For social workers to disregard this was a major blow to their perception of themselves, and women at times reacted defensively and angrily. The following woman felt the double, and related, exclusions of not being provided with information, and having her views disregarded:

> It would help me to help my daughter, and I have told them from day one that [she] needs to be in foster care with no other children. Just the adults, because she has no real friends, she don't get on with other kids. She would sit with adults for hours. She would rather be with adults. Yes, I have told

her social worker. The social worker, to my eyes, has been a prat. I told them everything about what she can be like, and until she does something they don't believe me. They thought they knew her.... I blew my top with them. I am quite a calm person, and I will listen to them and what they are doing, and I will agree to anything, but they can only push me so far, and I felt they were putting things on me that they shouldn't have. They were putting me in a corner.

Many women felt that this was not simply a matter of social workers ignoring them. They had a pervasive sense that the social worker focused on their children and excluded them at the same time. This reflected comments made by the social workers themselves: that they were the social worker for the child, not the mother. There were practical consequences as far as the mothers were concerned: being social worker for the child and mother were mutually exclusive. One woman made comments, without acrimony, about the social worker, which nonetheless showed the extent to which she felt excluded:

Because social workers must be there for [son] they are concentrating on what he has to say and the problems with him. And he does need to do that, so he can think how best to help him, and how best to help our situation. So it would be nice to have two social workers, one for the children and one for myself...because you have got someone to listen to who is here a lot. And because he is not here very often, he doesn't get the whole picture.

Like the previous woman, she felt she knew her son and had something to contribute, but expressed this less angrily. This was not the case with one mother, whose daughter made an allegation (which later turned out to be untrue) that she had been sexually abused by the mother's partner:

[Social worker] was quite unbelievable. I mean she didn't believe what I was saying — what [she] could be like...she said, but we have got to believe the children...we have got to let the children know we believe them. I said, 'Yes, fair enough, you are social workers, but surely you have got to listen to what we say. She is my daughter, not yours. I know my daughter, you see her once every now and again and think you know her. You don't know her like I do, so you should be listening to what I have to say. She is my daughter and I love her dearly, but I am telling you what she is really like', and it wasn't a few months down the road that she came to me and said, 'You were right, I didn't believe she could be like this'.

This was obviously an extremely difficult situation for both mother and social worker. With many mothers having distorted, negative and blaming attitudes towards their children, the social worker could not be sure that the mother was wrong. Likewise, they would be aware that for many young women who reported abuse the need to be believed was crucial, in circumstances where others would discount what they said. Perhaps inevitably there will be occasions, like this one, when the child is lying. Nevertheless, this lay within a wider issue: that mothers were often marginalised by social workers who saw themselves to be 'for the child'.

Contact

Contact with the social worker, or the lack of it, could be a bone of contention. Where contact was seen as poor, some women felt this had a disabling effect on them, and made it difficult for them to exercise any influence over the direction of the case. Occasionally, there was a delay in the social worker visiting, following the allocation of a family, and this could be discouraging where they felt they were in crisis. Women were also aware of reductions in contact as the situation appeared to improve. In these cases the social workers were reacting to the pressure of work and the need to prioritise cases, but the mothers, not themselves involved in the process of setting priorities, at times felt they needed greater social work involvement. One of the problems cited by mothers was the difficulty they had getting hold of social workers, and this could cause considerable frustration and could have a demoralising and alienating effect. One mother found the difficulty contacting her social worker was compounded by developments at home:

> Yeah, it gets very frustrating 'cos I can't do phone calls from here any more. I'm on incoming calls only. Even though social services is only up the road, it is still a nightmare when you have got so much going on indoors...he doesn't come here much, he's only come here twice.

> It's a rigmarole. You've still got to make an appointment. When you want to speak to her you can't just go in there. You have to make an appointment. I don't really want to talk to her now.

This frustration could occur in less routine situations. One woman, who was imprisoned for drug and shoplifting offences, complained bitterly that the social worker did not contact her once while she was in prison. In this case, she was concerned about her son's behaviour and she subsequently found that he also had been offending. She blamed the social worker for the deteriorating situation of her son, because he had not contacted her (a case, perhaps, of someone throwing stones in glass houses). A surprising situation, given the general support orientation of practice with this group, was the failure of one social worker to retain contact with a mother with learning difficulties, whose child was accommodated. This woman could recall only one meeting with the social worker, who had promised to return, but had failed to do so. However, she was 'understanding' of the social worker because she had been convinced by arguments that the social worker was primarily 'for the child':

> No, fair enough, he is social worker for my children, and he'll talk to my sister, which is fair enough. But I'm not involved in any aspect of what's being said, and different things like that.

This was a particularly unfortunate case, since she was especially vulnerable because of her learning difficulties, and it is arguable that, because of this, even greater efforts should be made to involve mothers. Although many women expressed frustration and anger at the social worker, with an alienating effect, occasionally women mentioned that they would like more regular contact, partly as a more effective means for involvement in the intervention process, but also, as in this case, for more general support:

> It would be nice to have contact with him at least once a fortnight. Just pop his head round the door to make sure everything is alright.... Just reassuring me really.... And if you have got a hard time at that time, then just to see if there are ways that they can help you out a bit.

The practitioner

Characteristics

The characteristics and qualities of the practitioner provided a further dimension of the women's judgements. These involved a range of issues. One was the experience and knowledge of the social workers themselves. Only a few mentioned this issue specifically and discretely. Nevertheless, those that did felt that, in order for the social worker to be competent, they needed also to have knowledge and experience. These two terms, furthermore, were largely indistinguishable in the women's accounts, giving some clue as to what, for these mothers, counted as knowledge. This was knowledge learned from life, not from some academic, or even practice learning, but most frequently from having been a parent themselves.

This was associated with factors over which social workers had little control. Some women, for example, expressed a preference for a female social worker, or an older individual with 'life experience'. At times this could be a very personalised issue of what the woman felt was good for herself in particular. One particular woman commented on how exceptionally nice her social worker was, but that she personally 'got on better' with people who were older than her, particularly those who were retired! Another commented on the combination of age and experience with children in a very positive manner:

> I have a new social worker. He has just started coming. I feel that I am able to talk to him, the times that I have spoken to him. He seems very sensible. He is older, and has lots of experience. Children of his own. I think I get on with him fine.

Another woman felt that a special understanding could exist between women which was inaccessible to men, and this made her more reluctant to have a male social worker:

> It's funny, I had a female social worker a few years ago. She was extremely supportive, absolutely wonderful. And that helped me, as it was somebody that I could talk to and who would see things from my point of view. So it is difficult, men, even when they have training, can't always see things from a woman's point of view.

The reverse could be the case, and women could be extremely disparaging about social workers on the basis of their youth and inexperience, and their imputed lack of knowledge. It became a means by which the woman could, in her own mind at least, undermine the social worker's authority, and legitimise her own difference of opinion with them. One woman felt she had a bad deal because of the relative youth of her social worker. She thought the social worker knew very little and was rarely able to answer her questions satisfactorily. She wanted one who was more experienced and who would, as a result, not just understand her point of view rather better, but support and agree with her more. Another was very disparaging of her social worker, and equated knowledge with experience:

> They read lots of books. I find young social workers very difficult to deal with. Because they haven't got a clue of what it entails to bring up a family, and the stresses. I find people who are older, lived life a bit, seen life and know more. They don't go by the textbook, they know a situation, instinct and experience.

This did not necessarily blind a woman to other qualities in the social worker, as was the case with another woman, but it remained a weakness: 'Generally she is good. She has got her heart in the right place, and she does listen ... in principle yes, she is a good social worker, but they have got to learn that life is not just a text book situation'.

Personal qualities and skills

Personal qualities and skills can be difficult to separate in the women's accounts since their language meant different characteristics could be either or both. If, for example, a social worker was described as 'warm', it could indicate a spontaneous element of their personality, or the consciously directed effort at empathy and understanding which came through to the woman as warmth. These were the kinds of qualities or skills, nevertheless, which under difficult circumstances, encouraged more positive relationships between social workers and mothers. Mothers could easily feel the potential threat of children being 'taken away', whether or not this was justified, or feel particularly sensitive because the involvement of social services was a visible indicator of their 'failure' as parents. They could also, more positively, provide the basis for constructive expression of feelings with potentially beneficial psychological effects. All but one of the women expressed a need to talk about their private feelings, and 17 felt this to be a considerable need. Likewise, all but one expressed the need for positive feedback, and 20 felt this to be a considerable need. About a quarter (7) of these women reported that they treated the social worker as confidant by expressing private feelings to them, and altogether a third considered they had either expressed private feelings or received esteem–enhancing positive feedback from the social worker. Although, then, some of the partnership aspects were considered by the women to be problematic, a considerable minority indicated positive dimensions in the quality of relationship with the social worker. This capacity to respond to women's private feelings could involve a delicate balance, whereby not being too intrusive could enable the woman more effectively to express her feelings:

> She was a woman who would if you wanted to talk, would talk, but she wouldn't ask, and to me, she gave me the respect, she wouldn't pry. If I wanted to talk, fine, it was alright. She was nice to talk to and there was a kind of privacy there.

Some of the personal qualities or skills were very similar to those identified by women in the disability group. Some women referred, positively or negatively, to the presence or absence of listening skills, and to other elements, which might be better termed human qualities rather than professional skills, such as being comforting or caring, and being responsive to their feelings and needs. One social worker was described as 'very good' because of the way she made the woman feel comfortable, a human quality which contrasted with other social workers who were 'on this plan, family plan thing'. Another described the importance of listening skills much like those in the disability group:

> She is very understanding, very. And she will sit there, and she will listen to you. And then she will maybe put her point, what she feels needs to be done.... The one I have got now, yeah, she is fantastic.

This is in marked contrast to the scathing judgement of one woman, who felt her social worker was cold, and never sought to understand how she and her family might be feeling in the face of social work intervention. This was not uncommon as a response amongst women who expressed negative feelings towards their social workers. Although these were in the family support rather than child abuse group, they still felt very strongly the potential power and authority which could be wielded by the social worker. This could make them rather defensive, as they feared the possible outcomes, the worst of which was 'taking the child away'. One woman commented on this 'sword of Damocles' hanging over her:

> I just want him off my back...he will let me go a couple of weeks, then he will start on to me again. He came out one Tuesday, because someone was here, and he was very nasty to me. He won't like it because my dad will be here on Tuesday — my dad won't let me be in the house with him because he thinks I might smack him in the mouth.

In these circumstances, considerable skills might be required to avoid confrontation or a pervading negativism. This was an unenviable position. One woman thought the social worker less knowledgeable than overbearingly arrogant; a negative cocktail of thoughtlessness, lack of understanding, lack of knowledge and an absence of respect:

> He thinks, just because he's a social worker, that he knows everything, and knows everybody, but he doesn't stop to think about other people's feelings ...he hasn't stopped to think about my feelings. He definitely hasn't respected me or my children.

Where social workers showed themselves to be particularly committed to the women, this was warmly received. A few, such as the woman who commented negatively on the care management orientation (in terms of 'this plan, this family plan thing'), were aware that the strictures of the job itself could make it difficult for the social worker to respond as positively and warmly as might otherwise be possible, because of limitations placed on them by time or agency expectations. When high levels of commitment were shown, this was appreciated. One woman referred to the considerable generosity of one social worker who visited the family one Christmas Eve and 'gave the children a fiver each out of his own pocket', some presents and £10 to the mother. She commented, 'I thought it was great'. Another social worker gave, perhaps more conventionally, of their time:

> He came round after I phoned him 'cos I was having such a hard time with my husband. He was actually quite good. He was here for three hours until eight o'clock at night. I know it is his time off. And he said that he could see that our relationship was in absolute tatters, and he suggested that we both have counselling.

These quotes show the lengths to which social workers were at times prepared to go, and *had* to go, in order to respond in a way which fitted with the seriousness of the family's circumstances. The circumstances of their practice, these women appreciated, meant that the social workers had to give considerably of themselves, going far beyond expectations of them as agency functionaries, in order to provide an adequate response to the families.

A few women alluded to the importance of trust, honesty and openness. Where these were absent, the effect on the relationship could be crippling. One woman commented on 'lots of promises that never happened' (in terms of resource provision), and she felt that she was 'this person who is pushed to one side all the time'. Where the social worker was perceived as honest and open, this could provide the basis for a working relationship, even where families were expected to deal with difficult issues. One woman drew attention to the need for this to be undertaken in an ordinary way:

> She is very straightforward. She is very nice, but straightforward. She would tell you what she was doing, why she was doing it. She would put you in the picture. Nothing was done behind your back. It took me a while to trust her...even when things weren't good and she said she might have to [accommodate son] she would put you in the picture.

Feeling helped

Women's sense of being helped provided a third dimension of their experience of intervention. There were four general themes which emerged in this group. The first involved the extent to which they felt supported. This related to specific things which the women felt the social workers had done for them, such as providing material help or emotional support at the right time. Secondly, it involved the extent to which they felt the social workers enabled them to cope, or to cope better, with their problems, and thirdly, the extent to which the women felt the social workers were more friends than simply professionals. The fourth theme would be difficult to imagine in the conflict situations which sometimes emerged in child abuse cases, and indicated the extent to which support, rather than control, was on the agenda (although control remained a latent issue). The issues of being a friend, and of helping women to cope when they needed it most, emerged clearly in some of the women's accounts. Two women, for whom social workers had provided clear support (both practical and emotional) at a crisis point, when they felt considerable difficulty going on with their parental responsibilities, commented thus:

> Yeah. That's how I see social services, more friends. Like they help you out. They are more of a friend. They have been a tower of strength to me. I can always ring him if I want to.

> I wouldn't have coped at all if I didn't have any social worker. They have made a difference. They have helped a lot. I could do with a bit more.

Another key issue related to the authority role exercised by the social worker. While these were currently cases of support rather than child protection–child abuse some of the women were aware of the fluidity of the situation. Although they may not have been child protection–child abuse cases at the time, they could easily have become so in the future should the situation deteriorate, or should the social worker judge this to have happened, and some women were acutely aware of this threat. This was more likely to be the case where the women were finding it most difficult to cope, or where there was a greater likelihood from some other source of an increased risk to the children. At times this threat could be clear, as social workers felt that openness on their agency function meant that this dimension of work had to be stated. However, women were aware, even where this was not stated, of the potential threat involved. On these occasions this might be called a 'latent threat'. One woman stated:

> My social worker, he ain't one of those social workers that comes around and checks up on you. If I needed him he is there. If I have got problems, he is there. He is not one that comes around every week. He was always there for me.

Similarly, another commented:

> She always said to me that it was her personal role, and that she would do all she could to keep the children and parents involved, not to split them up, and that it would only be in extreme cases that she would take the child away.

This clarity, while recognising the authority to remove the children when circumstances required, nevertheless gave women reassurance which was realistic, and enabled the social worker to present a fundamentally supportive demeanour to the woman. However, women could feel the threat of removal as the overwhelming feature of social work intervention. In this case, the mother herself gave some indication as to why the social worker might become concerned by her disciplining behaviour, should any further deterioration occur, but was very angry at her social worker:

> I mean, like social services say you can't touch her. You hit her, and then we take her away. You hit her, you lose her, that is what I got told by the social worker, you will lose her. I just let go. Normally I just bodily pick her up and stick her in the shower and turn it on, so that she has to have a shower, because she is wet.

A further dimension was the sense of being undermined by the social worker in a variety of ways in the course of intervention. Some were obvious ways: by not keeping the woman properly informed, or not involving her properly in the decision making, both of which related to the quality of partnership, or by suggestions that the woman was neglecting her child. These issues could involve disagreement and anger: over a quarter of the women stated they disagreed with the social worker 'most or all of the time' (8/27), while 70 per cent (19/27) disagreed with the social worker 'some, most or all of the time'. Only eight stated they disagreed with them 'rarely or never'. There was an undercurrent of anger against the social worker in many cases: just under a fifth of these women (5/27) described themselves as angry with the social worker 'most of the time', and a further half (14/27) some of the time. However, the social workers were often in difficult positions in this respect, because of the sensitivity of the women, combined with their lack of confidence. In one case, a woman was trying to put over that she felt she was not coping properly, a message which the social worker was not picking up. Her response was to try to encourage the woman, and this left her feeling undermined, and losing hope that she would get the help she felt she needed. The problem, she felt, was in part:

> ...because I appear to be coping. But what I appear to be doing, and what I am doing, are two different things. Because I do, I do have a lot of pride, and I won't let myself get so down, for a long time.

One of the ways women felt undermined was in the way they feel they were directed to act as a parent:

> I think, basically, he's my children's social worker, but I'm the mother, and I seem to be shut out.... I'm not getting involved with children aspect of life or anything like that, because they think I'm not capable.... It doesn't make me feel very good. It makes me feel below the standard of everything that's going on. I mean, really, I'm a 35 year old woman, and I'm being treated like a 15 or 16 year old child.

The final feature was a feeling, amongst some women, that they needed a social worker for themselves. This is not surprising in view of the frequency with which the social workers themselves said they were the 'social worker for the child', and some women felt social workers paid attention to the child to the exclusion of the woman herself. One way of responding to the attention provided to the child was anger, and this featured in some of the cases. In a few cases, the woman came to the conclusion that she should have a social worker. One woman put this clearly:

> Maybe someone coming in and just sitting down and talking to me. Not directly for [daughter]. How I am coping, and how I am going to deal with this situation. Five minutes of their time would have done it. While they were here with her, they could have said, just nip out, while we have a chat with your mum, and stuff like that.

This reflected an optimistic and positive views of the possibilities, rather than the negative conclusions drawn by some women who felt they were not involved in the intervention, or decisions relating to it.

Key points

There were a number of key facets to these women's experience of intervention:

1   This group showed some differences from the child protection-child abuse group. The central feature of much work with the CP-CA group related to the issue of authority and the associated issue of compliance, arising from the risk to the child. While authority, and the fear of losing the child, remained a concern within the CP-FS group, a key issue was the extent to which partnership could be achieved, and how depression, and the women's situation, made this difficult.

2   There was a high degree of negativity among women towards social workers, particularly a sense of exclusion, and anger, which a considerable minority felt most of the time. However, there were also some very positive elements, such as the third of women who felt strong emotional support from the social worker, including their capacity to act as confidant. Negativity was surprising in view of the 'support' orientation of the work. However, the issue of control was an ever-present threat, which became overt whenever they were in danger of becoming child protection cases.

3   The social workers regarded themselves as having acted positively in consultation and the provision of information, in sharp contrast with the views of the women themselves. At the heart of the problem was the mothers' sense of inclusion or exclusion in the process of decision making and intervention. Only a minority of women felt they were kept fully informed or that they were consistently consulted before important decisions were made. Where women suggested the social worker made little or no attempt to initiate contact , this was particularly disabling, and the social worker could be unfairly blamed for a deteriorating situation.

4   For women who felt they had not been consulted, consultation frequently meant 'consultation *and* agreement'. Where the social worker did not agree with the woman after consultation, she could feel that they were 'going through the motions'.

5   Some mothers felt the focus on the child meant that they were marginalised. The fact that their views of their children were not sought was a blow to them, since they felt that they knew their children best. Some women felt that being the social worker for the child and mother were mutually exclusive. A few commented that they would have liked either a specific focus on themselves, or a separate social worker, who could consider their needs independent of the child's.

6   The characteristics, human qualities and skills of social workers were important for some women, and lack of these qualities contributed to their sense of exclusion. Many women had set ideas about the appropriate characteristics of the social worker, related to age, sex, experience (particularly of childcare), to which the social worker either conformed, or did not. Where they did not, some could be quite dismissive, regardless of any formal knowledge the social workers possessed.

7   The mothers' experience of intervention was related to the extent to which they felt either supported or undermined by the actions of the social worker. These involved not just issues of partnership, but also the way women felt they were treated, or labelled, in terms of their competence as parents.

8   Many of the women's comments held the social worker responsible for their sense of inclusion or exclusion in the intervention process. The claims of exclusion made by some women are consistent with social workers' accounts in some cases. This is particularly clear where the women considered that social workers tended to focus exclusively on the child. However, it is evident that the women themselves were finding it difficult to engage actively in the intervention process since the majority felt they lacked the energy, confidence and motivation in presenting their views. These were women whose depression severely dented their morale in relationship to partnership.

15 Families with disabled children

Women with disabled children were involved with social services not primarily because they had children at risk, or because their parenting competence was called into question, although they could feel under intense pressure because of their children's disability. Their relationship with the social worker was not one which was based on authority, with its inherent potential for conflict. Theirs was a situation defined by the needs of the child rather than blame which might be attributed to an abusing parent.

Nevertheless, these women's experience, although varied, was characterised by considerable disquiet. This was generally related to matters which have been discussed earlier, in particular the resource limitations which meant that these families were frequently given the lowest priority, and a consequent tendency for them to be seen, if at all, at times of crisis only. The kinds of feelings which could be engendered by caring for a disabled child were made clear by one woman:

> Disability will not go away. It will not disappear. It does not get better overnight. Yes, sometimes it will plateau and he [child] will have a few weeks, or, you just don't know what is around the corner. I have friends who have had children who have died. That is the end of disability – death. This is the living hell for children like [my son].... It's no fun.

Such families may have competent parents. They may not have children significantly at risk. Yet their feelings of need for support, which do not relate to those key criteria for resource provision, were nonetheless great.

There were two key dimensions to women's judgements about interventions: the services provided, and the personal qualities and professionalism of the social workers involved.

Service provision

Service provision was fundamental. Sufficient contact between the social worker and mother was a prerequisite for any real level of partnership between the two, and where the contact was sporadic and infrequent, many women expressed feelings of neglect and abandonment. Service provision was far more frequently mentioned when women were describing the social services response negatively, than when they were positive. It was an issue, in other words, in its absence, rather than presence.

Occasionally, services were mentioned positively, and referred to specifically. Thus for one woman, it was the provision of a kids' club that was important, and for another it was transport for her children:

> She gets the funding for [daughter's] kids' club.... They run a kids' club for holidays which is wonderful...nine to three...it means she is not at home all day, causing absolute disruption... brilliant, brilliant. It was such a relief.

> I had a bad accident...and I was bedridden for three weeks. [social worker] very kindly arranged for lifts to school and someone to pick him up. I couldn't cope with him at home because I couldn't move — he was more demanding then.... I appreciated it so much.

Services were much more of an issue, however, in their perceived absence or inadequacy. The women were generally very negative where they saw that services were not being provided for what they perceived to be their real needs. Women sometimes received only a single assessment visit, or, indeed, no response at all. Having got practically nothing, the onus to contact social services on a purely duty basis was often left to them. For most, therefore, it was not a personal issue; they were not refused a service because of the particular circumstances of their family. Rather, it was a priority issue; they were in a group which was not considered as important as other groups within social services. This was clear to one woman:

> [the social worker] came once. He could see that my son had problems, he was jumping all over him. He says to me, 'He's a very hyperactive child'. I said, 'You haven't seen nothing yet'. I was being honest with him. What he had seen in that 20 minute visit was nothing to what I see in 24 hours, and he is taking down these notes and everything and he goes back again, and then I get a letter saying the same as before. You are not a priority. If you need help, contact the duty worker. But duty workers can only do so much.

This awareness of general rules, rather than individual preferences, which underlay allocation of priority was evident to some women: 'I think that if you are a single parent, you would get more help, and there is more available...maybe he [son] is solely for the disability aspect'. Some also felt the social workers were under great pressure, simply because of the amount of work they were expected to do:

> Well, when he came in I could see that he was under a lot of stress, because there are a lot of kids, and I can imagine the position he is in. Well, when he didn't come back for months, I thought, that is it, he must be doing a lot of backlog work.

This low priority had a number of knock-on effects, outlined by the women. One was aware of long waiting lists:

> Well I had the stair lift put in — I had to wait a long time for that. And that was through the occupational therapist, not the social worker.... There is Crossroads and Service, and so on, but it doesn't sound permanent enough, and there is always such a long waiting list.

Even where there was something more than an assessment, some women felt that it was difficult to engage with social workers at all, as they could be very elusive:

> We were sure that through social services, I would get respite care, because he was able to go back to nursery. Nothing happened. I was spending every day, all day, on the phone, chasing all these people. They were never in, or they were on holiday, and that's not the right person, and you get fobbed off.

Negative views were not confined to the absence of a service, but also to the lack of an *appropriate* service. Where this happened, one woman was quite contemptuous, since it indicated that the social workers had little real understanding of the position of her child or family. Their lack of professionalism suggested to her that they would always tend to make the wrong decision:

> If he needed it, then fine. But if he needed it, they probably wouldn't say it. But now he doesn't need it, they're saying it. You can't win with them. They're stuffing it down your throat, which he doesn't need, but the things I need, he's not covered.

The practitioner

The conduct of the social workers was another dimension. Women's views of social workers were secondary to those of services. Women were positive about social workers only when they felt they received necessary resources. They were always negative when they felt they did not. There was little that was esoteric or exceptional, in terms of skills, which these women demanded. Although depressed, there was no sense that they were looking for therapeutic skills which would help them deal with their depression. This was perhaps largely because their depression was, for them, mostly a product of external factors of their social situation — their feelings of desperation, guilt and entrapment arising from their child's disability — rather than internal psychological conflict. Women tended to be concerned primarily by the social worker's responsiveness to their concerns, and courtesy when conducting themselves in direct contact with the mothers.

Positive responses

The professional and personal qualities of practitioners dominated over the issue of resource provision amongst those making positive comments. Where women commented positively about the social worker, this was in the context of feeling they were getting a service which at least addressed some of their needs. This could include the social worker simply being prepared to visit and listen to their problem. The women tended to identify two key elements of commitment and basic skills in working with others, which formed the basis, as well as the provision of a service in the first place, of any form of effective partnership with these depressed mothers. At the heart of the relationship was a preparedness to share information and advice, which could be done relatively easily, by, for example, using the phone: 'She often phones to tell me where to find him after school activities, and what have you — I never ever really have to ask, [she] always comes and tells me'. Another woman commented on the way information was imparted: 'It wasn't just that she told us what had happened and when and everything, but it was the way it was worded'. A third woman referred to the way that partnership could emerge not simply through the provision of information and advice, but the way this could be used as a catalyst to help women to help themselves:

> She does [direct us where we can go], but we are quite resourceful in finding things out for ourselves...[she] will, sort of give you a bit of an idea, and then we will track it down...she gives us the name and that of the person to chase, and we are quite happy to chase...and if you say, if we do this or that, how is this going to react and that, so you know what is going to happen without jumping in and upsetting anybody.

This is a partnership of equals in which the social worker acts as enabler of the women.

The human qualities of the social worker were of particular significance. Some of the most frequent of positive comments included references to the 'warmth' of the social worker, to their genuineness, whereby they presented themselves as a person rather than in an officious manner, that they were like a friend, and even that they were like a 'mum'. One effusive comment linked the human qualities of the social worker with the actions she took:

> She was so special. She was kind, she was warm, she glowed. She would only have to smile and you felt better.... She was so bubbly. She was loving. She was so good. For her the room just sparkled when she walked in. She got us money for travelling through the DSS. Spoke to her colleagues in the social services...she couldn't do enough...she was always there...she was superb.

Another way one mother tried to describe the extent of the social worker's warmth and involvement even analogised the social worker to her parents:

> It's like having a parent. It's somebody you can actually moan at, so when she comes on the phone I just moan, and it is always important to have someone who can understand, perhaps, where you are coming from,,,, She is sympathetic to what you are going through. If you try to explain that to a friend or neighbour, you feel they are saying, what are they making a fuss about? They can't actually see the pressure you are under from the mental aspect...she does know.

While positive comments at times sought to portray social workers in terms of their human qualities, such qualities could involve the use of skills. It would be rather too much to expect these mothers to have detailed understanding of technical terms denoting skills (although appropriate analysis can show that client accounts can enable the identification of perceived skills (Sheppard 1991). Nevertheless, they went some way in this direction. They were, for example, able to identify, to their satisfaction, social workers who were knowledgeable, who listened, and who were able to give sound advice:

> He is a good listener. And if I suggest something, he tells me if it cannot be done, and why it can't be done.... Very helpful, very understanding. A very good listener, and able to give practical advice which is not always the same thing...he does not promise what he can't deliver.

His listening skills could not be divorced from his other qualities, and the response he was prepared to make to deal with the problems. This is not simply 'listen and know what I mean' (England 1985), but 'listen and help me do something about it'. Active listening entailed, where appropriate, making responses which made it clear they had heard.

One woman commented on the difficult task for social workers of knowing when to give of themselves in order to provide a sense of reciprocity without seeming patronising or trivialising the women's problems. This was no easy task, since few social workers were likely to have experienced directly the degree of stress and pressure suffered by these women. One woman linked this skill to experience:

> I think that she has more experience. It is easier to talk to her...she sits there and tells you experiences about her family as well...so it makes it easier for you to share your family.

> ...quite knowledgeable about things, and to put you in an area that perhaps you hadn't thought of, like Family Fund, for the washing machine...she knew where the family fund was and how to access that...she knew the lady and her name, and how to get into the house with a clipboard.

The other main area generating positive comments related to perceptions of professionalism. Women responded positively to the social workers' conscientiousness, thoroughness in going about their business, and a real, role–based sense that they were really interested in the women. One woman referred to just such qualities on the part of her social worker:

> She always covers every point. Before she make any decision she says she has to go and speak to her manager first. If she comes here with my duty review, she makes sure the consultant gets one, the GP gets one, her manager gets one, but she always makes sure I get one first. Then she will drop me a little note saying 'Are you happy with the care plan?' Is there anything you need and that? I imagine she does her job very thoroughly and doesn't overlook anything.

This conscientiousness was not seen simply as professional, but also opened the way for a good working partnership. In the above example the social worker provided appropriate and timely information, but also sought to engage the woman as far as possible in decision making.

Negative responses

Where there was limited or no response, it was difficult for even the most basic form of partnership between social worker and mother to emerge. There was little in the accounts of women who felt negatively about the social worker to suggest a sense of partnership. Indeed, the prerequisite for this – basic and sufficient contact with the woman – was simply not present in some cases. Following an initial interview, one woman commented:

> After that [social worker] just left and I didn't hear anything again.... He said he would have to go back and check, and then I didn't hear anything at all until April, April this year!...he said to me, you realise your son was not registered.... i didn't know what he meant by being registered.

Social workers were at times perceived not to be listening. This was not simply a matter of failing to hear the pain and needs of the children and parent, but failing to respond in a way which matched their sense of desperation for a service. Where this happened, they described the social worker as 'not listening': 'He wouldn't really listen to what you have to say. He was just telling you what the rules are ... and you can't do this, and you can't do that'. Another woman described going through the motions:

> If he has got the time to listen...I can tell him, but if he has the time. So I don't know if he's going to have the time or no, because the way I tell it he could be here for days – I could offer to put a bed up for him! I could try, though not many people listen. What I want is that people who are there to help me to listen to me. You know, instead of just sitting there and taking notes.... If I am sitting here and all you do is write and write, and then I say something and you are not concentrating...I'm not stupid you know...I have a good mind to go to social services and get them together and say this is me and I need help and do something about it.

A failure to respond to their particular case could be seen to indicate a lack of concerns, and could elicit negative views regardless of any generalised pressure on social work time. One woman was exasperated when a social worker was late for an important meeting about resource provision, but supposed to be on her side, acting as advocate for her:

> [social worker] said I should try and have a review. So he said, you write a letter for a review. At the time we had moved, and it was a mess, so I put it in writing. They wrote back and said they were looking into it, and they called me up there. He said that he would go and represent me, but when we got there...he was 15 minutes late. The lady in the office asked if I had

anyone representing me, and I said yes, my social worker. She asked where he was, I said not here yet. They did point the way to him when he got there, but I said, we don't need him. We were getting on all right.

Another bugbear for these women was where the social worker seemed to lack knowledge or expertise. Women at times felt they knew more than the social worker about the kinds of problems associated with their child's special needs or disability. To some extent, this was a right they claimed, in that they were the mother, and they expected to know their particular child the best. However, where they felt the social worker generally lacked knowledge or experience about the area they could feel let down, for example, 'It was weird, because I thought it would be something he would know about really. But no, he didn't.' Another women commented:

> And you could tell that she just wasn't experienced, no-one was experienced, and it was a waste. I thought it was just a waste of time because I was saying that I could have found someone to come in and they could have paid for that person.

Effects of intervention

Positive effects

Where women made positive comments, they were always eulogistic. Their accounts indicated that involvement could have fundamental effects on their lives. One woman referring to the beginning of social work involvement, said, 'I don't remember how it came to be. All that I know is, it was most probably the best time of my life when she came on the scene'. Another, who had become ill and was unable to cope properly with her disabled child, found the social worker quickly organising support services:

> Brilliant. I can't believe that somebody done that for me. Because like no-one else had done that sort of thing. My GP wouldn't have gone in, or the hospital or that, but she did.

The effects could be quite profound. Clearly, social work action did not resolve these women's depression, since they were still depressed, but they described themselves as feeling more supported and secure, felt that intervention had a calming effect, and that they were able to take a more optimistic view of their lives. One woman commented, in this spirit, on the regular contact and response of the social worker:

> She has said to me on many occasions, that if you have got any worries, problems, anything at all, just give me a ring. What more can you ask for? ... I have not as yet. But one day, it might be that bad, perhaps I will need to do that. And she will be there. And if she is not she will get back to me. I have got no doubts about that at all.

Another, in the same vein, drew attention to the security that the support of the social worker gave her, and its calming effect, as well as giving her some sense of hope:

> If I say that I just can't cope with this and this, she will say well, we will find a way out. When we was waiting for [son's] operation and I was getting myself in a state...she phones me to make sure everything is OK. She seems to have a calming effect on you in a way.

The women also described how the social worker could act as the basis for moving forward and gaining greater control of (though not resolving) their problems. The women described the social worker as providing a boost to their morale, of giving them a sense that, at least in part, their problems were more controllable, of acting as a catalyst for ideas, and even of being therapeutic. In relation to the last of these, one woman commented that 'I found it sort of therapeutic. I, I enjoyed just sitting down for an hour and talking things through, and I found it very helpful'. Another woman commented on the sense of progress the social worker was able to give her, because she knew the family, and contrasted this with her GP:

> My GP keeps changing...you haven't aired your views that you have come for, because you have been so busy discussing about the past.... At least you can cut through that. She knows where you have come from, and what point you are at now.... She can turn and say, 'Look how far you have come', because when you are in the middle of it, you can't always see the progress.

This progress could be encouraged by the discussions the women had with their social workers, where they were able to consider alternative ideas together:

> We sort of knock about ideas, of how we can make it easier...I feel she does listen...I feel quite confident with her that you can say what you want.

Acting as a catalyst for ideas was one of the strong dimensions of effective partnership which these women identified when making positive comments. A good, often excellent relationship, a sense of security and support, and an approach which enabled women to progress, all bespoke the basis for a proper partnership with social workers who were supportive in responding to their difficulties.

Negative effects

For those with negative comments, the poor service provision was the basis for equally negative effects. The difficulty in getting resources was matched, in some cases, by the determination of some women to get a service. This, arguably, reflected one of the aspects of the women regarded by social workers as 'stoics'; however, they were clearly more demanding. Their determination reflected a belief in the right to receive some kind of service, and a real concern that the children should get the support needed through helping the family. This was voiced strongly by one woman:

> So at last we got the disability social worker.... That's what we were fighting for [disability social worker]. So we've got him now.... His [child's] needs have obviously got worse, he's obviously changed.... I was phoning everyone, never let them forget who I was, never let them forget my voice, never let them forget my child's name. I was never going to let that happen.

However, such effort did not always end positively: 'I end up in tears.... It doesn't do no good anyway...because I know that I have been fighting for over three years. I have tried and I have got no further forward. It is stressing... I am fighting for a social worker, but they won't do nothing'.

Occasionally women expressed real anger about the ways they felt they had been treated, and the low priority they received in the context of other kinds of childcare cases:

> I get more angry than anything else. Because you know that there's a system out there, that's supposed to help, and you know, if I phoned up and said, 'Oh, I'm losing it, I want to batter my child', you can believe that it would be less than 24 hours, the police would have been on my door, with social services. Probably shouting child abuse at me.

Others, some of whom were regarded as 'stoics' by social workers, registered the seriousness of their plight. In truth, they were not stoical in the sense social workers understood it. They were not able women who refused to let their troubles get them down. These women were wilting under the pressure, but refusing to give up. The feeling of getting nowhere was taking its toll. The women expressed clearly and widely the emotional cost, one talking about 'running around like a headless chicken', and another talking of the sense of being 'isolated and overwhelmed' as she found she was, in turn, not responded to, given unhelpful advice and, in her view, 'fobbed off' with encouragement to contact inappropriate services. Women felt a loss of dignity as they sought desperately to get help that was not provided. One woman felt she ended up begging for the help she thought she needed, and her general sentiments echoed those of other women:

> He said I would just have to wait, to be put on a waiting list, as there were other children, and this wasn't that serious...we just needed a couple of hour [respite] a week, that's all.... So I was trying to say to them was that I would only be asking for help when I was desperately in need, because they said it was money problems, why couldn't they do something for him?... I don't know how it works. They agreed at the time, but now they say no, I can't have it.

A gamut of emotions, including desperation, perplexity and the humiliation of begging were brought together because services were absent.

These circumstances did nothing for the women's health, or their capacity to run their lives effectively. Women talked of lacking sleep, of feeling tired and exhausted, feeling nauseous, having headaches, being generally more run down and prone to minor illnesses. The absence of support, arising from the limited social service help, left this woman in a state of physical and mental turmoil, affecting her parenting capacity:

> I had blood pressure, really high blood pressure. Sometimes I feel nervous. If the kids are upstairs and calling me, I go like this you know. It's not because they are shouting, it is just the nervousness I get. And I keep everything to myself, and feel that I am getting more stressed.

This was accompanied by a loss of morale which was typical of many of the women:

> I am already under stress and I have all these problems and then there is another one that comes on top and so it goes on. I am constantly going over and over the same problems and getting nowhere. They think I am getting a head start...but they do not know what I am talking about. I have sent them all these notes, and I am sure they are going in the bin.

Social workers could underestimate the devastation wrought on these women, when faced not just with their child's disabilities, but also the bureaucracy required to get any service, followed by the services not being provided. This woman suggested it could endanger her child:

> I have filled in all the forms [for respite care]... a massive lump of forms. And he just waits. They have got nobody who can look after him [son] because his needs are so diverse.... I just fill in another form every couple of years. When I get to crisis point — I am going to tell you what scares me — is that sometimes I get to breaking point.... I can see myself losing it all and killing him. Just frustration now, I am trying to control his tantrums, and hyperactivity, and trying to control myself, and it clashes.

Key points

These women's perceptions were not affected by the authority role of social workers working with child protection families, with its power imbalance arising from the concern about risks to the children. The overwhelming issue for this group was one of resources: how were they to be able to get the help they felt they needed in an environment which systematically disadvantaged them because priority was allocated to other groups? Limited resources where therefore the key to understanding women's responses in this group.

1 The fundamental aspect affecting the views of these women was whether or not they received services they felt they needed. When they did not, the women's views were strongly negative. However, when they received a service that helped them with their needs, they rarely referred to the resources they had been given, but focused on the personal and professional qualities of the social worker. Resources were an issue in their absence, rather than their presence.

2   The women's accounts show a strong disjunction between social workers' perception of them as frequently stoical, and the reality of the desperation they felt when they were not being adequately supported. The 'stiff upper lip' imagery which pervaded social workers' perceptions contrasted with the women's experience of being at breaking point, and hanging on to their emotional stability by their finger tips. Some responded with determination to obtain the appropriate services, which nevertheless frequently did not get anywhere. Others' desperation showed that they were only just managing at great emotional cost, and felt they were losing control, unlike the calm, controlled, determinedly able women described by social workers as 'stoics'.

3   The absence of services led to circumstances liable to reinforce the women's depression. Where social workers did not respond in a way women felt sufficient or appropriate, strong feelings could be evoked. Women could be very angry or dismissive of the social workers. However, the key to their experience was their desperation, and the isolation and hopelessness they felt in the absence of support.

4   Where women felt they received little or no service, they were often highly critical of social workers, who appeared unresponsive and uninterested, lacking in basic courtesy. This greater tendency to personal and professional criticism may in part have reflected the priority which social workers felt they had to give to other work.

5   The women who praised their social workers made comments which were extremely positive: brilliant, wonderful and so on. The positive qualities valued by the women were, in many respects, the mirror image of those on the basis of which they criticised social workers. The women highlighted the human warmth of the social workers, their capacity to listen and respond to their concerns, and to provide useful and relevant information and advice. Persistence and expertise were also valued.

6   Women's perceptions of partnership were first and foremost based on whether they felt they received an adequate service. Where they received little service, there was no basis for partnership, since there was no communication. Such basic elements as information provision and consultation were not possible where there was little or no contact. Where they needed help, but received little or none, they were even reduced to supplicant status, with a major imbalance in power and actions between mother and social worker, which had nothing to do with the potential conflict which their authority role could generate in risky situations, and everything to do with rationing resources. Where services were not provided, in other words, frustrations were high and partnership non–existent.

7   Positive views of partnership occurred at many levels. The favourable views of women frequently presuppose that information provision and consultation were taking place. However, effective partnership did not simply arise from these, or the provision of resources alone, although that was a prerequisite. Partnership

also emerged through a combination of human qualities which made the social worker seem 'real' and concerned for the mother. The basic skills important for social work, such as listening and provision of appropriate information and advice could contribute to positive developments in women's lives.

Overall, poor or absent social work support was not merely neutral, but actually diminished the woman, and caused her emotional state to deteriorate. Where adequate support was provided, it usually freed the women to have positive views of social workers. They did not demand advanced, highly skilled therapists (although this may be what they got occasionally), but warm, human and courteous individuals.

Part six
Epilogue

6

16 Conclusion and recommendations

Conclusion

This research shows a complex set of factors which influence the conduct of social work practice with depressed mothers in child and family care. In a difficult situation, with an environment which did not always help them in their practice, there is clear evidence of high levels of commitment on the part of many social workers. However, the main concern here is identifying areas where improvements could be made in the light of problems relating particularly to work with depressed mothers.

Notwithstanding the fact that many of the mothers presented a threat to their children, a picture emerges of many depressed mothers who were marginalised, and felt threatened and undermined in their involvement with social services. These factors produce clear features, such as exclusion, absence of control and blame, which are known to engender and maintain depression. Their circumstances as service users therefore, are depression–inducing and maintaining. In seeking to understand this, the strongest emphasis should be placed on the organisation, aims and culture of the service, rather than on the commitment of the social workers as individuals. This does not mean there was no variability in practice, or that practitioners never undermined the women. However, the practitioners were in many respects working in adversity, some of which is perhaps inevitable, because of the child protection orientation of much of their work. However, if the service is to be improved, the strongest emphasis needs to be placed on its structural–cultural dimensions.

Social workers' attributions and intervention strategies

The starting point is a group of mothers whose life experiences provide a context for their depression. Their vulnerability is understandable and is evident in a number of ways: their social disadvantage, disrupted social relations, their own experiences of maltreatment and abuse in childhood as well as the pressures of childcare (something of a chicken and egg situation). Nevertheless, depression can impair women's capacity to care for their children and to cope with other responsibilities, and there is evidence from the women themselves to confirm this. These were women with high levels of needs in their own right for a range of very deeply entrenched reasons. It is already understood, for example, that those subject to maltreatment and abuse in childhood, are highly vulnerable to depression (Bifulco and Moran 1998), and also likely to have high dependency needs. This, furthermore, can be both a brutal and brutalising experience.

There are clear and important links between the women's self-reported experience of abuse as children, the social workers' mental health attributions, and their intervention strategies. The association between experience of child abuse and those defined as 'troubled and troublesome' is consistent with ideas which connect child maltreatment and high dependency needs discussed in the Introduction. The descriptions provided by social workers of women in the 'troubled and troublesome' group – which in some cases are consistent with features of personality disorder – include egocentric, chaotic, and sometimes malicious behaviour, particularly towards their children. Their own high needs, often dependency needs, were a major feature of the threat to the child, and were further linked with agency responses which placed them in the child protection–child abuse group. Some of these were alcohol dependent, and many were involved in a series of poorly functioning, often abusive relationships.

In other cases, the depression was manifested in a greater sense of despair, where the egocentric dimensions were less apparent, and a concern for their children, and their own shortcomings as parents, was more obvious. These were characteristics of women in social workers' accounts of the 'genuinely depressed'. These too, it is interesting to note, contained a high proportion (though significantly fewer than 'troubled and troublesome' women) of mothers who reported having been maltreated themselves as children. Where there was a connection with childhood maltreatment it was, in social workers' accounts, more about internalisation and self-doubt. Such women, despite their already existing disadvantages, were liable to experience guilt and self-blame, individualising and internalising their problems, although some could reflect upon the context in which they emerged. These were women who were disadvantaged in several ways. An obvious question, particularly ironic for those with their own experience of child abuse, is why are these women considered less deserving of support services than their own children?

The third group, of 'stoics', also contained a considerable proportion of women who reported maltreatment as children, very similar in this respect to the 'genuinely depressed'. Their response, however, according to the social workers, was a response of stoicism in adversity, rather than dependency, aggression or self-doubt. Nevertheless, the women's own reports, while confirming that they just about manage childcare, suggest that this was a far more traumatic process than that described by the social workers. It is worth noting that in this group, as with the others, a considerable proportion had not reported experiencing childhood maltreatment, and the relationship between this and mental health attribution remains a tendency.

One of the most marked features was the link between mental health attribution and intervention strategy. Although the relationship was far from perfect, they were nevertheless highly significant. 'Troubled and troublesome' women were significantly more likely to experience CP–CA intervention, 'genuinely depressed' were more likely to feature in CP–FS intervention, and 'stoics' tended to be in the disability intervention group. The strategies pursued were markedly different, which meant that there was a strong tendency for different 'types' of mothers to have quite different experiences. The combination of control, assessment, monitoring, and support were central elements of the CP–CA intervention, where the danger to the child (often presented by acts of omission or commission by the mother) was the key concern for social workers. The supportive tendency of CP–FS intervention involved a greater concern with parental coping and competence, with the support provided mainly through management of care, though without excluding some direct work. Rationing was the key issue for disability interventions, and limited help was accompanied by crisis responses in much of this intervention.

This link between definition and intervention arises through the underlying concerns of the social worker, which formulated into a 'hierarchy of riskiness', concentrating on the mother. At the highest level are cases where protecting the children became the priority, hence the child abuse dimension. At the next level, parental competence, and supporting the mothers to this end, became the prime focus, although of course such cases were not devoid of risk. At the lowest level, where mothers were considered to be reasonably competent, the main issue became one of quality of life, and at the most serious, preventing the problems becoming so great that the mother's competence as parent was being threatened. These different dimensions relate specifically to the mother, and helps us to make sense of social workers' judgements of them. They have differing response and resource implications, providing some understanding of different intervention strategies.

This link, which represents a general tendency, can be broadly presented in Table 16.1:

Table 16.1 Relationship between mental health attribution, risk and intervention strategy

Mental Health Attribution	Risk focus	Intervention strategy
'Troubled and troublesome'	Danger to child	Child protection–child abuse
'Genuinely depressed'	Parental competence	Child protection–family support
'Stoics'	Quality of life	Disability

This provides some representation of the relationship between mental health attribution and intervention strategy, through an overarching notion of risk, which indicates the dominant focus. There will always be some risk to children, as no situation is completely risk–free, even where parental competence is the priority. The higher order risk tends to incorporate the lower order risk, rather than each being mutually exclusive. Thus, for example, the danger to the child does not exclude a concern about parental competence. It shows also, through this notion, the way in which mental health attributions are understandable in terms of the central concerns and agency expectations of social workers. Such attributions are understandable in a context where social workers needed to consider the women in terms of the kinds of intervention required.

Exclusion and partnership

One important concept requiring understanding is that of 'exclusion', which describes much of the experiences of these depressed women. These bring together key related issues of intervention strategy and partnership. There was an underlying culture of concern for the child, which to a large degree excluded concern for the mother as an individual in her own right (as distinct from as a parent). Although individual social workers were frequently sympathetic, a focus of concern on the child was a general feature, recognised by both social workers and mothers, and accompanied by a neglect of the woman's own needs. The focus on the child involved an implicit conflict of interest thesis: that to pay attention to the mother's needs is more likely to place the child at risk. This may well have been the case with some families, particularly those in the 'troubled and troublesome' group, but social workers tended to apply this principle across the board.

Women, as a result, often felt a profound sense of exclusion. Social workers who prioritised mothers' needs for themselves, were the exception rather than the rule. There is considerable evidence that the processes of social work intervention were, for many women, profoundly undermining, and rather than being supportive, seemed only add to their problems. One way in which they felt excluded was through what they perceived to be an overwhelming emphasis on the child, with very little attention given to them in the process of decision making. Where there was already inbuilt potential for conflict – through, for example, fear of losing the child – an orientation to the child simply reinforced that potential.

A consequence of this central concern with the child, and a major contributing factor to their sense of exclusion, is that women were generally seen as mothers, rather than an individuals in their own right. The role, rather than the person, was for social workers the crucial issue. The undermining effect of this is significant, since despite their shortcomings, these mothers are those upon whom social workers tend to be most reliant for the care of the children. There is evidence that social services not only attracted a group at high risk for depression, they also contributed to its generation and maintenance.

In this there are key structural factors. The move towards care managerialism has tended to place an emphasis on the management of resources, rather than more extensive and direct involvement of the social workers themselves. Social workers were reminded that they were the care managers of the case and not to spend too much time working directly with the family in general, and the mother in particular. Those who wished to focus more on the mother were forced to 'go the extra mile', which placed a large burden on them, and we might speculate, made burnout more likely. This limited the attention given to the mother herself. Priorities, which reflected agency expectations, meant that social workers frequently simply had no time to devote to the women as they might have liked.

The exclusion, however, had different components according to intervention strategy. A further organisational dimension related to the child protection orientation of the agency. This is reflected in the distribution of resources and priority given to different types of cases. However, it exerted an enormous impact on the interaction between social worker and mother. Mothers in the disability group were most affected by the limited resources available to provide support and suffered the consequences. This impacted so much on relationships with social workers that, regardless of the personal qualities or helpfulness of the social worker as an individual, women had negative views of them when they felt support was inadequate, and gave them glowing testimonials when they received resources. This reflected the reality of resource limitations. Work with the child protection–child abuse group was overwhelmed by the child protection responsibilities, and the resulting conflictual relationship was difficult for social workers to overcome. The issues of authority and control, as well as mothers' fear of losing children, made the task of forming a trusting, open relationship extremely difficult. The child protection processes created a very hostile environment for practice, making women feel blamed and threatened, and contributing to their depression.

Even in the child protection–family support group, there was a strong dimension of the 'latent threat' of losing the child. This was so powerful that at times it obliterated the other message which social workers sought to get across: that they were there primarily to support the family, and only if all else failed, and the risk became sufficiently great, to arrange accommodation or care. Where they tried to communicate this message, the women's feeling of 'latent threat' was so strong that women became extremely cynical, and treated the support message as one being communicated in bad faith. In both the disability and the child protection–child abuse groups, these organisational–structural dimensions exercised an overwhelming influence on interactions between social workers and mothers.

With CP–FS intervention, however, another dimension came to the fore, where organisational factors had less influence in defining the social worker–mother relationship. This involved what might be termed 'interpersonal dissonance' which arose in the context of the woman's depression. In these cases, the feeling of non–involvement by mothers was accompanied by diffidence, and, on the part of the social workers, a lack of awareness of dissatisfaction, accompanied by an absence of sufficient skills to engage the women properly. In this context the particular features of depression, associated with low confidence and motivation, made the effort for partnership difficult. Many of these women, as a result, felt alienated from the processes of intervention, while the social workers felt they had engaged them adequately in partnership.

The concept of 'entrapment' has been developed here to describe many of the ways these women experienced intervention. This reflects the sense of lack of control over what is happening, a feature both of depression, and their life experiences prior to involvement with social services. Because of the organisation, expectations, and culture of social services, the practice of social work seems to be condemned to produce feelings of entrapment on the part of many mothers. The result of this was an inbuilt tendency for relationships and practice to be disrupted by this sense of entrapment. Some of these women expressed considerable distrust of social workers, and not just those receiving CP–CA intervention. They were reluctant to give them information about themselves, for example of their own depression, for fear of the social worker's response. As a result, social workers were working with information which was avoidably imperfect. Some women felt frustrated and angry, and this could be expressed in extremely personal ways. Where there is so much disruption it is difficult to develop constructive relationships, and there are considerable impediments to achieving positive outcomes. All this, of course, could affect social workers' perception of mothers who could come across as uncooperative, angry, aggressive and defensive. How does one disentangle this from assessment of risk?

At the heart of all this are serious features of 'blaming' the mother. Blame was not necessarily the intention of social workers, but it is the consequence of the culture and organisation of the service. This might be referred to as systemically produced 'felt blame', that is, blame felt by mothers even where not attributed to them by social workers. Their very involvement in an agency whose role is largely child protection, is a badge of failure on their part. These, we should remember, were women who had stayed with their children, while their partners were no longer there, and who laboured under considerable long term disadvantage. However, involvement with social workers was in many cases only likely to exacerbate their sense of self–blame. The moral–predictive dimensions of their assessments of mothers (into 'stoics', 'genuinely depressed', 'troubled and troublesome') meant there was a moral dimension to definitions of their situation, which invited feelings of self–blame. The child orientation did not help women develop a sense of self–worth. Indeed, women explicitly referred to the way they felt undermined and undervalued by this practice. Their constant fear of losing their children left them with an implicit indictment of their own parenting.

In these circumstances, women become the primary victims of the system, and social workers, in some respects, become its secondary victims. It is quite clear that social workers were forced to experience abuse, aggression and anger, and at times became quite fearful (one social worker had changed their name by deed poll, assuming a new identity to escape the threats of one parent). While this is perhaps an inevitable consequence of involvement in child protection, the organisation and culture of the service, with its lack of interest in the mother as an individual in her own right, almost certainly exacerbated the problem.

One of the key issues to be addressed, and which emerges from this study is: how far can social workers act in the interest of the welfare of the child, unless they are able to focus also on the welfare of the mother, as an individual in her own right? The tendency to compartmentalise matters ('I am the social worker for the child') means that there tends to be an interest in the mother only as parent, rather than as an individual herself. Yet we have seen how this is self–defeating: mothers who feel there is no interest in them as an individual feel alienated from the process of intervention. To focus effectively on the mother as parent requires, it would seem, an interest in her as an individual. This general theme permeates the findings and recommendations which are presented here.

Although there are signs of a growing interest in social work and social services in the link between childcare and mental health problems, it is not clear that most social services departments (or health authorities) have begun to get to grips with this issue and its multifaceted implications. This research has shown something of the breadth and depth of problems. Amongst the key issues are: the way social workers seek to make sense of the women and their depression; their degree of training in this area; the link between social and mental health services; the culture of exclusivity in relation to the child; the very organisation and expectations of childcare services; the nature of, and skills involved in conducting partnerships; and the way in which agency conduct and expectations influence the women's own capacity to involve themselves positively in the work of social workers, and, indeed, conduct themselves as parents.

Recommendations

The need for mental health knowledge

A central feature of the findings is the extent to which depression was a pervasive facet of the circumstances of women in child and family care. There is not a single specialism of 'childcare social work', but mental health issues are a major feature of this practice. There is considerable evidence that depression played an important part in the interaction of social worker and mother, yet there was little consistent appreciation of the part it played. The mothers' depression can be understood, in large part, as a psychosocial phenomenon, involving multiple disadvantages, at times lifelong maltreatment and needs, sometimes as severe as those suffered by the children. The key recommendations arising from the research are as follows:

1 The fundamental need for all childcare social workers to have some degree of training in the understanding of, and response to, mental health problems in general, and depression in particular. This is not to suggest that judgements of mothers and families should not be concerned with risk, but they would benefit from a more detailed mental health knowledge in order that the assessments of risk and parental competence may be made in a more informed manner.

2 Beyond this, there is a strong case for a hybrid mental health–childcare social worker, with specialised knowledge in both areas. It is arguable that the very complexity of the cases, and the significance of the mother to childcare, mean that quite high level skills and knowledge are required. These might operate as a reference and consultation point for other workers who have less specialised mental health knowledge. Whether having only a proportion of workers with these levels of skills would be sufficient depends, at least in part, on the extent to which the other recommendations, made below, are successfully incorporated into practice.

3 There are two possible models. Model A would combine a small group of consultants with high levels of expert mental health and childcare skills and a majority of childcare workers with some knowledge, and Model B would entail all childcare social workers being mental health–childcare hybrids. The kinds of knowledge which would need to be widely available would be:

❏ depression recognition skills

❏ awareness of origins and consequences of depression, particularly for childcare

❏ understanding of appropriate case management techniques

❏ knowledge and skills of effective intervention

❏ understanding of ways of effectively engaging with depressed individuals.

Of considerable interest here is the psychosocial context of depression, including disadvantage and social relations, and the need to understand the effects on adults of abuse in childhood, a feature of some women with strong dependency needs and considerable childcare difficulties. One of the most basic and long standing skills of the mental health social worker, the capacity to take and apply the social history, would seem to have obvious use here.

4 In the absence of appropriately knowledgeable and skilled practitioners, a system of swaps and exchanges might occur, in which childcare practitioners change places for a period of time with mental health social workers. Although this could incur some cost in the temporary loss of particular expertise (for example of an experienced childcare practitioner), immediate gains would be team access to specialist mental health knowledge, and the long term development of mental health knowledge and skills in the childcare teams.

Organisation of mental health and family services

The small proportion of depressed women with access to specialist mental health support, which was identified in this study, is a cause for considerable concern. Underlying this was a fragmentation of services – adult/childcare, social service/NHS, statutory/voluntary – arising from a specialist orientation which took little account of the connectedness of problems in the real world. The bizarre outcome was that many cases, with the highest priority, and greatest risk to children, missed out on a mental health service because they did not fit with the eligibility criteria operated by the mental health services. The following recommendations are made:

1 There is a strong case for revision of some of the most fundamental aims and objectives of both mental health and childcare services. These would need to be wider ranging and more inclusive, in particular allowing that, where a childcare case is one with high priority, and a mental health problem is present, it will be given priority amongst mental health cases. This could sensibly be applied both to NHS services and adult social services.

2 A more open access to mental health services is required with the opportunity for direct referral from childcare social services to mental health services. This is currently the exception rather than the rule (Sheppard 1991). The current configuration of services provides barriers to childcare–mental health collaboration, in particular the need to refer through the GP.

3 Where childcare and mental health services remain separate, there should be provision for a more systematic and routine connection between these two services. This would need to occur both at organisational level, between managers at the appropriate strategic and operational levels, and at practice level through appropriate channels of communication, which could be both formal (for example as periodic meetings) and informal. Strategies for 'working cases' would need to be jointly developed.

4 A more radical solution would be to create a hybrid agency which would enable appropriate childcare and mental health professionals to work together directly. A comprehensive family service would involve the combination of childcare and mental health expertise for both children and their parents, and include child psychiatry.

5 Whether a hybrid service is created or services are kept separate, where voluntary sector facilities exist, such as NEWPIN, there should be a clear identification of when and how these should be used, how far they duplicate other services such as family centres, and their 'added value'. Clear processes for working with drug and alcohol services would facilitate case management where substance abuse is a feature.

Focusing on the child, focusing on the mother

Social workers in general sought to focus primarily on the child and the resulting sense of exclusion felt by many mothers had an undermining effect on positive relationships and practice. Some of this was based on an implicit conflict of interest thesis. The following suggestions are made to give due attention to the needs of the mother:

1 It is important for social workers to distinguish between families where there appears to be a real conflict of interest, requiring a more exclusive focus on the child's interest, and the majority of cases in which the interests of the mother, in the form of her well–being, are consistent with the interests of the welfare of child. A much greater emphasis on the possibility of mutual (mother–child) interest is required than is currently the case, together with processes which give expression to this.

2 It may be important not just to emphasise parents' fundamental responsibilities, but also their rights – to services which enable them more realistically to carry out their responsibilities. This should enable, at the level of principle, their needs as individuals to be recognised, for it is through this recognition that we are able to develop their capacities as parents.

3 On this basis there is also a case, at least for some mothers, for a social worker for the mother as an individual, consistent with a more comprehensive childcare and mental health service.

Partnership and exclusion

In view of the undermining effect of depression, a key issue is the extent to which the women were able, of themselves, to engage in meaningful partnership with social workers. Two facets, which underlie various elements of social work–mother interaction further affected partnership: the focus on the child, and the latent authority dimension of social work. The following measures could be taken to improve partnership:

1 A clearer and more overt focus on the mother herself in the process of intervention would improve the quality of partnership. The sense of exclusion is widespread, and without some direct interest shown in the mother she is likely to feel undermined and disabled.

2 Specific provision should be made for situations which women find formidable, such as review meetings. There is nothing novel about this suggestion: that women should have support within meetings, and clear opportunities to express their views outside meetings. However, a further force is applied to this argument by our knowledge of the effects of the depression on women's capacity to engage.

3 The findings indicate that developing the capacity of women to engage effectively in partnership should be a routine and discrete aspect of practice. It should, however, also be regarded as an aspect of practice which requires high level skills taking into account the disabling and undermining effects of depression. The most useful technique, in this respect, would involve the use of Task Centred Practice.

This is designed to be carried on alongside other elements of practice, and partnership itself could be viewed as the specific issue to be worked on. It would enable a short piece of focused practice to be undertaken, the effect of which would be to enable women to take part more effectively in partnership. As a 'side effect', women would discover an effective problem–solving method which could be transferred to other areas of their lives.

Organisation structure and agency function

One of the main problems for social workers was the way in which bureaucratic and service delivery dimensions affected their capacity to work directly with mothers. There was also a problem for some social workers with a care management orientation, which saw social workers primarily as managers of care, rather than the providers of direct work. This meant that when social workers wanted to carry out direct work with mothers, this involved extra work and very high degrees of commitment.

Organisational and agency function issues, furthermore, could exercise such a pervasive and negative influence, that they overwhelmed any potential for positive partnership relationships. The lack of control and power felt by women had a pernicious effect on relationships, particularly with regard to fear of losing children. The depth of mistrust on the part of the mothers suggests there is little chance of resolution of this problem within the current structure and ethos of service delivery, and the following changes are recommended:

1 The care management orientation of practice has tilted the balance unhelpfully towards indirect work at the expense of direct work. It is necessary that there is greater recognition of, and scope for, direct work by social workers with the mothers if they are to respond better to their needs, without excessive demands being placed on the practitioners.

2 A recommendation is that in these cases a mediator who is both independent of the social services department, and experienced and knowledgeable in child and family care, should be able to work with women themselves, at least for defined periods. Their role would be to mediate between the social worker and the woman. This could be particularly important at an early stage in intervention. Their independence is crucial, since it would be self–defeating for the woman to perceive the mediator as another agent of social services. This mediator would need to be able to advise the woman herself, and to represent the social worker to the woman, and vice versa. They could provide the basis for a clearer and appropriate understanding of the positive potential of the childcare social worker's role.

The system creating depression: blaming the mother

It is not easy to identify the extent to which depression was the product of social services intervention, rather than the reverse. It is apparent from this research that there were at least three groups of factors which individually and collectively would contribute to the generation of depression:

- ❏ past lifetime experiences of being undermined and abused

- ❏ current circumstances of disadvantage, limited support and fractured social relations

- ❏ the experience of social work intervention, which has clear alienating, controlling and resource dimensions.

Vaughn and Leff (1976) have shown how significant even relatively limited criticism is to the generation of depression in vulnerable individuals. The sense of blame and criticism felt by women, notwithstanding the best efforts of the social workers, were significant aspects of the women's experiences of intervention. There is some suggestion that depression may play some part in the loss of contact between child and mother when the child is placed in care. Certainly there is graphic evidence of the psychological trauma of involvement with social services, and of at least some women's attempts to conceal it because of their fears of the consequences. Social workers should be aware of the following:

1 The extent of depression, and the emotional turmoil which these women feel in view of their involvement with social services. In particular, they need to recognise that elements of the child protection processes can induce depression, and this is particularly the case with the loss of children into care and cessation of contact with children. An important recommendation is that social workers are acutely aware of this demoralisation, which might appear as indifference, and specifically focus on this issue where children are received into care or accommodated.

2 The issue of blame. Despite the criticism voiced by some of the women about social workers, few women were able to avoid blaming themselves directly or indirectly for their involvement. Notwithstanding the welfare issues for the child, these were women for whom social services' involvement was frequently an additional burden in a life characterised by disadvantage. On top of this was the moral–predictive dimension of the ways in which the women were defined by social workers. Whether they were sympathetic or otherwise, this meant that women were invariably involved in circumstances where moral judgements were made about them and their childcare capabilities.

3 The feelings of guilt, self–blame and low self–esteem amongst mothers, which are major facets of depression. Social workers need to take positive action to counteract the strong tendency to negativism occurring as a result of social services' involvement, and in the women's oppressive environment of disadvantage. It is also important that social workers are able to communicate to

the women an understanding of the oppressive context in which their childcare problems have emerged. This is not to dilute their childcare responsibilities, but to create more auspicious circumstances for a more constructive relationship with the woman, and a more positive outcome for the family.

Disability

The disability group were at a permanent disadvantage because of the terms in which childcare resources were allocated. Despite the distress and despair which many of these women felt, it was, in the end, not the tribulations suffered by the parents which counted, but the degree of risk to the child. For many of these women, social services *were* the problem. Many of their difficulties could be resolved through an increase in resources, but resources are perhaps the most intractable and difficult issue. Nevertheless, certain observations should be made:

1 For depressed mothers of disabled children to obtain a more supportive service, greater priority should be given to the travails of the parents, and mothers in particular. This is a general message of this research, but unlike other areas, risk and parental competence were not considerations which would enable these women to obtain more support.

2 The location of these cases in the wider child and family services context may contribute to their difficulties in obtaining services. Although they are not universally located thus, the guidelines which emphasise (for good anti-discriminatory reasons) that children with disabilities should be considered 'children first' place them logically within children and families' services. The problems caused by the allocation of priority in case by case resource provision are such that they are always liable to be disadvantaged by their current location. The mothers' serious mental health needs are not being addressed: a greater focus on their needs, and particularly their depression, would be a simple route to improved service provision.

3 The logical course, in the light of this evidence, would appear to be a realignment of services, with a service set up specifically for families with disabled children. This would be a hybrid social and health services agency, separate from other services for children and families, which would be able to address the social, physical and mental health needs (as well as other issues, such as education) of the family as a whole, unencumbered by competition for resources with child protection cases. Allocation of priority would occur between like cases, rather than with disparate groups, and where criteria were weighted in favour of those in other groups.

Concluding comments

Until recently, the issue of mothers' depression has been surprisingly marginalised in research on childcare social work. This, perhaps, reflects the mothers' own sense of exclusion and marginality which has been identified in this research. Understanding the implications of the very high rates of depression for the conduct of practice has been a complex process, and this arguably has profound implications for the organisation and conduct of practice. It is clear, however, that depression as a major aspect of childcare social work will not go away. If we are to be concerned for the adequate performance of practice, this is an issue which cannot be ignored, and which should be placed at centre stage in the organisation and conduct of practice.

References

Abramson, L., Seligman, M. and Teasdale, J. (1978) 'Learned helplessness in humans: a critique and reformulation', *Journal of Abnormal Psychology*, **87**, pp. 49–75

Aldgate, J. and Tunstill, J. (1995) *Making Sense of Section 17*, London: HMSO

Barbaree, H. E. and Davis, R. B. (1984) Assertive behaviour, self expectations and self evaluations in mildly depressed university women, *Cognitive Therapy and Research*, **8**, pp. 153–72

Barnes, M. and Wistow, G. (1992) *Researching User Involvement*, Leeds: Nuffield Institute for Health Service Studies, University of Leeds

Barrera, M. (1981) 'Social support and the adjustment of pregnant adolescents: assessment issues', in Gottlieb, B. (ed.) *Social Networks and Social Support*, Beverley Hills: Sage

Barrera, M. (1985) 'Informant corroboration of social support network data', *Connections*, **8** pp 9–13

Beck, A. (1976) *Cognitive Therapy and Emotional Disorders*, New York: International Universities Press

Beck, A., Steer, R. and Garbin, M. (1988) 'Psychometric properties of the Beck Depression Inventory: twenty five years of evaluation', *Clinical Psychology Review*, **8**, pp. 77–100

Becker, E. (1973) *The Denial of Death*, New York: Free Press

Bibring, E. (1953) 'The mechanism of depression', in P. Greenacre (ed.) *Affective Disorder*, New York: International Universities Press

Bifulco, A. and Moran, P. (1998) *Wednesday's Child: Research into Women's Experience of Neglect and Abuse in Childhood, and Adult Depression*, London: Routledge

Birchall, E. (1995) *Working Together in Child Protection*, London: HMSO

Blackburn, I. (1988) 'Cognitive measures in depression', in Perris, C., Blackburn, I. and Perris, H. (eds.) *Cognitive Psychotherapy: Theory and Practice*, Heidelberg: Springer Verlag

Blackburn, I. and Davidson, K. (1990) *Cognitive Therapy for Depression and Anxiety*, Oxford: Blackwell

Bowlby, J. (1977) 'The making and breaking of affectional bonds: 1. aetiology and psychopathology in the light of attachment theory', *British Journal of Psychiatry*, 130, pp. 201–10

Bowlby, J. (1988) *A Secure Base*, London: Routledge

Brewer, J. and Hunter, A. (1988) *Multi Method Research: A Synthesis of Styles*, Beverley Hills: Sage

Brown, G.W. and Harris, T.O. (1978) *Social Origins of Depression*, London: Tavistock

Brown, G.W., Ni Brolchain, M. and Harris, T.O. (1975) 'Social class and psychiatric disorder in women in an urban population', *Sociology*, 9, pp. 225–54

Brown, G.W., Andrews, B., Harris, T., Adler, Z., and Bridge, L. (1986) 'Social support, self esteem and depression', *Psychological Medicine*, 16, pp. 813–31

Bulmer, M. (1979) 'Concepts in the analysis of qualitative data', *Sociological Review*, 27, pp. 651–77

Burgess, R. (1993) *In the Field*, London: Routledge

Caplan, H., Cogill, S., Alexandra, H. and Robinson, K. (1989) 'Maternal depression and the emotional development of the child', *British Journal of Psychiatry*, 154, pp. 818–22

Chodoff, P. (1974) 'The depressive personality: a critical review', in Friedman, R. and Katz, M. (eds.) *The Psychology of Depression: Contemporary Theory and Research*, Washington DC: Winston

Cohen, J. and Fisher, M. (1987) 'Recognition of mental health problems by doctors and social workers', *Practice*, 3 pp. 225–40

Colton, M., Drury, C. and Williams, M. (1995) *Children In Need,* Aldershot: Avebury

Cooper, B., Harwin, B., Depla, C. and Shepherd, M. (1975) 'Mental health in the community: an evaluative study', *Psychological Medicine*, 5, pp. 372–80

Corney, R. (1984a) 'The mental and physical health of clients referred to social workers in local authority and general practice attachment schemes', *Psychological Medicine*, 14, pp. 137–44

Corney, R. (1984b) *The Effectiveness of Attached Social Workers in the Management of Depressed Female Patients in General Practice*, Cambridge: Cambridge University Press

Cox, A.D. (1993) 'Befriending young mothers', *British Journal of Psychiatry*, 163, pp. 6–18

Cox, A.D., Puckering, C., Pound, A. and Mills, M. (1987) 'The impact of maternal depression on young children', *Journal of Child Psychology and Psychiatry and Allied Disciplines*, 28, pp. 987–28

Cox, A.D., Puckering, C., Pound, A. and Mills, M. (1991) 'Evaluation of a home visiting befriending service for young mothers: NEWPIN', *Journal of the Royal College of Medicine*, **84**, pp. 217–20

Dartington Social Research Unit (1995) *Matching Needs and Services*, Totnes: Richard Smith

Davies, M. (1984) *The Essential Social Worker*, Aldershot: Gower

Denzin, N. (1978) *The Research Act*, Second edition, London: McGraw Hill

Department of Health (1989) *Introduction to the Children Act*, London: HMSO

Department of Health (1991a) *The Children Act Guidance and Regulations: Volume 2. Family Support, Day Care and Educational Provision for Young Children*, London: HMSO

Department of Health (1991b) *Child Abuse: A Study of Inquiry Reports*, London: HMSO

Department of Health (1995a) *The Challenge of Partnership in Child Protection*, London: HMSO

Department of Health (1995b) *Child Protection: Messages from Research*, London: HMSO

Department of Health (1998) *Partnership in Action: New Opportunities for Joint Working between Health and Social Services*, London: Department of Health

Department of Health/Social Services Inspectorate (1994) *The Health of the Nation. Key Area Handbook: Mental Illness*, London: HMSO

DHSS (1985) *Review of Child Care Law: Report to Ministers of an Interdepartmental Working Party*, London: HMSO

Dingwall, R., Eekelar, J. and Murray, T. (1983) *The Protection of Children, State Intervention and Family Life*, Oxford: Basil Blackwell

England, H. (1985) *Social Work as Art*, London: George Allen and Unwin

Farmer, E. and Owen, M. (1995) *Child Protection Practices: Private Risks and Public Remedies*, London: HMSO

Fisher, M., Newton, C. and Sainsbury, E. (1984) *Mental Health Social Work Observed*, London: George Allen and Unwin

Fisher, M. (1983) *Speaking of Clients*, Sheffield: University of Sheffield, Joint Unit for Social Services Research

Forehand, R., Brody, G., Slotkin, J. and Fauber, R. (1988) Young adolescents and maternal depression: assessment, interrelations and family predictors', *Journal of Consulting and Clinical Psychology*, **56**, pp. 422–446

Freden, L. (1982) *Psychosocial Aspects of Depression*, Chichester: John Wiley

Fuller, R. and Stevenson, O. (1985) *Policies, Programmes and Disadvantage: A Review of the Literature*, London: Heinemann

Ghodsian, M., Zajicek, E. and Wolkind, S. (1984) 'A longitudinal study of maternal depression and child behaviour problems', *Journal of Child Psychology and Psychiatry and Allied Disciplines*, 25, pp. 91–109

Gibbons, J. and Little, M. (1993) 'Predicting the rate of children on the child protection register', *Research, Policy and Planning*, 10, pp. 15–18

Gibbons, J. with Thorpe, S. and Wilkinson, P. (1990) *Family Support and Prevention: Studies in Local Areas*, London: HMSO

Gibbons, J., Conroy, S. and Bell, C. (1995) *Operation of Child Protection Registers*, London: HMSO

Gilbert, P. (1992) *Depression: The Evolution of Powerlessness*, London: Lawrence Erlbaum

Goldberg, D. and Huxley, P. (1992) *Common Mental Disorders: a Biosocial Approach*, London: Routledge

Goodyer, I., Cooper, P., Vize, C. and Ashby, L. (1993) 'Depression in 11 to 16 year old girls: the role of parental psychopathology and exposure to recent life events', *Journal of Child Psychology and Psychiatry and Allied Disciplines*, 34, pp. 1103–15

Hammersley, M. and Atkinson, P. (1995) *Ethnography: Principles in Practice*, second edition, London: Routledge

Hardiker, P., Exton, K. and Barker, M. (1991) *Policies and Practice in Preventive Child Care*, Aldershot: Gower

Fox Harding, L. (1991) *Perspectives in Child Care Policy*, London: Longman

Henderson, A.S. (1984) 'Interpreting the evidence on social support', *Social Psychiatry*, 19, pp. 49–52

Home Office (1998) *Supporting Families: A Consultation Document*, London: The Stationery Office

Huxley, P. and Fitzpatrick, R. (1984) 'The probable extent of minor mental illness in the adult clients of social workers: a research note', *British Journal of Social Work*, 14, pp. 67–73

Huxley, P., Korer, J. and Tolley, S. (1987) 'The psychiatric 'caseness' of clients referred to an urban social services department', *British Journal of Social Work*, 17, pp. 507–20

Huxley, P., Raval, H., Korer, J. and Jacob, C. (1989) 'Psychiatric morbidity in the clients of social workers: clinical outcomes', *Psychological Medicine*, 19, pp. 189–97

Isaac, B., Minty, E. and Morrison, R. (1986) 'Children in care: the association with mental disorder in the parents', *British Journal of Social Work*, 16, pp. 325–39

Kelmer-Pringle, M. (1978) 'The needs of children', in Smith, S.M. (ed.) *The Maltreatment of Children*, Lancaster: MTP Press

Klein, M. (1975) *Envy and Gratitude and Other Works*, London: Hogarth Press

Kuiper, N., Olinger, L. and Macdonald, M. (1988) 'Vulnerability and episodic cognitions in a self worth contingency model of depression', in Alloy, L. B. (ed) *Cognitive Processes in Depression*, London: Guildford Press

Layder, D. (1993) *New Strategies in Social Research*, London: Polity Press

Lynch, M. and Roberts, J. (1982) *Consequences of Child Abuse*, London: Academic Press

Miles, M. and Huberman, M. (1994) *Qualitative Data Analysis: An Expanded Source Book*, Beverley Hills: Sage

Moss, P. and Plewis, I. (1977) 'Mental distress in mothers of pre school children in inner London', *Psychological Medicine*, 7, pp. 641–52

Murray, L. (1992) 'The impact of post natal depression on infant development', *Journal of Child Psychology and Psychiatry and Allied Disciplines*, 33, pp. 543–61

Murray, L. and Stein, A. (1991) 'The effects of post natal depression on mother-infant relations and infant development' in Woodhead, M., Carr, R. and Light, P. (eds.) *Becoming a Person: Child Development in Social Context, Vol. 1*, London: Routledge, pp. 144–66

Murray, L., Kempton, C., Woolgar, M. and Hooper, R. (1993) 'Depressed mothers' speech to their infants and its relationship to infant gender and cognitive development', *Journal of Child Psychology and Psychiatry and Allied Disciplines*, 34, pp. 1083–1101

Packman, J. (1981) *The Child's Generation*, Oxford: Basil Blackwell

Packman, J. with Randall, J. and Jacques, N. (1986) *Who Needs Care? Social Work Decisions about Children*, Oxford: Basil Blackwell

Pannacione, V. and Wahler, R. (1986) 'Child behaviour, maternal depression and social coercion as factors in the quality of child care', *Journal of Abnormal Child Psychology*, 14, pp. 263–78

Parker, R., Ward, H., Jackson, S., Aldgate, J. and Wedge, P. (1991) *Assessing Outcomes in Child Care*, London: HMSO

Quinton, D. and Rutter, M. (1984) 'Parents with children in care, 1: current circumstances and parenting', *Journal of Child Psychology and Psychiatry*, 25, pp. 211–29

Reder, P., Duncan, S. and Gray, M. (1993) *Beyond Blame: Child Abuse Tragedies Revisited*, London: Routledge

Reder, P. and Lucy, C. (1991) 'The assessment of parenting: some interactional considerations', *Psychiatric Bulletin*, 15, pp. 347–8

Rees, S. and Wallace, A. (1982) *Verdicts in Social Work*, London: Edward Arnold

Richman, N. (1977) 'Behaviour problems in pre school children: family and social factors', *British Journal of Psychiatry*, 131, pp. 523–7

Richman, N., Stevenson, O. and Graham, P.A. (1982) *Pre School to School: A Behavioural Study*, London: Academic Press.

Rowe, D. (1983) *Depression: The Way Out of Your Prison*, London: Routledge and Kegan Paul.

Sharland, E., Jones, D., Aldgate, J., Seal, H. and Croucher, M. (1995) *Professional Intervention in Child Sexual Abuse*, London: HMSO

Shaw, M., Maston, J. and Brocklesby, B. (1991) *Children in Need and their Families: a New Approach*, Leicester: Department of Health, University of Leicester School of Social Work.

Shepherd, M., Harwin, B., Depla, C and Cairns, V. (1979) 'Social work and the primary care of mental disorder', *Psychological Medicine*, 9, pp. 661–9

Sheppard, M. (1982) *Perceptions of Child Abuse: A Critique of Individualism*, Norwich: University of East Anglia Publications

Sheppard, M. (1991) *Mental Health Work in the Community: Theory and Practice in Social Work and Community Psychiatric Nursing*, London: Falmer

Sheppard, M. (1993a) 'Maternal depression and child care: the significance for social work and social work research', *Adoption and Fostering*, 17, 2, pp. 10–17

Sheppard, M. (1993b) 'The external context for social support: towards a theoretical formulation of social support, child care and maternal depression', *Social Work and Social Sciences Review*, 4, 1, pp. 27–59

Sheppard, M. (1994a) 'Maternal depression, child care and the social work role', *British Journal of Social Work*, 24, pp. 33–51

Sheppard, M. (1994b) 'Child care, social support and maternal depression: a review and application of findings', *British Journal of Social Work*, 24, pp. 287–310

Sheppard, M. (1994c) 'Post natal depression, child care and social support', *Social Work and Social Sciences Review*, 5, 1, pp. 24–47

Sheppard, M. (1995) *Care Management and the New Social Work*, London: Whiting and Birch

Sheppard, M. (1996) 'Depression in the work of British health visitors: clinical facets', *Social Sciences and Medicine*, 43, 11, pp. 1637–40

Sheppard, M. (1997a) 'Social work practice in child and family care: a study of maternal depression', *British Journal of Social Work*, **27**, pp. 815–47

Sheppard, M. (1997b) 'Double jeopardy: the link between child abuse and maternal depression in child and family social work', *Child and Family Social Work*, **2**, pp. 91–109

Sheppard, M. (1997c) 'Depression in female health visitor consulters: social and demographic factors', *Journal of Advanced Nursing*, **26**, pp. 921–9

Sheppard, M. (1998) 'Social profile, maternal depression and welfare concerns in clients of health visitors and social workers: a comparative study', *Children and Society*, **12**, pp. 125–35

Sheppard, M. (1999) 'Maternal depression in child and family care: the design, development and use of an instrument for research and practice' in Ulas, M. and Connor, A. (eds.) *Mental Health and Social Work*, London: Jessica Kingsley

Sheppard, M. (2000) 'The parents' concerns questionnaire: evaluation of a mothers' self report instrument for the identification of problems and needs in child and family social work', *Children and Society* (forthcoming)

Sheppard, M. and Woodcock, J. (1999) 'Need as an operating concept', *Child and Family Social Work*, **4**, 1, pp. 67–77

Silverman, D. (1985) *Qualitative Methodology and Sociology: Describing the Social World*, Aldershot: Gower

Thoburn, J., Lewis, A. and Shemmings, D. (1995) *Paternalism or Partnership? Family Involvement in the Child Protection Process*, London: HMSO

Vaughn, C. and Leff, J. (1976) 'The influence of family and social factors on the course of psychiatric illness: a comparison of schizophrenic and depressed patients', *British Journal of Psychiatry*, **129**, pp. 125–37

Weissman, M.M. and Klerman, G. (1977) 'Sex differences in the epidemiology of depression', *Archives of General Psychiatry*, **34**, pp. 98–111

Weissman, M.M., Paykel, E. and Klerman, G. (1972) 'The depressed woman as mother, *Social Psychiatry*, **7**, pp. 98–108

Welner, Z. and Rice, J. (1988) 'School age children of depressed parents: a blind and controlled study', *Journal of Affective Disorder*, **15**, pp. 291–302

Welner, Z., Welner, A., McRary, M. and Leonard, M. (1977) 'Psychopathology in children of in-patients with depression: a controlled study', *Journal of Nervous and Mental Disease*, **164**, pp. 408–13

Whipple, E. and Webster-Stratton, C. (1991) 'The role of parental stress in physically abusive families', *Child Abuse and Neglect*, **15**, pp. 76–82

White Paper (1998) *Modernising Social Services*, London: The Stationery Office

Williams, M. (1997) *Parents, Children and Social Workers*, Aldershot: Avebury

Zuvarin, S. (1989) 'Severity of maternal depression and three types of mother to child aggression', *American Journal of Orthopsychiatry*, **59**, pp. 377–89

Index

women's experiences of
interventions 187–202
child protection register 15, 79, 128,
178–9
childcare
maternal depression and 4–5,
12–14, 217–18
women's expectations of 80, 174,
175, 185
childcare services, collaboration with
mental health services 28, 31,
112–14, 122, 224–5
childhood experiences 175, 228
effect on mothering 46, 47
relationship to depression 17, 19
children 15, 16
effect of depression on 13–14,
50–3, 54
fear of losing 171–2, 182, 184, 221
mothers' care for 57–8, 79, 80, 82,
156
problems with 81, 88–9
social workers' focus on 88–9, 94,
95, 103–5, 132, 158, 161, 193,
202, 220, 223, 225–6
women's views of social workers
and 192–4
Children Act 1975 10
Children Act 1989 10–11, 103
children with disabilities 28, 78, 153,
219, 229
intervention strategies with
families 99, 153–64
women's perceptions of
interventions 203–14
Chodorow, P. 17
Christmas hampers 86
Cohen, J. 21
Colton, M. 15, 16
commitment of social workers to
mothers 102, 198
compassion 58–9
confidence, lack of 188, 189, 200
confidence–building 87, 95, 143
conflict, with social workers 36, 168,
169, 174, 184, 220, 221

conflict of interest 103–4, 110, 158–9,
193, 226
consultation 190–2, 201, 202
contact
with children in care 180–2, 185
with social workers 194–5, 203,
205, 208, 213
control 167, 168, 184
and risk management 133–4
women's lack of 17–18, 217, 222,
227
Cooper, B. 22
coping
difficulties with 51, 135–6, 199, 200
help with 144–5, 150
Corney, R. 21, 22
council housing 73, 74
counselling 89, 94, 101, 106, 149, 160
court work 99
criminal behaviour 74–5, 82
crisis responses 121, 154, 155–6, 163,
219
cycle of abuse 53–4

decision-making, women's part in 168,
187–8, 190–1, 201
dependency 18, 218
depression 3–5, 14–16, 37
awareness of 41–3, 53, 54
effects of 48–50, 54
need for knowledge about 223–4
and negative world view 16–19
produced by child protection
process 8, 182–4, 185, 228
social workers' identification of 5,
22, 55–6, 63–4, 106, 189, 223
social workers' perceptions of
56–67
women's experiences of 41–54
desperation, of women 211, 212, 213
Dingwall, R. 21
direct work with mothers 140–1,
143–5, 150, 227
with disabled children 158–60, 164
see also support for women
drug addiction 64, 74, 178